Advance Praise for *The Mommy Group*

"If you read only one parenting book this year, make it *The Mommy Group*. Elizabeth Isadora Gold has the chops, the wit, and the heart to take it where few dare to tread; this book is incisive, insightful, and downright delightful. I did not mean for that to rhyme."

—Adam Mansbach, #1 *New York Times* bestselling author of *Go the F*ck to Sleep*

"Elizabeth Isadora Gold's *The Mommy Group* is a mordantly funny, deeply poignant look at the pleasures and perils of early motherhood. It is also a testament to the power of female friendship, and a wake-up call to policy makers that this nation must do more for its moms. *The Mommy Group* is a must-read for anyone who is a mother or cares about one."

—Amy Sohn, author of *Motherland* and *The Actress*

"When women get together to tell the truth about their lives, amazing things happen—as you shall see when you read Elizabeth Isadora Gold's funny, touching parenting memoir!"

—Jennifer Baumgardner, author of *Manifesta* and *Look Both Ways*

"Like the very best friends, *The Mommy Group* is warm and witty, reassuring and generous, and always so refreshingly honest. It should be required reading for all expectant parents."

—Kimberly McCreight, *New York Times* bestselling author of *Reconstructing Amelia*

"This vital, comprehensive book is effectively a mommy group unto itself: a glorious, harmonious, companionable chorus of voices. It's a consciousness raising, a rallying cry, the drum of our collective heartbeat. It's also an essential reminder that the struggle for reproductive justice encompasses much more than birth control. Gold has done humankind a solid. Are you a mother? Did you *have* a mother? Read it."

—Elisa Albert, author of *After Birth*

"Part memoir, part cultural exposé, *The Mommy Group* lays bare our lack of support for those who bear our children, while also celebrating the remarkable—but not uncommon—determination of new mothers to support one another in our post–*Lean In* country, a land of unsubsidized childcare and unpaid parental leave. Touching on topics as diverse as envy, Cry It Out, and what it really feels like to have sex after pushing out a baby, *The Mommy Group* is the perfect guide through the uncharted postpartum jungle."

—Miranda Beverly-Whittemore, *New York Times* bestselling author of *Bittersweet*

The

MOMMY GROUP

Freaking Out, Finding Friends,
and Surviving the Happiest
Time of Our Lives

Elizabeth Isadora Gold

ATRIA PAPERBACK

New York London Toronto Sydney New Delhi

ATRIA PAPERBACK
An Imprint of Simon & Schuster, Inc.
1230 Avenue of the Americas
New York, NY 10020

First Atria Paperback edition March 2016

ATRIA PAPERBACK and colophon are trademarks of Simon & Schuster, Inc.

For information about special discounts for bulk purchases, please contact
Simon & Schuster Special Sales at 1-866-506-1949
or business@simonandschuster.com.

The Simon & Schuster Speakers Bureau can bring authors to
your live event. For more information or to book an event, contact
the Simon & Schuster Speakers Bureau at 1-866-248-3049
or visit our website at www.simonspeakers.com.

Interior design by Renato Stanisic

Manufactured in the United States of America

10 9 8 7 6 5 4 3 2 1

Library of Congress Cataloging-in-Publication Data
Gold, Elizabeth Isadora, author.
    The mommy group : freaking out, finding each other & rediscovering
ourselves / Elizabeth Isadora Gold.
        pages cm
Includes bibliographical references.
    1. Mothers—United States. 2. Motherhood—United States.
3. Mother and child—United States. 4. Women—Identity. I. Title.
HQ759.G586 2016
306.874'3—dc23
2015030713

ISBN 978-1-4767-8586-8
ISBN 978-1-4767-8587-5 (ebook)

To Clara, Danny, Larry, and Vicky.
In no particular order.

All the children were there. Among the trees, in the arms of statues, toes in the grass, they hopped in and out of dog shit and dug tunnels into mole holes. Wherever the children ran, their mothers stopped to talk.

—GRACE PALEY, "FAITH IN A TREE," *ENORMOUS CHANGES AT THE LAST MINUTE* (1974)

Contents

While this is a work of nonfiction, I have changed names and identifying details to protect the privacy of the many mothers, fathers, and children whose stories are in this book. Thank you all for your generous candor.

The
MOMMY
GROUP

Meet the Mommies

Anna was the group's founder, married to Stephan. Both were brilliant (they met in college), attractive (she was flaxen blond and he was Bavarian handsome), and madly in love. But when Anna became pregnant with Isabella, their fairy tale went dark. Anna's dedication to preserving her family, her honesty, and her humor showed us all that we could get through anything—with a little help from our friends.

Jane seemed a prototypical Brooklyn crunchy type: a social worker from the Pacific Northwest, the daughter of hippie dropouts, and a card-carrying member of the Park Slope Food Coop. Happily married to Carl, an architect, Jane's sarcasm and emotional acuity save her from being a sancti-mommy stereotype.

Antonia was Australian and fiercely smart, with a newly minted PhD in comparative literature. Her Augustus (Gus) was the first-born of the group (and so "energetic" he'd broken two front teeth by his first birthday). Her husband, Dillon, was a filmmaker who took a day job when they got pregnant. Living in a tiny one-bedroom rental with a very old dog, Toni obsessively worried that she'd never sleep through the night again.

An administrator at a school for students with special needs, Heidi lived three doors down from us with her musician husband, Josh. Walking by, I would peek into their ground-floor window, marveling at her seemingly calm demeanor. Half Danish and half Jewish, Heidi exercised her anxiety by bundling Clay in clothing befitting a Nordic winter and feeding him whenever he cried. The first of us to return to full-time work, we looked to Heidi as we navigated our own postbaby professional lies.

Renée's son, Charlie, was a toddler when she had her daughter, Emme. Her husband, Benji, had a thriving practice as a therapist. To me, they seemed the most financially stable of the group, owning a comfortable house in a great school district, and not agonizing over the cost of a full-time nanny. Even so, the toddler/infant combo was crazier than Renée expected. Though she was often unable to come to meetings for Emme's first year, her emails reassured us that no baby problem would last forever.

Seemingly demure and shy, Melissa was actually a fierce mother and accomplished painter (though she worked as a graphic designer to pay the bills). I became obsessed with the immaculate loft she shared with Patrick, her art director husband. After she told us she used to have pink hair and confessed to taking Patrick to a gun range to "spice up" their marriage, I no longer felt so intimidated. Her daughter, Sofia, led the way for the other kids in potty training and My Little Pony obsession.

I'm Elizabeth. You'll soon hear enough about me. . . .

Introduction

From Anna

May 7, 2010

For August, September, and October Expectant Moms,

A small group of women are getting together at my house on Tuesday, May 18 at 7 P.M. The purpose of the pregnancy circle is to offer support and friendship to each other as we enter into this exciting time! Also, it can progress into a new mother's group. If interested in coming, please RSVP.

Best,

Anna (expecting in early September)

I was hugely pregnant, buying apples at the Saturday Greenmarket at Grand Army Plaza, when I ran into Anna, holding her newborn daughter, Isabella, tight in her arms. It was late September 2010, and the leaves on the trees at the border of Prospect Park were beginning to curl with yellow. Those leaves and the apples for sale at the market—tart, juicy, and crisp, perfect for my last month of pregnancy—epitomized a picture-perfect Brooklyn fall day. My husband, Danny, and I were out to enjoy one of our last solo weekends before our lives changed forever.

"Hey!" I called out to Anna, happy to see such a new mama out of the house. Isabella was two weeks old, and Anna had been having a rough recovery from her emergency cesarean. Even though we'd only known each other a few months, I considered her a close friend. Anna was the leader and organizer of our mommy group.

An email on Park Slope Parents, our local parenting Listserv, brought us together as our bellies were beginning to show in our second trimesters of pregnancy. Anna, Renée, Antonia, Jane, Melissa, Heidi, and I were all in our mid- to late thirties and (with the exception of Renée, who already had a three-year-old son) new to motherhood. From our first meeting, we shared a sensibility: supportive, sardonic, and terrified.

Since that spring, the seven of us had gotten together every few weeks, then more often as our babies were born. We exchanged tips on choosing electric breast pumps and hiring nannies, complaints about varicose veins and weight-obsessed OB-GYNs. We confided our fears and hopes about labor, marriage, and maternity leave.

Though we were all thrilled about our impending parenthood, mommy group was always a place we felt safe exploring the less sunny side of our new lives. Seeing a post about Heidi's baby shower on Facebook, I was feeling surprised that she looked so happy in the photos. Had we been reserving the adoring photo-ready moments for people who already knew us—and who we didn't want to worry?

Because of this intimacy, I was hurt and surprised when, in response to my enthusiastic greeting, Anna gripped Isabella closer, turned around, and actually ran off into a cluster of trees behind the artisanal cheese stand.

Only two weeks earlier, I'd visited Anna and Isabella when they were newly home from the hospital. Swaddled in a pink blankie and lying in a tiny pink hammock, Issie looked like a rosebud. Anna was so swollen with retained fluid I was sure she had some kind of terrible illness.

"It's an extreme reaction to the C-section meds," she told me, with strange (to me, looking at her) good cheer. "Stephan's been great," she added. "I've barely been able to get out of this chair since we got home."

Stephan stuck his head into the room. I'd never met her husband before that afternoon, but he fit her adoring description for sure: tall, dark, and handsome, but with an intimidating (and somewhat sexy) German accent.

They were both attorneys, though as Anna had explained to us at our first meeting, "I'm the do-gooder, and he always knew he'd go corporate. The balance is great. With his salary, I can take as much pro bono as I want. Lots of domestic violence, ugly custody battles. Pretty hard-core stuff. And then he's on these crazy zillion-dollar real estate deals. It's really long hours, though," she added. "I can get pretty lonely, especially now."

"What do we need, babe?" Stephan asked now. "I thought I'd do some shopping since you have company."

"More paper towels. And red Gatorade?" Anna looked up at him with so much love, her china-doll blue eyes bright. He blew her and Isabella a kiss.

"It was nice meeting you," he said to me. But before I could respond, he was gone.

Anna said, "The birth was kind of a nightmare, but he was so calm and loving and present. He made me feel safe."

Eight months pregnant myself, I was terrified by her words, her body, even the accoutrements of newborn life (so many containers for the baby and her various liquids). Nevertheless, Anna, swollen legs, stitches, and all, seemed determined to normalize her experience, and for my benefit. Her personality—real talk, emotional presence, empathy—was one of the reasons I, usually the last person to "join" anything, felt comfortable in this group. From the first meeting, she'd led by no-bullshit example.

Now, watching Anna disappear into the forest like Bambi's mother, I revisited the details of that visit. Had I offended her? My history of female friendship dynamics shuffled through my head. I'd never been good in groups, my relationships with women always worked better one-on-one, maybe this was some kind of pregnant-lady *Heathers* (and here I dated myself—a "young" mother would have thought of *Mean Girls* or *Clueless*—God, I was old). Had the other mommies decided to cut me out because I couldn't eat brownies and croissants with them, my gestational diabetes preventing me from eating carbs? That seemed unlikely, even in my excessively paranoid advanced pregnant state. Perhaps Anna simply hadn't noticed me as I longingly browsed the raw honeycomb (I could eat no honey because of the GD, no raw honey because of botulism risk). Yes, that must be it. She hadn't seen me.

In the midst of my emotional ramp-up, a white-haired woman who looked exactly like Anna (but with a practical hairdo and crackly warm-up suit) walked over to me. I recognized her as Anna's mother, from Kentucky. We'd met earlier in the summer. But Anna'd told me her mom wasn't coming back to New York for another month.

"You're Elizabeth, right? From her mommy group?" she said with a twang.

"Yeah," I said. "Wasn't that Anna over there? I thought I saw her . . . Is everything okay?"

"*No.*" Anna's mom pressed her lips tight and shook her head. "Her husband walked out on her three days ago."

I thought I'd misheard her. Was she really talking about that guy I'd just met? Who held his wife while she mourned a miscarriage, and held her together when she was almost hospitalized from severe morning sickness? Stephan was supposed to be the love of her life. Did he never come back with the paper towels and Gatorade?

Interrupting my thoughts, Anna reappeared at her mother's side. As she clutched Isabella to her chest, tears rolled down her cheeks; her face was red and raw. When she finally looked at me, her eyes were unfocussed. "I'll call you later, Liz," she managed to say. Her mother put a firm arm around her shoulders and led her away.

I wondered if this would be the last time I'd ever see her. If so, I felt really sad.

The following Monday morning, the mommy group planned—as we had for the last few weeks—to meet at the Tea Lounge, a neighborhood coffeehouse with worn, overstuffed sofas and decent salads. The place earned its nickname, the Teat Lounge. Even our circle of incompetently nursing new mothers (maximal nipple flashing, minimal lactation) didn't warrant so much as a side-eye from the other patrons or the hipster coffee jerks. Danny and I were expecting our daughter, Clara, around Halloween, which meant that my due date was the last in the group. So even though I didn't have my own baby in arms, I came to hold the other mommies' tiny squishy people, hear their week's war stories, and check out my near future.

The others were already there, sitting on the least ratty (and therefore least potentially bedbug infested, we hoped) circle of sofas. Jane waved at me first. She was a social worker and Portland expatriate whose two-month-old daughter, Katie, had an adorable perpetually surprised expression and a silky cap of strawberry-blond hair. I already loved Jane because she always seemed to say aloud what I was thinking, no matter how awkward or inappropriate.

Renée was our soft-spoken maternal authority, as she already had a three-year-old son, Charlie. Her baby, Emme, was a petite six-week-old who slept constantly. (I'd been shocked when Danny and I ran into her husband, Benji, in Prospect Park, and Emme snoozed through our whole forty-five-minute chat.) I loved to marvel at Emme's delicate eyelids and the long lashes that reached halfway down her rosy cheeks.

Antonia and Heidi, and their boys Gus and Clay, were my recruits to the gang. Toni and I knew each other from a stint as adjuncts at the same state college, and we'd bumped into each other (almost literally, considering the size of our pregnant stomachs) at a former colleague's party. Antonia was smart. Her writing about the connections between Australian and American colonial literature had brought her to the States on a Fulbright, and she'd always been two steps ahead of me in classroom dynamics and curriculum. Now her emails to the mommies were as clever and profound as her criticism of pioneer myths had been. And Gus was one of the most beautiful children I'd ever seen, long and lean even at two months, with features that looked drawn on with pen and ink. The tricky bit: he never slept.

Heidi lived four doors down from Danny and me in a ground-floor apartment. Though we'd shared the same block for over a decade, we'd never met until our husbands got us together. Both musicians, they'd chatted at a professional function and were delighted to realize that a) they were neighbors, and b) both had pregnant wives due at around the same time. Within days, we were knocking on each other's doors (or her street-level window) to grab an iced tea or take a slow walk to look at baby gear together. Clay was also two months old, with a melon of a head and the chubbiest legs I'd ever seen on such a small person. Heidi was convinced he and Clara (even in her current unborn state) were destined for love.

Melissa, the most recent member of the group, was a painter and web designer. She came via Antonia's husband (she'd built the website for the film library he worked at). Her girl Sofia was the biggest (though not the eldest) of the baby gang, with enormous blue-gray eyes and a passionate attachment to her Sophie the Giraffe chewy toy. I didn't know Melissa well yet, but she seemed cool, especially if I was judging by her accessories (which I will admit I was). Silver Converse sneakers and delicate rose gold earrings were a *good* combination. Most of all, though, Melissa was nice, really listening when the other women talked. I wondered what her story would be, once she felt comfortable enough to tell it.

I already imagined (though perhaps not with Heidi's fervency) a future for these kids together. I'm an only child, and grew up without close kid neighbors. Already, I wanted this to be my daughter's gang, and I was ready to be the grown-up with a supply of Band-Aids and juice boxes.

In the midst of my fantasy, Anna arrived: our leader, a family law attorney in dire need of her own services. Issie was still tiny, a pup beside giants Gus and Sofia. Anna wouldn't—couldn't?—put her down. But she also couldn't—wouldn't?—stop crying. She sat in the center of the middle couch, and we huddled around her, bringing her hummus, coffee, and an enormous glass of water.

"Thanks, girls," she said. "I needed to see you all. You're the only people who know me without him." Between bites of pizza bread, Isabella's mewls for milk, and her own tears, she told us what had gone down with Stephan. "He kept saying he didn't want to be married anymore. I think he's having a nervous breakdown."

We hugged her and cried with her. We held Isabella, offered to babysit, make her lasagna, and beat the living shit out of that asshole. And right there in the Teat Lounge, our mommy group transformed into the Mommy Group, our force and sisterhood, our emotional succor for the next two years.

Mommy groups had always seemed cheesy to me. "Go to Mommy and Me classes! You'll meet other women with adorable babies who have pink bows pasted on their bald heads!" Not for an urban bohemian free spirit such as myself. Danny and I already had friends. Sure, they were mostly child-free gay men, but we knew they'd love hanging out with our little girl when she was finally born.

Candide-like, I thought I would be raising my putative child in the best of all possible parenting worlds. We live in Prospect Heights, Brooklyn, a few blocks from infamous Park Slope, one of the most child-friendly urban neighborhoods in the country. I moved to Brooklyn twenty years ago because it was cheap. By the time I "matured," met and married Danny, and decided to have a baby, my corner of New York had become a living cliché of hipster parenthood.

Park Slope Parents, the Yahoo parenting Listserv on which the Mommy Group members and I found each other, boasts more than 7,500 members. Stroller pushers outnumber "civilians" on the sidewalks. Within a few blocks of my stoop are five playgrounds, two "best in the country" ice cream shops (it's all about grass-fed milk versus house-baked mix-ins), a fancy toy store, the Brooklyn Museum, the Brooklyn Botanic Garden, the Central Branch of the Brooklyn Public Library, and the beautiful and wild 585-acre

Prospect Park. Then there is Amorina, our local Italian-style pizza joint (Danny calls it "the artisanal Chuck E. Cheese"), several play spaces to spend rainy and cold days, kids' art and yoga and music classes, and excellent public transportation. All of this is within the larger universe of New York City's resources and diversity. If you live in a big city, raising a kid in Brooklyn should be pretty close to perfect.

Of course, there is a dark—and, often, annoying—side: the Park Slope Food Coop is so notoriously PC that it was the subject of a *Daily Show* episode. A humor piece in the September 2014 *Vanity Fair* bore the headline: "From Brooklyn to Buckingham Palace: Park Slope Moms Offer Kate Middleton Parenting Advice," explaining that "Park Slope moms are revered—and reviled—as some of the most doting, kale-eating mothers around." The neighborhood's $30-an-entrée restaurants feature high chairs and gourmet mac 'n' cheese (economically reprehensible *and* delicious). And please note essentials I did *not* mention in the "pros" paragraph above: reasonable rent, affordable childcare, and consistently excellent public schools. Brooklyn now ranks as one of the most expensive places to live in the country.

I'm a city girl, born and bred; I hate driving, and (much to my raised-in-the-burbs husband's amusement) believe serial killers lurk behind every tree in the suburban forest. Yes, New York is expensive and can be stressful, but it's home. Danny and I belong to that crazy Food Coop, buy most of our clothes and household furnishings secondhand, and accept that we'll always work three jobs each and have one bathroom in our apartment. But we also go to museums and the opera, walk two miles for the best bowl of pho, and love living here.

But, no matter how excellent our coping skills, we didn't predict what would happen when we procreated in a city without family living nearby, with little experience in newborn care, while living in a walk-up rental apartment without a washer and dryer or even a second bedroom.

Call me naive, but I thought adding Clara to our lives would be easy. Danny and I were a solid, happy couple, with professional lives that already offered flexibility. We'd both earned prestigious degrees in our fields, and we were accustomed to working at odd hours, on little sleep. Most important of all, we loved children, and we couldn't wait to have this little girl. Every night of my pregnancy, we got in bed together and sang the same lullaby my parents had sung to me when I was little: a tune by Brahms with changing lyrics about our day, and what we were going to do tomorrow, taking turns to come up with the silliest or most banal verses we could. Once the baby was born, we thought, life would be like the lullaby, only real. Sleep deprivation, spit-up—we could handle those. Pregnancy had been difficult. Once our baby was here, it would get easier.

I don't want to say we were idiots, but . . . Enthusiasm aside, we were almost completely unprepared for the reality of parenthood. What we didn't know and couldn't imagine: there is no life experience as transformative as the birth of a child. The baby is a bomb that goes off in the middle of your living room, affecting all aspects of home life, marriage, body, and sense of self—especially for mothers. And if you lack the traditional structures and support of close family or have little experience with babies, it's shocking.

I—and the other members of the Mommy Group—assumed we'd "just know" what to do with our infants. We'd been running our own professional and personal lives, paying bills, being grownups for decades. Why was this so hard?

Perhaps our confusion, our lack of power, had something to do with how strong we were *before* having children. This is the alienation of the contemporary not-quite-pre-middle-aged parent: old enough to have found a career and to have begun to excel at it, to have lived away from your childhood home for as long as you were in it, but not too seasoned to not need help.

We're all members of Generation X and children of the Baby Boomers. Many of our parents divorced after starting families, and many of our mothers found themselves through feminism in the seventies and eighties. They fought for our rights to plan our families via contraception and abortion, to go to graduate school, to find partners who would co-parent with us when the time came. They taught us to choose work that we loved, and to hold off on marriage and babies until we were *ready*.

Having such choices did make it easier for us. If our pregnancies had been unplanned, if we'd been poor, if having children had interrupted our career paths in more substantial ways, then we would have felt even further marooned on the dark side of the moon.

As much as we adored our babies, we knew what we were missing. Working late without worrying about (or paying for) childcare. A slow Saturday morning in bed with our partners. Reading novels, staying in hotels, attending conferences and events, ordering one more cocktail on a night out with friends. Mature, child-free independence. When these noisy, damp, transfixing creatures came into our lives, all of that was gone, at least for the near future. When you're a sleep-deprived, adoring, terrified new mother covered in spit-up, it's hard to imagine past the next feeding.

The first few months of motherhood were overwhelming for all of us. I can only imagine how scared and tired we seemed, each of us holding our babies tight to our swollen chests when we met at cafés. We ate our croissants and slices of quiche, drank endless cups of sugar-sweetened coffee, and talked.

There's much made in the media about "Mommy Wars" and "parenting styles." Stay-at-home versus working moms, attachment parents versus free-rangers, unschoolers versus flash-card devotees. The Mommy Group showed me that such differences should be immaterial.

I now believe that almost any group of mothers who meet once a week for a few months, and who consciously go beyond chatting about stroller brands and whose baby sleeps in an organic bassinet, will feel the same sense of sisterhood that we did. And its powerful effects.

Our Mommy Group didn't only save Anna when her marriage collapsed. It saved all of us. I am well aware that the word *saved* implies we were dying or drowning. It sounds final, maudlin. Weren't we supposed to be magically in love with our babies, cherishing this special time (especially according to whatever celebrity just lost all her baby weight while simultaneously founding a chain of green preschools)? But *saved* is the right word. Without the Mommy Group, I think I would have lost my*self* in new motherhood, going crazy without knowing if I'd ever feel better. Instead, I had these women, this community, to help me find the ring, complete the quest, make the journey home.

Our struggles did not take place in a vacuum (though we all ended up doing a lot of vacuuming). The personal decisions of parenthood have never been more political. It's a sad, oft-reported and oft-repeated fact that the United States doesn't fully support parenthood, or the decisions surrounding it. Our abortion and contraceptive decisions (Hobby Lobby, anyone?) play out in the voting booths in every election cycle. The United States is one of the few developed countries without paid family leave or subsidized child-care. This country's shameful maternal policies meant we had to return to work before we felt as if we knew our babies well enough to leave them for a full day. It's no surprise half of us were on psychiatric meds within the first six months.

This was not how new motherhood was supposed to look according to the baby industrial complex of parenting magazines and BPA-free teether manufacturers. We were supposed to sail past the dragons and monsters of early parenting with only the internet and inborn wisdom to guide us. Magazines and advertising push otherwise self-aware women on an idea of perfect motherhood: baby bumps to flat abs, rapture in the nursery and ecstasy in the marital bed, a seamless transition back to work. Even if we know these messages are as bullshit and Photoshopped as ads for cellulite-busting cream, it's almost impossible not to internalize them. And, therefore, to wonder if we're doing something terribly wrong as mothers all the time.

The Women's Liberation slogan of the seventies "the personal is political" has never been truer. As daughters of the women's movement, contemporary mothers may have missed official consciousness raising, but we can still organize (and with better wine and fewer leaflets). We have to, if we want to effect the change American mothers so desperately need.

Women spend about twice the amount of time per day caring for their children that men do. Single mothers are the heads of household for more than 9.6 million American families. One in ten women experience some kind of postpartum mental illness in the first year after giving birth. One out of six children are diagnosed with a disability.

We should organize for: national parental leave policy and

subsidized daycare; consistent screening for and treatment of post-partum mental illness; subsidized parenting support and counseling for low-income and working-class families; better education (from preschool on) about diverse families—single-parent, adopted, and/or LGBT. What better way to understand these issues, to organize, and, frankly, to politicize, than through mommy groups?

I do feel compelled to acknowledge the privilege that my particular group enjoys, and I am well aware of our demographic advantages. We are all college educated, and while we don't all own apartments, houses, or cars, and most of our kids will be attending New York City public schools, we are by no means poor.

Many mothers with fewer resources might not have the same kind of time and energy to devote to finding and maintaining a group, especially in our increasingly economically polarized country. Which is why it's so crucial to note that our Mommy Group initially bonded almost as much via email, texts, and social media as in person—and we maintain those "virtual" bonds today. In fact, they're often the only regular way for us to connect. Five years after our babies were born, every one of us now works full-time (several of us as our families' breadwinners).

As I researched and reported for this book, I wanted to include many varieties of mommy groups and parenting experts, and hope I have done so within the limits of time and logistics: a "nonviolent parenting group" in Echo Park, Los Angeles; Freda Rosenfeld, a lactation consultant known as the "Breast Whisperer," in Brooklyn, New York; Kate C. and her neighbors at their weekly "plastic picnic table party" in Minneapolis, Minnesota; Katherine Stone, founder of Postpartum Progress and a trailblazing activist about maternal mental illness.

Across class, geographic, and racial boundaries, I discovered we had more in common than politicians or news editors would like us to believe. We were mothers, all searching for the same thing: a way to raise our children while retaining—or remaking—our Selves.

The mommies about whom I have written here have generously given their precious time (and we all know how precious time is when you have a small child or children) to talk to me, to open up their lives and homes. I am moved and honored every time a mommy group invites me to sit in on their personal time and space, and I'm thankful that they have allowed me to share their stories. This is especially true for the mommies of my own group. Jane said to me when I started this process, "We all needed the book you're going to write." Here are our stories. Make them your own.

1. First Meetings

Why Did I Need a Mommy Group Anyway?

From Elizabeth

May 5, 2010

Hi, Anna,

I'm due at the end of October, and interested in attending your group. I'm in Prospect Heights, and am a writer. This is my first child, so I'm definitely looking to meet other neighborhood moms. Thanks for coming up with this!

I read the notice on the Park Slope Parents Listserv with a mixture of fear and cynicism. Twenty weeks into my pregnancy with Clara, I was feeling far from radiant. The last thing I wanted to do was talk about my emotional and physical changes with a bunch of strangers, even if we were all harboring the same adorable species of parasite.

Still, I told Danny about the email. I must have known he would urge me to go against my instinct to close off and shut down. I was right.

"Sweetie, go," he said. We were curled up on our couch, an enormous brown ultrasuede sleeper we bought off craigslist when he moved into my Brooklyn apartment seven years earlier. It was like a marshmallow boat that took up most of our living room: soft, puffy, worn shiny in places. But it could fit both of us lying down if we squeezed, which is what we were doing at that moment, eating take-out Mexican food out of my favorite green vintage pottery bowls.

"*Whyyy?*" I whined at him, in the way that only a pregnant woman can to her long-suffering husband. "I don't have swollen feet or heartburn, which is all they'll want to talk about. They're probably younger than me, own their own brownstones, and aren't going to go back to work. And I'm too busy."

Danny looked at me, serious even as he piled guacamole on his chicken taco. "You need the support. *We* need the support. I want you to meet some friends to talk to and not just surf the internet all night."

"Okay, but if I go, will you . . . ?" I couldn't think of anything I wanted, except a healthy baby.

"I'll buy you an ice cream," he said.

"Deal."

We did need support—for many reasons. The first and most obvious were logistical. How did we intend to pay for and care for this baby? I'm a writer, and Danny's a composer. We both make a living with a Rube Goldberg–esque combination of part-time teaching (tutoring, private lessons, adjunct positions) and freelance work (writing and editing for me, music journalism and the occasional piano man gig for Danny). In preparation for the baby, we were working as much as we could. With no full-time employment status, and therefore no maternity or paternity leave, we'd both need to go back to work ASAP after Clara's birth. Money would be tight, but we were used to that.

Childcare was a mystery. All we knew was that we couldn't count on family. As I've mentioned, I'm an only child, and Danny's sister lives in Las Vegas, which feels like a world away. I have three cousins with whom I'm almost sibling close, but they live in Oregon, Texas, and DC. Danny's parents are in Los Angeles. Mine are in Philadelphia. They were planning frequent visits, but we wouldn't be able to text them to pop by for a few hours of impromptu babysitting.

Luckily, we felt we had a great "friend family" for support. Danny and I have lived in New York for a combined three decades. I attended college and graduate school here; Danny's community of musicians and performers is both wide and close. We know current-day NYC is a world capital of money and materialism, but our close friends are, for the most part, artists (or those who work with them), with DIY schedules and imaginative ideas.

We decided to designate a few godparents: my oldest friend, Chris, and his longtime partner, Randy; Danny's BFF/surrogate kid sister, Stacy, and her husband, Jayson; and Stephanie, another of Danny's oldest friends and the mother of James, one of our favorite and most beloved kids. They'd be lining up to babysit, right? We hoped so, but knew it might be useful to at least hear about less casual childcare solutions.

Logistics aside, we also needed emotional support. Our path to parenthood hadn't been what we'd expected. We'd known the process could be challenging, of course. Many people we loved had had or were having a difficult time. My best friend, Tara, had been through several rounds of in vitro fertilization (IVF). About a year before we started trying to get pregnant, Stephanie developed life-threatening preeclampsia (maternal high blood pressure) at the end of her second trimester. James weighed less than one and a half pounds at his premature birth and spent four months in the Neonatal Intensive Care Unit (NICU) before being discharged to a developmentally complex future. My cousin and his wife have two beautiful sons, but between the boys' births, they endured five miscarriages.

But when I got knocked up on our first try, we forgot those stories. I felt pregnant so quickly, with nausea, cravings, and shocking exhaustion in the first few weeks. We bought *What to Expect When You're Expecting*, came up with a list of names, and bickered over how we'd split up childcare.

At our seven-week prenatal appointment, Dr. Bosch, my OB-GYN, inserted the transvaginal ultrasound probe as I blithely asked, "When do we get a heartbeat?"

Dr. Bosch, usually chatty, went quiet. "Hang on . . ." She was rummaging inside me with her wand, her cursor bouncing all over the ultrasound screen. "I'm afraid I don't see a heartbeat," she said.

"What do you mean?" I said. There are few things sadder than an ultrasound screen where a week before there was a little visible blob of something, and then seeing the opposite: an empty circle, surrounded by fuzzy, blurry, blank space.

"Our timing might be off," Dr. Bosch said.

But I was sure about the date of the night we'd conceived, glasses of wine half finished by the bed, after a luxurious swim in Chris and Randy's heated pool at their house in the Berkshires (sorry, guys, if that's TMI about the conception part in your guest room). I'd been tracking my basal body temperature, and (just like the book said it would if we conceived) it stayed high the next morning and never dropped. Our timing was not off.

Danny interrupted my spiraling thoughts. "Do you have an estimation of the odds?" He's a doctor's kid and doesn't break down around a white coat.

"About fifty-fifty," Dr. Bosch said. She paused, and added gently, "If a pregnancy ends this early, it's the body's way of saying it wasn't meant to be. Come back in a week and then we'll know for sure."

During that week of waiting, my nausea disappeared, my cravings abated, and I cried more than I thought was physically possible. On my next visit, Dr. Bosch's confirmation that I was miscarrying was (almost) a relief.

The next morning, I inserted two oversize white pills into my vagina and popped the first of many painkillers. For the next twelve hours, I writhed on the bed and couch, feeling as if my insides were the part of the garbage truck where the trash gets ground into bits.

My thirty-fifth birthday—coincidentally also my tip into official "advanced maternal age"—was two days later. Trying to celebrate, Danny took me to our local fancy flea market, but then we had to rush home in a car service. I was still bleeding and cramping.

None of this was what *What to Expect When You're Expecting* had led me to expect. Miscarriage, I discovered, is a prolonged event. It takes weeks for the bleeding to stop and months for the body to recover. Why hadn't anyone warned me?

People don't like to talk about death, and miscarriage is a confusing version of mortality. It's sex and blood, but not in a "fun" horror movie sense. Friends recited the same well-meaning platitudes: Once you have a baby, you won't remember. Statistics say you'll have a healthy child soon. Reduce your stress.

I obsessed over how the miscarriage was my fault. I drank a

glass of wine before I knew I was pregnant, ate tuna sushi, carried groceries home from the Food Coop, took the subway, smoked a single cigarette, inhaled truck exhaust on Atlantic Avenue, stepped on sidewalk cracks, slept too little, flew across the country and back in an airplane, rode in a car with my bare feet on the dashboard, worked. I hadn't seen myself as a delicate mechanism, or the new life inside me as fragile as a butterfly.

It didn't matter that Danny, Dr. Bosch, and every book and expert said there was nothing we could have done. Like so many women who suffer difficulties with conceiving or carrying a pregnancy to healthy term, it was as if I *wanted* to blame myself. Without a cause, the loss felt too random.

Looking back now, I recognize that magical thinking, and that my feelings of guilt and self-blame were an integral part of the trauma that accompanies miscarriage.

Back when I was happily pregnant, I'd signed up to attend a writing workshop in upstate New York. While we hadn't actually using the term *babymoon* (too cheesy), Danny and I rented a little cabin in the woods, imagining a cozy time together.

By the time we got to Woodstock, I was still bleeding, bloated, and emotionally and physically unsteady. The other students were so young they were writing about boyfriends and dorm-room epiphanies. I hung out with the instructors, their husbands, and the visiting authors—all of whom were my age. I'd been dying to meet Emily, the final night's reader and the author of several weird and fiercely intellectual novels. Emily brought her one-year-old son, Toby, to the reading. After dinner, he climbed into my lap, as if he knew. With my hormones in free fall, I blurted out my story to his mother.

Emily's eyes were wet when she told me, "Go to my acupuncturist back in the city. She got me pregnant."

This was, I now realize, my first experience with a mommy I didn't know treating *me* like a mother. I would have followed Emily's advice if she'd told me to burn five eagle feathers at the top of a mountain to get pregnant again. A few needles? Easy. Danny and I may have spent the rest of the summer watching *The Wire*, pausing only to cry or fight, but I went to acupuncture every week.

That summer of 2009, it was almost impossible to find narratives about miscarriage and pregnancy loss beyond message boards and blogs. Dr. Bosch was kind and clear, but offered little help. As Danny put it, "We didn't even get a brochure." I could read the stats: up to 25 percent of pregnancies end in miscarriage, and the majority of women who miscarry go on to bear healthy children. Still, I craved voices I could relate to. I wanted a friend.

Emily Bazelon is a senior editor at *Slate*, and the author of the excellent book *Sticks and Stones: Defeating the Culture of Bullying and Rediscovering the Power of Character and Empathy*. She is also the big sister of my best friend from fifth grade. When I found a correspondence she wrote with fellow *Slate* editor Dalia Lithwick about miscarriage, it was like advice from, well, my best friend's older sister. Bazelon notes that it is a "common assumption . . . that it's better . . . to grieve for the loss of a pregnancy in private. . . . Shouldn't we be talking openly about this much more often, so that we're better prepared for the grief when it hits us?"

Amen, sister, I thought. And nodded my head even more fervently reading Lithwick's response: "[H]ospitals that offer massages and hot tubs and music for new mommies also need to provide spaces—both physical and psychological—for the almost-mommies as well."

Reading these words didn't make my pain go away, but they did give me more of a context for my feelings. I wasn't alone.

. . . .

In October, after weekly acupuncture and diligently timed sex, I saw two pink lines on an EPT stick again. After a couple of weeks, it was over. A "chemical pregnancy," Dr. Bosch called it, explaining that this time the egg didn't even implant. "You probably couldn't tell you were pregnant," an acquaintance and the mother of two healthy children said to me. Tell that to my body, which had certainly felt pregnant as it told me to eat yogurt, cheese, and pudding like a dairy-only vampire. Tell that to my heart. Tell that to my marriage.

Structure helped. More acupuncture, hours at the gym, a daily writing word count. Once again, I yearned for the veil of secrecy around miscarriage to be lifted. I didn't think my experience was private. It was as public and important as an illness—or a healthy pregnancy. Still, most people didn't know what to say when I bluntly told them what I was going through. A simple "I'm sorry" would have sufficed. As would the offer of a margarita.

I got pregnant for the third time in early February and, true to my supersensitive system, by Valentine's Day, I could tell. Danny and I went out for dinner, cautiously celebrating with a virgin cocktail for me (he had the real stuff) and fried chicken.

At our "heartbeat" appointment with Dr. Bosch, I refused to face the ultrasound screen until Dr. Bosch and Danny both exclaimed, "*Look!*"

Turning my head, I saw her for the first time, a fuzzy vibrating ball on the black-and-white screen. This image was my child: all heartbeat, all heart. My heart, my love, my Clara.

Then heartbreak, though not for us directly. Tara was finally pregnant, and due a few months ahead of me. Though she lived in

Berlin (her husband is German), she'd decided to have her baby in New York, her former home. We were loving being pregnant together, finally, feasting on carbs, shopping for secondhand maternity clothes, and planning our new baby time.

One afternoon she called me, weeping, "There's no more heartbeat." She'd been twenty weeks along.

Tara's loss occurred just as I approached the end of my first trimester. I was days away from my nuchal fold test, the standard ultrasound and blood work to check for markers of chromosomal abnormalities, including Down syndrome. This was the first time we'd be able to confirm that everything was "right" with the pregnancy. Yet all we could think about was how terribly wrong it had gone for my friend.

On the morning of my nuchal, I woke at five in the morning, my inner thighs sticky with bright red blood. Waking Danny, I tried not to be hysterical, but it was hard. Whatever was going wrong felt inevitable to both of us by now.

"It's probably fine," Dr. Bosch said over the phone. "But come in for a check."

We were at her office by the time it opened at eight.

She was right. "There's that heartbeat!" she said, pointing to the vibration on the screen. "Everything's perfect."

"Then why am I bleeding?"

"Hmmm . . ." She slid in the good ol' speculum and went down for a peek. "Looks like a cervical polyp. Just a little growth of extra tissue. Very common, no big deal. Go have your nuchal and we'll talk about it more later."

Danny and I were so relieved, we went out for a lavish breakfast, followed by an early show of Tim Burton's *Alice in Wonderland* and an even more lavish lunch.

The nuchal test wasn't in Dr. Bosch's office, but in the "real" ultrasound lab in the hospital a few blocks away, with a waiting room full of pregnant ladies who made my barely-there bump look silly.

"Are all of those women having twins?" I asked the tech as she walked us into our room.

"No, darling," she said in an Eastern European accent and with a smirk. "Don't worry, you'll get that big soon enough."

The room was dark so we could see the screen.

"Is everything all right? I've been bleeding and I miscarried twice and I'm worried . . ." I was so nervous I was babbling. Danny stood silently by my side, holding my hand.

"Look, Mama, there's the spine," the tech said. "And the brain."

"It's good?"

"I'm not allowed to say because I'm not doctor," she said. "But . . . don't worry."

The doctor confirmed her all clear. We cried then, with relief and joy. Another bridge crossed. Now, what to do about the bleeding?

When we returned to Dr. Bosch's office, she explained more.

"Cervical polyps are very common and should not affect your pregnancy or delivery," she told us. "But we don't want you bleeding. No exercise or sex for the whole second trimester, and you get extra monitoring." She paused and looked me meaningfully in the eye. "Stay away from Google."

(As soon as I got home, I disobeyed her last command and regretted it forever. Especially noteworthy cervical polyps look like witch fingers or carrots poking out of their hosts' vaginas. Three years later, when Heidi had a cervical polyp with baby number two, she also didn't take her doctor's advice and I finally got to "process" those images, both of us shrieking and sputtering together. Google is not always your friend.)

A few weeks later, Danny and I were cooking dinner when I suddenly felt a gush of blood. Heading to the ER in a car service, I told Danny that if this pregnancy didn't stick, we'd take a trip and get a dog.

"Okay," he said, staring straight ahead.

Everything, thank God, was fine. *Take it easy*, the doctor said.

By the time we had our anatomy scan at twenty weeks, my bleeding had indeed stopped. We also got the best news: we were having a healthy girl. We dared, finally, to think this was real.

"How about Clara?" I said to Danny. "Because it means 'light.'"

"And Clara Schumann," he added.

"I want her middle name to be Yetta," I said.

"Of course."

Yetta, my beloved paternal grandmother, had passed away five years earlier. She would protect our girl. She knew how important this was.

Still, things kept going wrong(ish). On a vacation to visit Danny's family in Los Angeles at five months pregnant, I tripped on the sidewalk, landing flat and hard on my stomach (note: do not even try to walk in LA). I called Dr. Bosch, who ordered me to the ER, again. At Cedars-Sinai, my adrenaline rush was so extreme that Clara kicked the fetal monitor off my belly from inside and the nurse asked if my husband beat me. The next day, I bought a bracelet of glass beads meant to ward off the evil eye. And I decided that this pregnancy was never going to be great. I'd just have to push through it.

. . . .

No wonder that when I showed Danny the email about the Mommy Group meeting, he wanted me to go. Danny's an insomniac, which means he's always visibly tired. Now he looked beat. Dark circles seemed permanently set under his sweet blue eyes, he'd stopped shaving more than once a week sometime in February, and his nails were bitten down to pink quick. Danny was right: I—we—needed the support.

On the appointed Tuesday night, I walked up the steps in a Park Slope brownstone, pregnantly gasping a little for breath as I reached the second-floor apartment.

"Hey, come on in. I'm Anna." The woman who greeted me at the door looked about my age (late thirties), with a bump twice the size of mine, blond hair, and extraordinary, seemingly painted-on blue eyes. She wore a psychedelic-print maternity tunic with frayed bellbottom jeans, her feet bare. I couldn't tell what I thought of her. Was she fancy? Cool? After following her into the apartment, I exhaled: the same standard renter's Home Depot fixtures as in my own apartment, and a decor of third-world tchotchkes and comfortably battered furniture.

Other women were already sitting in a circle of chairs in the living room. Anna had laid out a spread and everyone was eating with the glorious unself-consciousness of visible pregnancy, plates piled with cookies, brownies, chips, cheese, fruit, and crudités. Sinking awkwardly into an armchair, I recognized the women next to me. She was Asian—Korean, I guessed—with dark hair in a shiny long bob, fancy maternity jeans, and a good bag hanging off her chair. I started mentally rolling through the places we could have met: college, the OB's office, a party back before my social life was limited to couch tacos and rooms full of random pregnant strangers . . .

"Hi!" she greeted me in a whisper. "Prenatal yoga, right? I'm Renée."

"Oh yeah. I kind of stopped going," I said with only a tiny bit of guilt.

"Me too!" Being pregnant yoga dropouts was not the deepest point of connection, but I'd take it.

Before we had a chance to chat more, Anna called the group to order. She'd settled on a rocking chair by the front window, her belly resting comfortably on her crossed legs. "I thought we could go around the circle and introduce ourselves. Maybe say what week we are, whether we know the baby's gender, where we're delivering, and our occupations? I'll start. I'm Anna, obviously, and I'm twenty-four weeks pregnant, due in September. I'm having a girl—which I'm so happy about. I'm a family law attorney. I recently opened my own practice here in Brooklyn. I'm not sure how it's gonna work after the baby. I guess if anyone has any nanny recs, I'm looking." *Nanny recs?* I thought. I was so not there yet. Should I be there yet?

"Obviously, this is my first baby." She gestured at her stomach. "I'm kind of nervous to have you all here." I felt my face form a polite party smile. "I'm delivering at NYU. I had a miscarriage before this, and they did my D&C, so I stuck with the same hospital and doctor." We all stopped chewing, watching Anna as she tucked a strand of blond hair behind her ear. "It's been scary," she added.

Even with my bleeding cervical polyp, my insecurity, and my fear of how I was going to manage a newborn, a marriage, and my life as an artist and make money . . . there, in Anna's messy, human apartment, I felt safe for the first time in a long time. The other women in the circle were nodding their heads at her words. These were not a bunch of Pollyannas crowing, "Once you're out of the first trimester, pregnancy is great!"

"I was so sick the first trimester," Anna continued, "I took a leave from work and went to my parents' house for a month to recuperate. I had to take drugs they give people who are having chemotherapy. If you saw someone vomiting in a trash can on Seventh Ave recently"—the main drag of the neighborhood—"that was me. Okay, I'm gonna shut up now. Next."

She turned to the woman to her left.

"Hi, I'm Jane." She had brown hair in a ponytail and wore a print skirt and plain sweater. No makeup, and she was knitting a complicated-looking beanie. "I'm a social worker. I'm going to quit my job when I have this kid. Which is probably crazy, because I hate feeling unoccupied." She gestured to her knitting. "I'm from the Pacific Northwest. Portland. I've been lucky. My pregnancy hasn't been bad. I'm much more nervous about having a baby!"

As the next few women spoke, I tried to listen, but I was preoccupied with Anna's and Jane's honesty. They'd been up front about their fears, more like we were in group therapy than at a party.

Renée went for more brownie (I was soon to learn: typical with her and the chocolate) before it was her turn to talk.

"This is my second baby," she said. "For my first, Charlie—he's three now—I was in San Francisco. I wasn't working, and I had my mom there. I forgot what a strange state pregnancy can be. It's alienating. In that, you feel like an alien. That is, I do." She took a huge bite of brownie.

I was up next. "I'm Elizabeth," I said. "I'm a writer, and I also teach. I'm due October twentieth, which is exciting because my husband and I can't wait to have Halloween birthday parties . . ." This seemed a little sorority girl to me, and not brave. "Um . . . I also had a miscarriage. Two actually. And I have also been having a hard time."

The women in the circle met my eyes, sympathetic, not judgmental. I breathed.

Before the silence became awkward, Anna spoke again. "I downloaded some questions for new moms' groups off the internet." She picked up a stack of index cards from the table next to her. "What is your favorite thing about being pregnant? I'll go first: I love the sex."

Jane snorted and Renée rolled her eyes. No one tried to answer the question. We were all laughing too much.

Even though there'd been a lot of honesty in the room (as they say) at that first meeting, I wasn't sure it would be a *thing*. It was summer now, and so bloody hot I rarely wanted to leave the house. Sure, a few of the other women had cheered me up, but it didn't have to *mean* anything. Maybe that get-together was like a good blind date that's fun at the time but doesn't go anywhere in the end.

Then I saw the women pushing newborns in their strollers around the neighborhood. They looked tired when they were alone, and happy when other moms were chatting and pushing beside them. I was relieved when Anna wrote again about a month after our first "date."

Her email was perky but with just enough complaint to make it interesting:

Hi Folks!

How many people have asked you about the heat??? It is rough heading into third trimester with the sun beating down on you while you are walking uphill. Park Slope needs a nice, big outdoor pool reserved for pregnant women! And a special air-conditioned cafe with recliners. I would love to see how you're coming along!

Almost against my own will, I responded with an equally chipper "I'm in! I can even host!" Maybe it was lucky when only Renée, Jane, and Anna responded. To round out the group, I invited Antonia, a friend I'd known since we taught Freshman Writing 101 at a local college and shared an office back in the early oughts. Her baby boy was due in July. From Melbourne, Australia, Antonia moved to the States as a sort of lark, fell in love with her now-husband, Dillon, and never left. I found her to be a salty yet comforting presence.

The day before the party, I cooked two whole boxes of pasta for a chilled salad, put the extra leaf in our dining room table, and happily watched Danny clean the bathroom (pregnant-lady privilege).

Anna, the first to arrive, fanned herself with a piece of mail; our living room was not air-conditioned. Renée and Antonia arrived together, introducing themselves to each other on my doorstep.

"I took a car service," Renée said. "I feel like such a wimp, but I can't walk two blocks anymore."

Antonia was stoic. "Well, it'll be better once we have the babies." She laughed. "Right?"

Jane arrived straight from a trip to Shelter Island with her mother. Though she didn't tell us at the time, she hadn't wanted to come but had forced herself. "I thought there might be something important for me to get from the group," she told me later.

Once they were all sitting around the table, no one wanted my pasta salad.

"I'm too pregnant to eat," Antonia told me. "No more room."

"Do you have anything frozen?" Anna asked.

"I already ate," Jane said.

We complained more about the heat, and then about who got seats on the subway.

"People told me no one would get up, and they were right," Antonia said.

"I always get a seat," I bragged. "I'm forceful. I ask people to get up! Okay, I did that once. But it worked."

"All I want to do is swim," Anna contributed. "Anyone want to go to the Red Hook pool with me?"

Sure, we all vaguely agreed. The Red Hook pool was a long bus ride away.

"What are you wearing for bathing suits?" I asked. "All I have is a bikini."

"Shorts and a tank top," said Jane.

"You have shorts that fit?"

Anna giggled. "I have the dowdiest, most stretched out hand-me-down maternity suit. Full-on eighties lady, with polka dots. But I'm rocking it, girls."

"Do you think it's crazy to go tubing?" Jane asked. "My mother is here for another few days, and she suggested horseback riding upstate." We all looked at her in horror. "Tubing is a compromise!"

Antonia changed the subject. "So let's get down to it. What are your birth plans? My sister had all of her babies at home. It's much more acceptable outside the States. I was thinking about a home birth, but it seemed a little too intense. We've decided on the Brooklyn Birthing Center. Anyone else going that route?"

We shook our heads, though we'd all heard about it. The only freestanding (as in, not inside a hospital) birthing center left in New York City, the Brooklyn Birthing Center is low-tech and midwife staffed. In routine—that is, uncomplicated—births (and the majority of births are uncomplicated), such an off-site center can provide an empowering and less "medicalized" alternative to the traditional labor and delivery experience. But if complications arise, the laboring mother must be taken via ambulance to the nearest cooperating hospital, where her baby will be delivered by an OB whom she's most likely never met.

"I want to use the birthing center at St. Luke's," I explained. I was big on my plan to deliver at the only *on*-site, *in*-hospital birthing center in the city. There would be a tub, and Danny could stay over without having to pay the astronomical private room fee in the regular labor and delivery ward. I'd be able eat and walk around with minimal monitoring. I hoped.

After dinner, we took a photo, standing in a semicircle. We'd chosen each other, and we wanted a record. When I look at the photo now, I think, *We were so young!* Maybe it was the softening effects of late pregnancy, the wider nose and fuller lips. Or maybe it's the look in our eyes: truly expectant.

Anna, Renée, and Jane left together, forming enough of a phalanx to flag down a bus on Seventh Avenue because there was no way they could run to the next stop. They all got seats.

Before starting a family, I'd thought about community, but mostly in the "friends as family" model of many urbanites who have left their hometowns. This is typical for a middle-class, college-educated Generation X woman such as myself. Generation X encompasses people born between 1965 and 1980. We're a sort of sad sandwich, "bookended by two much larger generations—the Baby Boomers ahead and the Millennials behind" (according to a study by the Pew Research Center). Gen X–ers are old enough to remember the Iran hostage crisis but too young for the Beatles. According to my nonscientific Facebook poll, current Gen X parents "grew up on Cheerios and Lucky Charms but feed our kids organic granola," remember "black and white TVs that got six channels" and bumping around free of seat belts in the "way back" of station wagons. Our children play with iPads and "sit in booster car seats until college." They also face potentially calamitous climate change and environmental destruction. No wonder we're so nervous for them.

Our mothers were second-wave feminists, breaking glass ceilings, taking advantage of the pill and *Roe v. Wade*, wearing power suits. My mother is a visual artist (a potter and sculptor, to be exact), and she taught full-time from when I was in first grade. She always seemed so confident in her work-life balance. If I complained about chicken for dinner again, or whined that I was always the last kid waiting to be picked up at school, she would say, "Tough shit. You're fine." Though she now admits she felt guilty seeing me sitting alone on the school steps, like many feminist Boomer women, she was invested in the idea that she could do it all, with no complaints and no regrets.

We were the latchkey kids (well, I wasn't—once again, I was waiting at school for my mom to arrive, NPR blasting from her battered Renault compact), and our parents did not "helicopter." We rode our bikes to elementary school and took the subway by ourselves when we were ten.

Even our children's books were about *not* always getting what we wanted. In Judith Viorst's 1972 picture book *Alexander and the Terrible, Horrible, No Good, Very Bad Day*, the titular character experiences bad dreams, bad breakfast, and bad sneakers. When he threatens to move to Australia, his parents don't stop to fix all his boo-boos with kisses and *Toy Story*–branded Band-Aids. They're having bad days, too, and he needs to deal. In Russell Hoban's 1964 classic *Bread and Jam for Francis*, the little badger's parents feed her just that until she gets sick and asks for different food. She's no wannabe princess whose parents accommodate her desire to wear only pink, as in Victoria Kann's 2006 bestseller *Pinkalicious*.

Our parents' benign neglect had a reasonable root cause: 50 percent of their marriages ended in divorce, a trend that Gen X is *not* continuing. A December 2014 piece in the *New York Times* by Claire Cain Miller explained that the divorce rate has been in steady decline since its peak in the seventies and early eighties.

This is in part due to feminism's success. "Marriage has evolved to its modern-day form," Miller explains, "based on love and shared passions, and often two incomes and shared housekeeping duties." The trend is most prevalent for middle-class marriages. Women with some means have more choices than their poorer and more marginalized counterparts, especially of the family planning and work-related variety.

My own story is both typical and not of my demographic. I was born in 1974, in Philadelphia. My mother, Vicky, is (as I explained above) a potter, and my father, Larry, is a musician; they've been married for almost fifty years. When they had me, they were in their midtwenties and barely knew anyone else their age with a kid, but they stayed in their hometown, close to family. My mother didn't have problems during or after her pregnancy.

Ever since I was a little girl, I knew I wanted to be a writer and a mother. I moved to New York for college in 1992 and never left. As I strode through my twenties, working a zillion weird jobs, going to graduate school, getting my heart broken, staying out until 3:00 a.m., I didn't think much about the motherhood part. I was ambitious, and parenthood would come after I found the right guy and wrote my first book.

Danny grew up in Southern California, came east to Boston for many years of graduate school, and then "immigrated" to New York in 2000. When we met, he was thirty-three and I was twenty-nine. I was working on a memoir and a novel, he wrote chamber music and operas. In order to make it in postapocalyptic, gilded-but-about-to-credit-crash New York City, we took every freelance gig we could find, worked odd hours on our own projects, and relied on the kindness and generosity of our families. We didn't get married until we'd been together for four years, and even after we were hitched in 2007, we decided to wait at least a year before trying to get pregnant.

I wouldn't have married Danny unless I was sure this was the guy I wanted with me as I tried to push a baby out of my body and, later, teach our kid to sing and dance along to the "Time Warp," or text her to come home *right now* from that no-adults party. Danny is one of the most reliable people I've ever known, as well the most brilliant and eccentric. Of course I wanted to have a baby with the guy who introduced me to the pleasures of operas by Arnold Schoenberg and *Buffy the Vampire Slayer* (the show, *not* the film). The guy who, on a cross-country road trip, insisted on stopping at every assassination and disaster site between Los Angeles and Miami (the grassy knoll in Dallas, Oklahoma City's Federal Building, Los Alamos, a fundamentalist Christian theme park—okay, that was my idea), but only asked me to drive for twenty minutes in two weeks.

Even so, before getting pregnant, we still felt as if we had things to figure out about how to live together. We were both independent, used to our eccentric bohemian lives and schedules. Neither of us is great about doing dishes or sweeping up crumbs. Danny didn't know how to cook, and I wanted him to learn before I was sidelined with morning sickness and swollen feet. Plus, we were having so much fun together.

One night, in our pre-Clara existence, Danny played the piano for a variety show of different musicians and writers. After the gig, we were at a bar in the Village with the other performers. One was a singer-songwriter who reminded me of Laura Nyro, all dark eyes and passionate lyrics. Another was a Jamaican-British woman who played her opera-in-progress on the piano, clad in a leopard print party dress. Our conversation was equal parts shop talk and tipsy gush. When I stepped out of the bar for a smoke, I looked up at New York's night sky and knew I was lucky. Being broke is okay when you stay out late drinking wine with brilliant people. The next day's slog of rewrites, rejections, and crummy money gigs are almost tolerable.

Two years later, I was a new mother, so confused and exhausted that the thought of going out to the wee hours, let alone to a concert, was paralyzing. The people from my pre-baby life didn't seem to miss me much, or even to think about me beyond clicking "like" on one of Clara's photos on my Facebook page. I'd always been the kind of person who hung out with my friends who had babies. I *loved* babies. Now I realized I was an exception.

It may be a cliché to say, "It takes a village to raise a child," but sometimes the clichés are right. For many women, the phrase raises a bigger question: Where do you find a village? My mother never had anything like a group. As she might have said, she was too independent for that shit. But my grandmother sure had one.

As I mentioned earlier, I was very close to my father's mother, Yetta Gold. Before I was old enough for kindergarten, I spent several days a week at her house, joining her life and routine. And that routine involved a community of women and families she'd known for more than three decades.

Yetta and my grandfather Lenny had their first son, Steven, during World War II, when my grandfather was in the US Navy (stationed on a battleship that never pulled out of Norfolk, Virginia). In the late forties, they bought a small storefront house in Kensington, a blue-collar neighborhood in North Philadelphia. Len's Yellow Front was an all-purpose joint of the kind that no longer exists, with inventory ranging from Mickey Mouse watches to (literal) nuts and bolts.

My dad was born in 1948, and my uncle Richard in 1953. As their family grew, Yetta's need for community did as well. Her own mother, who immigrated to the States from Russia alone when she was nine, died young. Yetta had no female relatives to pass on secrets of childrearing or to help her find her place as a mother in a new era and culture.

But even had her mother lived, she wouldn't have fulfilled all of Yetta's needs—and not just because she spoke only Yiddish and was semiliterate. A new mom's mother might help her get her infant to latch, or might know the special soup that's helped generations of women recover from the blood loss and exhaustion of childbirth.

But a new mother's mother loves her baby like her own. She can't be the repository of her daughter's frustration or fears, or hear how she might—God forbid—feel out of control.

Yetta's mother would not have been able to tell her where (based on photo evidence of my pregnant grandmother) to find a flattering Lucy Ricardo–style maternity smock, or how much TV is too much for a three-year-old boy (a lot, in my uncle Ricky's case). For that, a new mother needs friends.

Yetta found them. The other Jews in the neighborhood were also shopkeepers: Dottie and Al Frost down the block had the children's shoe store, Nate and Gloria Lipschitz were the pharmacists, the Ostroffs were chocolatiers, and the Elkans sold underwear. Throughout their years of early motherhood, my grandmother and the women of these families helped each other navigate a world that had completely changed since their own Depression-era childhoods.

My father was in the first class of Philadelphia's first magnet middle school for gifted children because Ida Shipley, two doors down, worked for the Board of Education and told Yetta about it. Dottie came from down the block to spend the night with the two older boys when Yetta went into labor with Ricky. In photos of bar mitzvahs and anniversary parties, my grandmother is standing next to friends as often as family.

Their community ties didn't fade when the kids grew up, either. Nate at the pharmacy tattled to Yetta when my twentysomething hippie dad kept refilling prescriptions for pharmaceutical cocaine. When Dottie's youngest son got divorced, my grandmother stayed friends with his ex, a "lovely woman." When they entered old age, they supported each other through mastectomies and dialysis, even death. These families are buried in adjacent plots at the same cemetery.

That's what my grandmother's mommy group meant to her. I hope it's what my Mommy Group comes to mean for me, as well. (Though not the death part; I hope we can all be cryogenically frozen or something by then.)

American women of my generation are tending to have our children later than previous generations. (As I searched for this data, and no matter how I rewrote my search terms, Google kept directing me to the Wikipedia entry for "Advanced Maternal Age." Nice.) We are also less likely to live in the places we grew up. According to a 1998 report from the Pew Research Center, "College education is a key marker of the likelihood to move." People who stay in their home-towns tend to do so because of family ties and the ease of raising children in the communities they already know; those who leave usually do so for professional reasons.

Everyone in the Mommy Group was (at least) college-educated, we were all in our mid to late thirties when we met, and we'd lived away from our hometowns for years. Only one of us, Heidi, even had a sister in New York City. We were, in many ways, building our own new culture of parenting in the big city. No wonder we needed each other so much.

It was late July when we had the final Mommy Group meeting before the first of our babies were due. A week earlier, I'd been diagnosed with gestational diabetes.

GD is a common pregnancy complication, but left untreated or uncontrolled it can have serious outcomes: babies too large for safe delivery, preterm labor, preeclampsia. The medical protocol wasn't easy. I had to prick my finger with a mechanized lancet five times a day to test my sugar, record everything I ate, and swear off ice cream, lemonade, and even fruit—during the hottest summer in New York history. My chances of making it to the Birthing Center were pretty much shot. My pregnancy was now "high-risk."

Physically, I was fine; GD was just a pain in the butt. But emotionally, in what I now realize was my already traumatized and anxious mind, this seemed like the final confirmation that I was bad at being pregnant, doing permanent damage to Clara and my own body.

The Mommies understood how stressed I felt. For the first time, our meeting buffet didn't feature cookies or chocolate. Instead, Anna and Renée set out nuts, cheese, and a rotisserie chicken. "We didn't want to make you feel bad because you couldn't eat treats," Renée said. Other, well-meaning friends were telling me, "One cupcake won't hurt you." These women, still so new in my life (and who were practically living on chocolate themselves), were so careful of my physical and emotional needs. I wept over the bowl of cashews.

We were all still pregnant then. By the next meeting, some of us had crossed the bridge into motherhood.

2. The Babies Arrive!

I Believe We're Falling in Love

From Renée

November 9, 2010

It does definitely get easier, but never easy. Those first few months are so unfamiliar and sleep deprived that I think no matter how much you might try to prepare, it could never be enough. What got me through last time, and is getting me through this time, is a group of friends to share all the craziness with. Thanks everyone.

It was August, an even hotter point of that hottest summer, and I was hosting Mommy Group at my house again. Renée couldn't come. She was home that night, having early contractions. Emme arrived a day later, with labor going too fast for the epidural her mama had been counting on. But I didn't know that yet. What I did know: Antonia and Jane were on their way with their babies! We finally had some babies!

Augustus and Katherine, who will forever be known as Gus and Katie, were born within days of each other: Gus on July 27, weighing eight pounds eight ounces (ouch!), and Katie on July 29, coming in at six pounds nine ounces. I'd seen their photos on

Facebook: squinty, wrapped in the hospital receiving blankets, and wearing those little stripy caps that all newborns get. But I hadn't met them yet.

"We have to feed people who are *nursing* now," I told Danny. "We'll need several chickens. We could get ice cream, even if I can only eat baby carrots. I hate gestational diabetes. Do you think Jane and Antonia will want special chairs, or will they sit on the sofa to nurse? What about footstools?"

"We don't have any footstools," Danny said.

Antonia had only had a few blocks to travel, but she took a cab, still unable to walk much. Carl tagged along with Jane to carry Katie up our steep stairs in her car seat, and then left to go have a beer and read a book by himself until she called him for pickup.

Once everyone was unpacked and set up, I dared to check out the babies. They were too small to even focus their eyes on each other less than a foot away, cradled in their mamas' arms. I couldn't decide if they were cute. Still, I was compelled to hold them, to feel their little bodies and their breath.

"Pleased to meet you," I cooed.

Jane and Antonia seemed different. It wasn't simply that their bellies were smaller, their breasts swollen to gargantuan size, and the purple circles under their eyes looked like tattoos. They knew things now that the rest of us pregnant ladies didn't, from their different spot in the space-time continuum.

Jane was still jazzed from drugs and sore from her C-section, holding two-week-old Katie in the crook of her arm, her boob out, trying to get her to latch on as she chattered. "I saw a lactation consultant at the doctor's office this week. She kept telling me Katie had birth trauma." She paused for a moment, blinked, and continued. "That was not helpful." Katie regarded her mother's nipple as a Victorian entomologist might examine a particularly rare species of Amazonian beetle: in astonishment, and with caution. "Come on, baby, you gotta eat! She still hasn't regained her birth weight, and everyone's freaking out."

"This nursing thing, it's bloody awful, right?" Antonia said, bouncing Gus in her arms. He squalled, almost soundlessly, scrunching up his face until it was bright red. "I don't know how we're supposed to do all of this, with sleep deprivation, after giving *birth*, for God's sake. Nature is an asshole."

I was glad Clara wasn't ready to pop quite yet. Jane and Antonia were talking like survivors or veterans.

"How did the births go? We want stories!" Anna and I were eager to hear.

"I'll go first," Jane said.

Jane delivered at a local Brooklyn hospital, rather than one of the fancier Manhattan institutions many of us chose. "I didn't want to seem picky," she said. "My whole idea about birth was that it was natural, and this would be good enough. I don't know if it would have made a difference, but I wonder."

Jane is small-boned but strong, with long dark hair and pale skin. As a social worker, she is sensible and educated about the ways of systems and protocols. True to her "Portlandia" roots, when it comes to her own care, she tends to a combination of medical and alternative.

It was a long labor. Her water broke at home, but when she and Carl got to the hospital, her labor didn't progress. The doctor induced her with Cervidil and Pitocin. Then she needed an epidural. By the time she needed to push, she was exhausted, and then the monitors started beeping too loud and fast. It was a "stat" situation, an emergency: the baby was losing oxygen. Time for a C-section *now*.

"You won't feel a thing," the anesthesiologist said, but she thought she did feel it, the incision, the opening of her body as the OB pulled her weakened daughter out. She hallucinated that she was a dolphin on the table, her arms flippers. Katie's APGAR—the score given to newborns to assess their health—was low initially, though they rose in a few minutes after she was warmed and washed. Meanwhile, too weak and medicated to talk, Jane heard the intern asking the attending surgeon how to put her uterus back into her body.

Katie had severe jaundice and was whisked off to the NICU while Jane was still in recovery. Having a baby in the NICU is one of the most stressful experiences imaginable for parents. It's a locked ward, and due to the premature and sick babies' compromised immune systems, only a few people are allowed in at a time. Visitors have to scrub their hands, surgeon-style. The preemies' domed and sealed bassinets are designed to imitate conditions in the womb, and the babies, clad only in diapers and hats and covered in tubes and tape, look even more like plucked chickens than most newborns. Katie and the other jaundiced beans basked under ultraviolet lights, wearing tiny sunglasses like miniature George Hamiltons.

As Jane talked, I flashed back to Danny's and my friend Stephanie's story. She's the one who, two years earlier, developed life-threatening preeclampsia and had to deliver her son James a full trimester early. Because of her own surgery and James's critical condition, Steph didn't meet him until he was two days old and she could walk herself into the NICU. By then, she was convinced the doctors were lying to her and that there was something far worse wrong with her son.

Katie's birth was not as dangerous as James's had been, but Jane still didn't get to see her baby for more than twelve hours.

Neither of them could be moved, and there was no way for them to be in the same room.

"I wish I hadn't had a C-section. If I'd had a little more time," Jane said. "These New York hospitals really try to get you in and out. I keep thinking it would have been different in Portland."

"Well, I had a natural birth," Antonia said, and we could almost see the quote marks around "natural." "And let me tell you, I am not feeling particularly in the pink."

Antonia is six feet tall, and she's run marathons ("*a* marathon," she's corrected me, but still). She has both an expatriate's sophistication and perspective, as well as a somewhat scoffing Aussie approach to danger. Just what she'd need in order to choose what for many women would be the intimidatingly no-frills, there-is-no-doctor-in-the-house Brooklyn Birthing Center.

That evening, she told us the whole story. Later on, I was able to interview both her and Dillon about Gus's birth as well. Their diverging versions clarified a crucial point about birth for me: what happens to the mother does *not* happen to her partner.

At first, Antonia's labor went according to plan. When she started feeling contractions, she stayed at home until they were close enough to warrant heading to the Birthing Center. Then all the rooms were full ("even though on the tour they told us that *never* happened"). She labored in the hall, bouncing on a yoga ball, walking when she could, in progressively worse pain. By the time a room freed up, she'd been awake for twenty-four hours and was dozing off between contractions. More hours passed.

"Finally, the midwife said, 'Okay, you're fully dilated. It's time to push,'" Antonia told us. Much later, after Antonia had her *second* baby, Verne, she understood: "I never had that 'urge to push' with Gus."

Still, she pushed. Like Katie, Gus went into distress.

"You need to go to the hospital now," the midwife said.

Antonia tried not to panic as she was rolled to the ambulance on a stretcher, an oxygen mask strapped to her face. When I asked Dillon about it later, he shook his head. He is even taller than his wife, and I imagined him crouching by her side as the ambulance bumped over Brooklyn's potholed streets. The hospital was chaotic. Maimonides Medical Center, in Borough Park, Brooklyn, is huge—their website boasts that they perform (host?) more than eight thousand labor and deliveries each year.

Waiting in triage, Antonia lay on a gurney, panting and pushing. A doctor she'd never seen before approached her and blankly told her, "We have to get you into surgery."

"'At least examine me,'" Antonia told us she said to the doctor. We were riveted, it was like a movie: *The Battle for Gus.* "I remembered what to say from birth class. Before they cut, find out how long you have. I asked her, 'Am I in danger? Is my baby in danger?'"

"What happened?" I couldn't help but shout. I was cradling my own belly, scared.

"She examined me and said, 'You can have another ten minutes.' He must have been coming out superquick, because all of a sudden, she said, 'Stop pushing!'"

Dillon was trying his best, stroking his wife's shoulder as she slowed down.

"Don't fucking touch me!" Antonia shouted at him.

"I backed off," he told me later.

Antonia explained, "What I needed was fierce animal energy. Not someone touching me like this . . ." She softly stroked her own arm to demonstrate.

I got it. In our birthing class, we'd watched endless movies week after week. They all looked to have been shot in the mid-eighties. The laboring mothers had permed hair and Princess Di–style maternity blouses. Their husbands were milquetoasts, stroking their wives' backs, gently encouraging them to breathe. "If you get in my face and touch me like that, I'm going to kick you across the room," I'd whispered to Danny.

But back to Antonia's birth: Dillon was worried about the doctor. "She didn't think that Toni was gonna be able to do it."

Neither did Antonia's mother, even though she'd delivered her own four children in her bed in a hippie cottage in the middle of the bush in Queensland. "Maybe you should go to the OR," she told her daughter.

Antonia disagreed. "I was like, *Fuck you all! I'm pushing out this baby!*" So she did. But the cord was around his neck.

Dillon remembers the birth from another angle. "Gus came out so fast they almost dropped him."

The doctor cut the cord away. He was blue, as many infants are at birth.

"Is he okay?" Antonia shouted. He was just fine, but Antonia didn't believe them.

Antonia was wheeled into the OR to be stitched up (at last receiving an epidural), still not having seen her baby. She added, "I had to get an episiotomy, which I wasn't even conscious of at the time. I think the OB was being scalpel-happy down there. I mean, I had all these lacerations." She lowered her voice conspiratorially, raised an eyebrow, and whispered. "And there's no sharp bits on a baby."

Eventually she was taken up to the maternity ward.

"And then there was Gus," she said. "Look at him. Gorgeous, right?"

We cheered the end of her heroic story, but Antonia delivered the last word. "In conclusion, again, this natural birth thing is for shit."

"We really should have hired a doula," Jane said, and Antonia nodded in agreement. "I mean, I don't know if it would have made a difference, but maybe Carl and I would have felt less alone."

Later that night I repeated their stories to Danny.

"A doula," he said. "What's that?"

"I think she does what an experienced sister or a friend would do," I said. "I don't know. She helps you during the birth."

"Can we get one?" Danny asked. "I want one. For me."

Our doula, Willa, had red hair and laughed at our jokes. She'd attended many births as well as having two of her own children. She promised not to rub my back in a tickling fashion while I had contractions, and that she wouldn't natter on about having an "orgasmic" or "peaceful" birth. I hoped she would do the trick, because as each of the Mommies gave birth, I was getting more worried.

In early August, Heidi labored for over twenty-four hours before her C-section. She'd known that Clay was supposed to be big (his head has turned out to be consistently large), and her doctor told her to prepare for a likely surgery. When she went into labor, "the hospital was so overcrowded, my OB was on her BlackBerry texting for backup between my legs while I pushed."

Once she came home, she felt better. Clay was healthy and strong, and because of their ground-floor apartment, she was able to take him outside for small forays even with her incision hurting (stairs make a big difference). Her mother and mother-in-law both stayed in apartments on our block, which meant she had food, laundry, and company covered.

Melissa's experience (which we heard about after the fact, as she joined the group when Sofia was already two months old) was simpler in many ways. Sofia was a breech in utero—butt first. She tried all the techniques to turn her, but no dice. So a few days before her due date, Melissa checked into the hospital and received a scheduled C-section. No labor, no pushing. Sounds dreamy, right? Not necessarily. Yes, she avoided the exhaustion and fear of natural, and complicated, labor. But she also missed the hormonal feedback that spontaneous labor triggers in a mother's body.

Anna gave birth in September. Like Jane and Heidi, she labored for over a day, then had surgery. *Hi girls*, she texted us from the hospital. *Not the easiest delivery. Ended up with cesarean. Can't win them all. It's been rough but she is beautiful and sweet.*

Within two weeks, she was writing us again, with shocking news.

3. Love and Marriage

Small People, Big Problems

From Anna

November 1, 2010

Can someone normalize my emotions? My husband seems to think that me napping a couple of hours will enable me to stay up with an inconsolable infant all night long. I DON'T THINK SO! Might take the edge off the evening hour but not the three-in-the-morning madness. Let him take care of an infant all day and I'll go to work full-time as a corporate lawyer. This is harder—to nurse, pump, change, nurse, pump, change. I don't think he understands what it is like to be the milk machine. Anyone with me?

Stephan and Anna had been together since they were undergrads at the University of Illinois, meeting in a literature class. She was a vocal major, and he was an international student, recently arrived from Munich. He needed English tutelage, and Anna was struggling to pass her German requirement. Kismet, it seemed. When they both decided to attend law school directly after college, their future together was bright and assured. She would be the fighter and he'd be the company man, yin and yang, adoring and adorable.

What Anna never wanted to see was that as the years went on, their interests diverged. Anna continued to be an accomplished amateur singer, active in a church choir as well as writing and performing her own alt-folk songs. Stephan was an avid European football fan who liked nothing better than a weekend skiing on snow or water, pausing to watch whatever games were on satellite TV. Still, they shared so much history and a close group of friends. What could possibly go wrong?

Even after being close with Anna for years now, I'd never heard the entire story of Stephan leaving. One afternoon I visited her office, and finally got the blow-by-blow. Unlike her often-overflowing apartment, the space is comfortable and simple. There are framed diplomas (University of Chicago Law, very impressive) on the wall, and only a few well-placed Latin American knickknacks. In a wrap dress and low heels, her hair back in a bun, glasses perched on the bridge of her nose, Anna looked warm, approachable, and serious. She radiated—not calm, exactly, but a sense of listening. I imagined this must help with her work, which consists almost exclusively (and ironically) of custody and divorce cases.

When she first started her practice, she and Stephan were newlyweds. The office was freshly painted and featured photos of them together. Stephan was on the partner track at a white-shoe firm, blah, blah.

After spending the better part of a year trying to conceive, she finally got good news. Then she miscarried. The depth of Anna's sadness and loneliness following her pregnancy loss surprised her—and her husband. "There's this whole thing about miscarriages where you're supposed to get over it, like it's just another part of life," she said.

"But you don't," I said. "I know."

She got pregnant again quickly, but was horribly sick.

"When our group met for the first time, I was coming out of the worst four months of my life," she explained. "There was one night when I couldn't stop vomiting. Stephan had decided we would go to Montana to some fancy ski resort, but there was no way I could do it. I was guilty about being this MIA partner. I told him to go by himself."

"And he took you at your word," I said.

She didn't say anything, but her face showed what she'd felt back then. Her eyes were big and liquid. Half smiling, she shook her head. "He went."

At the height of her sickness, she went home to her parents in Colorado for a month. "I needed someone to take care of me," she explained. "When I got back, Stephan seemed distant and withdrawn. When I asked what was going on, he told me he wasn't sure if he was in love with me anymore. We'd been together for twelve years, and he'd never said anything like that before!"

"What did you say to him?" I tried to imagine what I would have done in the same situation, but couldn't.

"I called our good friend back in Chicago, hysterical, and he talked to Stephan."

"Did he take it back?"

"No. But he didn't mention it again either."

"But there was never any acknowledgment of the fact that he had put you, in this vulnerable state, through something terrible?" I asked.

She shook her head.

As we were talking, I remembered something Anna had said at our first Mommy Group meeting: "I'm worried my husband isn't attracted to me anymore."

We'd reassured her then. It's a normal pregnant-lady fear. Who doesn't worry that her partner is no longer attracted to her hugely changed body?

Now I reminded her of that conversation.

"I remember," she said. "I knew there was more going on, but I didn't want to deal."

Her due date was in September. As it approached, Anna thought her marriage was improving. In fact, she felt closer to Stephan than ever. They did a pregnancy photography session together. A week before she was due, he put together the crib and tried on the Ergobaby carrier with a stuffed bunny rabbit in it for "practice."

Then, one night, sitting at their shared desktop computer, Anna noticed that Stephan had googled the phrase *How to leave your wife*.

"I'm looking it up for a friend," he told her when she confronted him. An hour later, her water broke.

Anna's labor didn't progress, so she needed an induction, and then surgery. After she delivered Isabella, she had an allergic reaction to the pain meds, breaking out in hives all over her body. She retained so much fluid that when she got home, she was too uncomfortable to lie down and slept in a chair for days—as I remembered all too well from when I visited.

Less than two weeks since her C-section, still mostly housebound, Anna noticed that Stephan once again seemed distracted and distant. She wrote the mommies her email about her husband not understanding what it was like "to be the milk machine" just before they visited his cousins upstate for the first time.

They were driving home from that trip when everything fell apart. Stephan was at the wheel of the BMW he'd insisted on buying when he started at his firm (Anna would have preferred an old junker or no car at all), with Issie in her rear-facing car seat in the back.

Anna brought up the Google search.

"I was sore from surgery, still wearing my maternity clothes," she told me. "We kept pulling the car over so I could nurse. I finally asked, 'Do you still want to be married?'"

He gave the wrong answer: "I want to see other people."

She didn't start crying right away because she thought he was joking. "Take that back," she said. "You cannot be serious!"

He was.

The next day, a therapist—"a kind, loving woman with children of her own," Anna recalled—came to their apartment for an emergency house call.

"You are having a crisis," she said to Stephan. But he didn't change his mind.

Two years later, Anna went to see that therapist again to confirm what had actually happened during the session. "She said it was rare to watch such devastating heartbreak, even as a seasoned couples therapist," Anna explained. "She said to me, 'You loved him so much, and he was just not there with you.'"

Though barely able to walk down her own apartment steps, Anna told Stephan that if he wanted to date other people, he couldn't stay in the house with her and the baby. He left. Isabella was less than three weeks old.

I bumped into her at the Greenmarket a few days later. That night, Anna wrote to the Mommy Group, *I'm a single mom.*

Immediately, we began emailing and texting each other like

bananas. Anna was our founding member; our loyalty was already fierce.

"That fuckface!" was the universal first reaction. Quickly followed by, "How is she going to do this?"

I knew what my first move would be in her situation: back home to my parents in Philadelphia. No way could I imagine living on my own with a newborn, and the other Mommies agreed. But Anna was inspiring.

She'd already hired a nanny, anticipating a quick return to work. That decision turned out to be prescient: she went back to part-time practice in less than two months, running home from her fortuitously local office to nurse Isabella between appointments, ordering Stephan to sleep on the couch a few nights a week to take early-morning feeds. Her mother came and stayed for a few weeks, friends watched Issie here and there so she could nap.

Stephan wanted to be a "good dad," and Anna actually supported him in that desire, agreeing to joint custody as soon as they could. But she couldn't forgive him.

In the first months after a baby's birth, mothers and babies are, in many ways, as biologically bound as they were during pregnancy. Babies' temperatures adjust when they're on their mothers' bodies; they respond to their mothers' smell, touch, and mood. By sundering his relationship with Anna, by introducing that level of stress and trauma into her life, Stephan destroyed part of her relationship with Isabella as well. She couldn't be a happy new mother, not like this.

One beautiful October morning, Anna wheeled Isabella to Prospect Park. The leaves were changing. On the Long Meadow, families picnicked on the grass in the fall sunshine, snacks arranged on blankets, wine in plastic cups, an idyllic picture of everything she'd lost. Issie started crying, wanting to nurse. Watching the perfect families and hearing her daughter cry, Anna felt as if she couldn't breathe. She had no husband to take the baby and try to shush her. Why did *her* daughter's dad leave? What had these women, sitting there as if a lunch on the grass was the most natural thing in the world, done that she had not? She'd been a good wife, tolerant and supportive. Running home to feed Issie in the quiet and dark of her living room, curtains drawn, Anna found herself in a full-blown panic attack.

Anna stopped going to the park. Or for walks. "I felt like I was going to die from heartache," she said. "I thought we had this epic storybook love. Isabella cushioned the pain a little, but . . ." Her contrasting emotions were vertiginous. She fell into a deep depression that would last most of Issie's first year. Four years later, she still felt guilty about it.

It didn't help that Stephan found a new girlfriend, and quickly. Anna would watch them walk away after their custody handoff, pushing Issie in her stroller. They took Issie on trips, strapping her into her car seat and driving away with their luggage, the new woman taking Anna's position with *her* baby, *her* husband, in *her* family.

"He got somebody who he didn't have an extensive history with," she said to me. "He could start over as an adult."

I thought she was being excessively nice. Then she summed it up. "He did *not* love me so much that he was willing to do this." The unthinkable.

Even so, she kept pulling it together. Every time it seemed that she was ready to curl up and give up, she steeled herself and found the strength she needed to raise her kid and keep on trucking.

The Mommy Group tried to meet at Anna's house as much as we could.

One Monday afternoon, her phone bleeped as we were in the middle of discussing nap schedules (fascinating).

"Oh, girls, get this," she said. "I told Stephan that we weren't allowed to fight in front of Isabella, because she's already going to be scarred by her father leaving her when she was two weeks old and doesn't need to see her parents in obvious conflict, right?"

"Right," we all agreed.

Anna continued, "So, instead of us yelling at each other and potentially damaging her further, I told Stephan I get to text him whatever I want, whenever I want, and he can only respond *Okay*, which is what he just did." Handing Jane her phone, she added, "Check it out."

Jane brought the phone close to her face, scrolling down a seemingly endless text with one hand while burping Katie with the other. She snorted with laughter.

"Pass it to me," I said, and then read aloud, " 'Stephan, you do realize that girls develop their feelings of self-worth around men in relation to their fathers, don't you? I don't know how you're going to make this up to her, but you better start trying. I can't believe what a fucking asshole you are, leaving me with your newborn child.' "

Antonia stuck out her arm. "Can I write one? When Dillon came home from work last night, he didn't understand why I hadn't walked the dog and Gus was throwing up on me. At. The. Time. I have some things to get off my chest."

Obviously, Anna's marriage represented the worst-case fear about life after baby. But we all wondered, was Stephan's the ultimate new-father bad reaction writ large? It must be natural for a new dad to want to run away from all the blood, milk, and tears, from the sleep deprivation, and from his wife's transformed body. Even if those fears, or one of the many other conflicts of early parenting, don't result in divorce, they still affect all couples to some extent. Marriage with a baby is hard, period. How do couples who don't experience the "worst case" get through the normal?

The early days of parenthood make couples doubt everything. Sleep deprivation leads to bad decisions, picking fights. As a new parent, your hormones are up and down all the time, and you may be overly sensitive or, worse, completely irrational. Unimportant details feel crucial. Later on, you balance, you seesaw, always wondering who's on the bottom and who's on top. Laundry is the game one day, dishes the next, sleep always and forever.

"When you're that tired, you don't even know what you want on your sandwich," Michele, Clara's first babysitter and now a doula, told me. We were discussing the need for postpartum doulas—people who will come to your house, do some dishes, and chat with Mom and Dad. "So how are you [and your partner] supposed to decide, *Should we renew this lease?*" She added, "And if Mom is going down, the whole family's going down."

Money and time are the two biggest immediate conflicts for couples. Almost 65 percent of women with children under the age of six work outside the home (for mothers of infants that rate drops to approximately 57 percent). Women, however, still tend to do the majority of the housework, including childcare. According to a 2014 article from *Time*, men are more likely to have time to participate in "leisure" activities such as "sports, exercise, or recreation." This is not to imply that all men are bon vivants or selfish bastards, shooting hoops while their wives scrub the bathroom tile with toothbrushes, crying babies strapped to their backs. But it does indicate a general truth that most two-working-parent families know too well: Mommy does more at home, even if both parents have jobs outside the home, and *especially* if Daddy makes more money.

What if neither parent makes enough money? I'm not talking about poverty, which is, of course, an extraordinarily important issue (as of the Census Bureau's 2013 American Community Survey, 21.8 percent of children under eighteen, or approximately 16.1 million American young people, live below the poverty line). I'm referring to the more genteel yet serious "money issues" with which so many ostensibly middle-class families struggle.

As mentioned earlier, Antonia has a degree in comparative literature. Before Gus's birth, like so many academics, she was unable to find a permanent job, and so taught as an adjunct (part-time, without benefits) at various colleges and universities. The spring before she had Gus, she'd only been able to teach one class, with a long and expensive commute over state lines. Her husband, Dillon, worked as a film librarian at a major New York City Museum, earning around $40,000 a year. They were always broke. So broke that when Gus was born, Antonia qualified for the Special Supplemental Nutrition Program for Women, Infants, and Children (WIC) program. "I used to buy organic sourdough bread and fresh fruit and vegetable smoothies with my WIC vouchers instead of the designated shitty products until the Key Foods supermarket stopped me," she told me.

Antonia was always honest in Mommy Group about her anger, which had a lot to do with her money woes. But she and Dillon, like Danny and I, had at least sort of known what they were getting into, having a kid in expensive New York City on low, bohemian-type incomes. The real *disappointment* for Antonia became the conflicts around co-parenting between her and Dillon. She'd walk into our Monday sessions furious. Her stories all shared a shape: Dillon let her carry the burden of childcare and housework and didn't seem to even notice, so they'd "rowed" and both of them were still too angry to apologize. After relating her latest tale of woe, she'd be laughing—but no less outraged.

She went back to work the September after she had Gus in July, juggling part-time hours with part-time childcare (a combination of a sitter and Dillon's mom, who lived in Manhattan). The result? Forty-plus hours a week of work in the gray area between full-time stay-at-home mama and full-time in-the-office worker. She managed to keep Mondays free, though; they were sacred Mommy Group time.

"The Mommy Group was important because it made me feel *seen*," she told me. "A lot of my anger when Gus was a little baby was about not being seen by my husband, in my new state of being a mother."

"What did you expect?" I asked.

"I was expecting equality!" she said. "It was a shocker that we fell right into archetypical gender roles. I had sole responsibility of looking after the childcare, running the household, managing the money—even though we were both working outside the home. How did things change for Dillon? He still slept through the night, went to work, was out in the world, being himself. I was having a complete revolution. Meanwhile, because we were so broke, my own obligation to earn increased!"

I do know that at the time it was hard to give Dillon a fair shake. Antonia was *so angry*. But we were hearing only her side of the story.

Over the last three years, Dillon and I have become friends independent of Antonia, logging many playground hours together with the kids, rolling our eyes during the endless preschool business meetings we've been required to attend. He's a great dad, and I wanted to know why Toni had felt so frustrated.

We decided I should interview him away from Antonia, and away from all of our children. So one summer Friday I took the subway into Manhattan to visit him at his office. The space was air-conditioned and practically silent. It was the opposite of his and Antonia's old one-bedroom, back when they shared it with baby Gus and an ancient Irish setter.

"I think dads, in general, don't get the whole 'parent' thing for at least three months," Dillon told me. "Mothers have this [automatic] bond. You're enmeshed with the baby, with feeding. It takes us longer."

When I listened to the interview later, I wished I'd pressed Dillon more about this "dads take longer to bond" thing. I didn't feel "naturally" bonded with Clara for months. I was, however, compelled to keep putting my nipple into her mouth, on endless repeat. Is that what eventually bonded me with Clara, or did I just get to know her better, easing my way into an acceptance of parenthood through sheer time and will? I'll never know.

"I was always *trying* to do the right thing," Dillon continued. "I wanted Toni to feel supported, but she was so furious all the time."

Looking back, I felt a little guilty for taking Antonia's side without at least asking for more detail. I think she does, too.

Back when I was still pregnant, I asked the other Mommies how, exactly, the co-parenting workload was breaking down for them thus far. I had this plan that Danny would take exactly half of the night feeds. Because he wanted to, and because it was fair.

"Carl gets up in the night all the time," Jane said.

The rest of the group made "Well, ex-*cuse* me" faces.

Antonia rolled her eyes. "Dillon has never gotten up—not once," she said. "He says because he has a full-time job he needs his sleep. When he gets to work, that's *all* he has to do! I just don't understand."

Many women have the biological responsibility—which can feel like a liability at three in the morning—to feed. We all know "breast is best," and waking your partner in the middle of the night may feel pointless if it means you'll have to pump milk during your precious daytime hours. To give fathers (and nonbiological mothers) agency, is it part of a breast-feeding mother's duty to pump as soon as possible, so that her partner can get an equal share of that early care? That seems like a lot of extra work just to make fathers feel like equal parents to their breast-feeding partners. Of course, it is possible to bottle-feed with formula (a decision that is by no means inherently inferior to on-tap or pumped breast milk). But many breast-feeding mothers feel as if a taste of formula will ruin their child.

So let's say, in the interest of egalitarian parenting, Parent A does most of the feedings, and Parent B changes all the diapers. That could work great for the first two weeks or so, when many partners are still on family leave after a child's birth. Mothers might stay home for another twelve weeks, usually without pay. When they get back to work, they're still focused on the baby more than their partners might be, because they spent a longer period establishing the new family routines and practices. What time are naps? Do they take place only in the crib, or are stroller or car naps acceptable? Is feeding on a schedule or on demand? When and how much is enough tummy time? It is okay to watch TV in front of the baby? What kind of shows? How many layers of clothing do you need for whatever weather? What goes in the diaper bag? And what's that weird rash on the side of Baby's face? Was it there yesterday?

These may seem like innocuous questions, one by one. In aggregate, however, they represent the complex twelve-dimensional Rubik's Cube of parenting.

Danny and I certainly had our share of fights about Clara's care, but I was lucky in this area. Because of our freelance schedules, the playing field, in terms of who knew more about Clara's day-to-day life, was pretty level. That is, we were equally likely to leave wipes out of the diaper bag.

That's not to say that Danny and I didn't fight about other things that first year. A lot. It is easy *not* to realize how much feelings—as opposed to facts—have to do with conflict between partners at this crucial early baby time. As Sarah, a freelancer friend of mine (and one mommy group removed, by association) explained, "I'm working from home right now, so doing the dishes doesn't feel so terrible. When I worked nine to five in an office, dishes were an imposition."

I would love to be the generous partner who has an easier time doing dishes when I've been in my apartment all day than when I've run around the city teaching, knowing my kid's going to be tired and cranky when I finally get home. But I hate doing the dishes, and so does my husband. They're *always* an imposition, for both of us. To extrapolate further: who knows, in the context of any particular, highly personal partnership, whose turn it is, really, to do the dishes?

So what should new parents do? Draw up chore charts? Immediately enter couples counseling? Build a primal scream therapy room in a spare closet? All reasonable options, but maybe start smaller and more logically.

Try to make various tasks with the new baby special for one parent. I nursed, and Danny was the chief of diapers. (Newborn poop smells like buttered popcorn anyway, so as shit work went, it wasn't bad.) Until Clara turned one, her favorite place in the house was the changing table, because that's where she and her father had all their little jokes and games. After Danny whisked her into the bathroom, I'd hear coos and giggles from both of them. When I went to change her, she looked at me stone-faced, like, *Where's the funny guy who usually does this?*

The nonprimary feeding parent should also be in charge of snacks for the nurser, as many and varied as possible. And be prepared to go to the drugstore at any time of the day or night. Yes, this sounds clichéd, but shake your head now and thank me later.

That first year with a new baby requires extra and conscious care from both partners. Settle for what works in the moment, rather than what you had before or wish you had now. That might mean more TV than sex, sleeping in shifts, and embracing the challenge of your in-laws' constant presence.

Ask for help, because having a baby is hard work, and you need backup if you and your partner ever want time alone or time together that is not all about chores. Call that old college roommate and ask him to make you dinner (and to fold some T-shirts while he's at it). Let your cousin take your husband out for a beer for half an hour. Ask your neighbor or the barista from the local coffee shop to come over for twenty minutes so you can nap. Order takeout again even if you've always been the type who churns your own artisanal butter.

Most of all: communicate, schedule date nights, and be considerate. Passion will probably return *after* backrubs. Try to go easy on each other. This is a discrete period in time, *not* your whole relationship.

"I don't think anyone with children under the age of five has a great marriage," my mother told me a long time ago, before Danny or Clara. We must have been talking about those bad old days of my parents' lives, when I remember my mother stealing time in her pottery studio, and my father always heading off to, as he put it, "work like a dirty jerk." I remind myself of my mother's words whenever Danny has done something I've deemed—in the moment—so irredeemably intolerable that I have to take deep breaths to keep from screaming. (PS: I am often—almost always, actually—in the wrong.)

Back in her office with me during our interview, Anna was able to reflect. "I take a lot of accountability now for the end of my marriage," she said. "Fifty percent. No—forty-nine percent! I'm able to look back retrospectively and say, *Okay, there were big issues in this marriage.*"

I asked if the Mommy Group had helped her at all. We'd all been so blurry back then. I didn't know if we'd offered real support to her. I did know that we might not have continued meeting if not for Anna, even though, as the months went on, she had the hardest time attending.

"You guys supported me on my journey where I was," Anna said. "If I was angry, you said, *Be angry.* When I was sad, you said, *It's okay to be sad.* And when I decided to *not* be in a conflictual relationship with Stephan because I wanted to make the best choice for Issie, you didn't give me pushback, or tell me I should continue to be angry forever." She paused, wiped her eyes, and then gave a wicked grin. "Or not date. When I told you I went out with a guy, you said, *Tell us about it! We wanna hear! You're gonna get more action than we will!*"

Reader, she did. But that's another chapter.

4. Away in a Manger, No Crib for a Bed

Clara

From Elizabeth

October 26, 2010

I've already gotten baby Clara Yetta to latch on for three good feeds! I got a pretty good night's sleep last night in spite of being woken every hour. No pain meds either since six last night. Today I get to eat, I hope, and try walking around untethered to machines as well!

Because of my gestational diabetes, I was scheduled for an induction the Sunday after my Friday due date. I'd check into the hospital in the evening, they'd hook me up to the meds, and Dr. Bosch would be on call for the delivery on Monday morning.

By the Wednesday prior to my scheduled induction, I began to feel skin-crawling-hyperventilating anxiety. I went for acupuncture, and that helped a little, though I had to spend my twenty minutes of relaxation time curled over a yoga ball with the needles sticking out of me because I couldn't lie on my stomach *or* my back.

At my last appointment before the birth, I asked Dr. Bosch if my nervousness was unusual.

"I could induce you today," she said. "Would that make you feel better?"

I responded with horror. "No! I have too much to do."

Like organizing wedding photos, a task I insisted to Danny was *absolutely necessary* and *not nesting*, until two in the morning on Saturday night.

I'd just fallen asleep after finishing with the wedding photos. In my dream, I heard and felt a *pop!* like a balloon, and then I woke up in the middle of a big wet spot on the bed.

"My water broke!" I called to Danny. (I'd kicked him out to sleep on the couch.)

We'd had a big day planned: last-minute errands, stocking up on food, putting together the bassinet we'd bought months before (I am Russian/Jewish/superstitious enough that I didn't want the bed to be ready too much ahead of the baby.) My parents were arriving from Philly that afternoon. They'd settle into their hotel, and then we'd meet up for dinner at a fancy-ish restaurant near the hospital where I liked the shrimp Caesar salad. I'd drink a glass or two of wine. After dinner, we'd stroll over to the hospital and I'd check in for my induction.

All that was not going to happen, I realized now, sitting on a folded towel in the middle of our entryway, giggling as Danny frantically threw random items into a tote bag. I wasn't feeling any contractions, but the steady seep of my "waters" continued.

"What do we do?" I asked him. Though we'd gone over the protocol several million times, I couldn't remember anything.

"We call Dr. Bosch, and then Willa," Danny said.

"Uh, come to the hospital as soon as . . . you can," Dr. Bosch said. We knew this was a coded order. She'd already explained to us that ideally she wanted me to labor at home as long as possible, but that the breaking water started a "timer" for a hospital birth: thirty-six hours, maximum, to get that baby out. If I stayed home longer, I'd have a better chance of progression before all of the medical paraphernalia potentially "scared" my body into stalling.

"Wait a couple of hours," Willa said when we woke her up, saying with more clarity what our doctor had implied. "And eat as much as possible now. You don't know if they'll let you eat at the hospital."

Danny made me my GD favorites and I gulped them down: peanut butter on one slice of seven-grain toast, and an egg with avocado and cream cheese on another.

"Let's go to the hospital," I said. It had been all of twenty minutes.

"Okay!" I could tell Danny was as relieved as I was to put me in the hands of medical professionals.

When the car service arrived, we piled in with our "minimal" luggage: a rollie bag of clothes, five novels each, my computer, DVDs, a few soft toys for Clara (in case she wanted to play), many adorable tiny outfits, my new bathrobe and PJs, a birthing ball (uninflated), the pump for the birthing ball, blankets for me and for Clara, a pillow (we'd been told to bring our own), and a tote bag of food.

"St. Luke's Hospital in Manhattan," Danny told the driver, who was looking at us as if he'd won the opposite of the lottery. "She's in labor, kind of."

"Don't worry. I won't have the baby in your car!" I said. He nodded nervously and started driving.

I still wasn't feeling contractions, I didn't think. I'd been having Braxton-Hicks for months already, so I knew the sensation of my belly tightening and releasing. Now, here I was in labor, officially, and I felt . . . nothing.

We got to the hospital by dawn on Sunday morning. All day, I hung out in my hospital room in my favorite soft maternity T-shirt, a pair of disposable underpants, and my new bathrobe, waiting. I wasn't effaced or dilated enough to have the baby. My parents arrived, bringing me miso soup—the only thing the doctor on call would let me eat. Tara was in for the week from Germany. She smuggled in egg drop soup (more solid than miso, and therefore forbidden), which I guiltily slurped. Though she was supposed to have a baby herself by now, she was happy and excited for me.

I texted the Mommies like crazy. *You can do it!* They wrote back. *We can't wait to meet Clara!*

But Sunday evening arrived, and my contractions remained AWOL.

I was still hoping for a "natural" birth (as in medication-free). After such a rough and tough pregnancy, I wanted *something* to go according to my plan.

"We'll start you on a low dose of Cervidil to induce you," said Dr. Simon, Dr. Bosch's partner. "It won't work right away. By the morning you should be ready to go." My induction was on time, after all.

As a "cervical ripener," Cervidil is the first line in the induction drug lineup. Over a year earlier, I'd taken it to bring on my physical miscarriage, and the very sound of its name still made me feel sick and scared. "*No* Cervidil" was the one point on my birth plan. Never mind that now.

Danny went out for a quick dinner with my dad. He'd been in the hospital for twelve hours, and he needed food and air. My mom hung out with me. I ate more miso soup.

I began to feel some pressure in my lower back. I didn't want to complain, but told my mom she should relax and go back to her hotel. I needed to concentrate.

By the time Danny returned, I was bouncing on the inflated yoga ball, screaming at my pain to go fuck itself. It turned out that I was having an extreme reaction to the Cervidil, going from zero effaced with no labor signs to 80 percent effaced with near continuous contractions in less than three hours.

"We'll give you something to help you sleep and relax," the nurse offered, as I bounced around the room on the ball like the Tasmanian Devil.

"Will it take the pain away?" I asked her through clenched teeth.

"Mm . . . No."

"Then I think I want an epidural."

Suddenly, everyone was in motion. This was a more complicated decision than I'd realized.

"Hold still. We need to put in a catheter," said one nurse.

"Now we're doing the IV shunt in your arm," said another.

"We'll need to put these bizarre swimmie-floatie-style compression cuffs on your legs, and they'll sound like Darth Vader breathing as they inflate and deflate," the first nurse said (or at least that's what she should have said).

When the anesthesiologist—a beautiful Indian woman who I estimated to be about six months pregnant—arrived, I remembered to quiz her about her credentials.

"How many of these have you performed?"

"Hundreds."

"Are you going to have one for your own child's birth?"

She smiled at me. "I chose an epidural for each of my three children's births."

I shut up.

Holding me gently but firmly, the anesthesiologist told me I'd need to bend over and lie perfectly still, in spite of my contractions.

I didn't think I could do it, but Danny held my hands and kept me steady.

Then . . . the sweetest relief. Ten minutes earlier, if I'd needed to point at the "pain level" chart of smiling to frowning faces, I would have bit the paper in two like a raging warthog. Now, nothing. I was floating.

However, with all the tubes, wires, and cords snaking out of parts of my body, I vaguely realized why this wasn't ideal. I was immobile, on my back. There would be no more food at all (not even miso soup), no more walking around or bouncing on the yoga ball. I was in this bed until I was deemed ready to start pushing.

Many buzzers, alarms, and beeps abruptly stopped my analysis. Again the nurses and the doctor on call surrounded me, and they were doing things.

"What's happening?" I asked, frightened.

"Your baby is fine, your baby is fine," Dr. Simon said, rubbing my back as if I was a baby myself. "We're just making sure you're getting enough oxygen." The nurses fitted a mask on my nose and mouth and wrapped me in blankets. I'd started shivering uncontrollably, a side effect of the medication.

Once all that calmed down, Danny and I were alone.

A *Keeping Up with the Kardashians* marathon was on TV. Danny never let me watch that show at home, but now he had no choice. The nurses brought him one of those awkward hospital chairs that recline partway, and he settled into it next to my bedside, close enough that we could hold hands. Then my insomniac, never-sleeping husband conked out, snoring, while I watched Khloe's husband, Lamar, learn to swim, several times. The notion that I was having a baby seemed perfectly ridiculous.

At around five in the morning, Dr. Bosch arrived and checked my cervix. No change since the night before—not ideal. Danny called Willa and told her to come in as soon as she could. They were going to give me Pitocin to speed things up "a bit."

Time passed. Dr. Bosch would pop her head into the room every so often. "You look great," she kept saying, "but you're still not dilated enough. Another hour."

At around noon, she said, "Still not quite there, but let's start pushing."

I pushed. A venerable and imposing Haitian lady nurse held one of my legs ("Something tells me you've done this for a while," I said to her; she chuckled and tightened her linebacker grip on my thigh), Willa held the other, and Dr. Bosch played catcher. Danny stood to the side, encouraging me, but not like one of the labor film's milquetoast husbands.

"Dads are in a uniquely weird situation," he said later. "We're obviously not the prime focus, but we're also becoming parents. And we have one job—to help you. But we don't know how!"

I pushed.

"I can see her head!" Danny said, beyond excited by hour three. "I see hair!"

"That's her head stretching," Dr. Bosch said, adding, when Danny and I both looked at her in alarm, added. "It's fine. Baby skulls are made to do that."

She muttered something about checking another patient, and left.

"That was a ploy, wasn't it?" I asked when she came back twenty minutes later. "You were hoping I'd progress without you."

"Yup."

Clara's position hadn't changed.

Everyone was calm, but I was frustrated. It was great having no pain, but I also had no marker for when the contractions were coming, nor any feeling of a need to push.

I kept at it.

By hour four, Dr. Bosch took a deep breath and stepped away from her post between my legs. "I could let you go for another three more hours, just to see if there's any difference, but I don't think there will be. Or we could do a C-section now."

Everyone cleared out of the room so that Danny and I could decide.

"I don't want to push for another three hours," I said. I was crying, in frustration and fear. I really didn't want surgery.

"It's up to you," Danny said. He was very calm. "Dr. Bosch has always given us the right advice."

I called Tara.

"Oh, honey," she cooed. "It's okay. You'll have a healthy baby—*and* a pretty vagina!" I cracked up. Surgery was not the end of the world. I would be fine.

As soon as we made the decision, there was another swirl and whirl of activity as seemingly a zillion people descended with equipment and supplies.

Reflecting on the moment, Danny recalled, "Birth is a process; surgery is an event. Medical people arrived, rather than just the Labor and Delivery people we'd been with for hours. A guy I'd never seen before told me we had to clear out of the room we'd been in for two days in like three minutes, but there were half-full containers of miso soup *everywhere*."

In a doula extraordinaire feat, Willa managed to condense our clown car of stuff back into our bags, moving them herself to what would be our recovery room.

Nurses changed my IV and shaved the top of my pubic hair, and then orderlies switched me from the bed to a gurney and wheeled me out into the hall. Flat on my back, I watched everyone rushing over me. A new (nonpregnant) anesthesiologist put a mask on my face, only to quickly pull it off when I vomited. I didn't see my husband, and I wanted him next to me.

"There were people I didn't know putting garments on me," Danny said.

Once suited up, Danny managed to tell the technicians not to strap my arms down to the table. A friend had told him to ask for that, which was good, because I would have freaked out with pinned arms. The experience was feeling enough like *One Flew over the Cuckoo's Nest* already.

"Your mask is way cooler than mine," Danny told me he joked to Dr. Bosch as they walked into the OR together.

"I've been doing this a little bit longer than you have," she said to him. "Bring your camera."

In the OR, they'd already put a surgical drape in front of my face; my stomach was painted with brown antiseptic (not that I could see it).

Dr. Bosch told Danny he could watch or not, his choice. He stood by my head. At some point she called out, "Daddy, take a picture!" Danny held his iPhone over the sheet and got shots of Clara being pulled out of me bloody and screaming. When I look at the photos now, I can't tell where my own body is in them, but I do see my girl.

When I heard Clara crying, I yelled, "Is that my baby? My baby needs me!" Yet in the first moment of what would later be, I now realize, my postpartum disregulation, I wasn't sure it was true.

"Do you want to come take a look at her?" a nurse asked Danny.

"Yes!"

Walking over to the scale, he turned around, and saw "more than I ever should have. You, not quite sewn up."

"What did I look like?"

"A big bloody protrusion out of your body. It was overwhelming. And there I was holding this beautiful Clara."

Through all the trials and difficulties of my pregnancy, I had reassured myself with the vision of holding my child's body still slick out of mine. I wanted us to smell each other, to have that full mammalian experience the baby books and yoga teachers said was essential for bonding. I'd carried her for nine months, terrified, pricking my finger, feeling her kick, not eating ice cream, worrying, and worrying some more.

When Danny finally brought Clara over to me and laid her on my chest, she was already wrapped up, cleaned, and swaddled. Someone else had touched her first. It didn't feel right. I was allowed to hold her, briefly, but then they took Clara away again. The worst part was that I didn't know if I cared.

Many women who've had C-sections experience similar feelings of loneliness and detachment after the birth. Here's something I could have been told, pre-op, that might have helped, post-op: that sense of depersonalization that I became convinced was due to my lack of attachment to my child? That was a side effect of the drugs. And, frankly, a sign of my impending postpartum mental illness. Maybe I shouldn't have felt so sad to be unable to hold Clara for what was really a relatively short period; I'd have the rest of my life to hold this girl. But . . . So many women experience trauma after surgery, it is clear that the current standard of care is not enough.

As I was finishing this book, a story on NPR.com blew up on my Facebook feed. In "The Gentle Cesarean: More Like a Birth than an

Operation," Jennifer Schmidt described a new "family-centered ce-sarean technique" being used in the UK. The idea, simple but revo-lutionary, is to let moms see their babies being born surgically if they want and to put newborns immediately on the mother's chest for skin-to-skin contact. This helps stimulate bonding and breast-feeding.

These new practices would require some modification of hos-pital protocol, but the potential benefits could be revolutionary: re-duced maternal trauma and sadness, more immediate bonding with the newborn, less of the weird drugged state in which C-section moms imagine bad things happening to their babies and bodies (à la Jane thinking she was a dolphin).

What do you do if you're a pregnant woman and you (reason-ably) fear surgery? Plan ahead for the birth you *don't* want. Ask your doctor about her C-section rate. Play out scenarios with her and your partner. Keep asking as many questions as you can before you're in labor. Don't be scared; talking about a C-section *won't* make you more likely to have one.

This theory worked for Heidi, whose surgery was not her first choice (obviously), but who felt considerably less traumatized af-terward than I did. When I asked her why, she replied via email:

> Since Clay was forecast to be big, I wrote to Park Slope Parents in advance of my due date, getting information from other mothers about their C-sections. Therefore, I knew some basics about the side effects of the medication, such as shivering and nausea. We also had an amazing anesthesiologist who talked to me during the whole surgery. He was probably making sure I was lucid, but also keeping me really calm and informed. He kind of cooed to me the whole time.

Heidi's comforting anesthesiologist was working within his own protocol. Why not codify that reassurance? A nurse or social worker could be present in the OR to talk to the mother: "Your baby is wonderful, and you'll get to hold her in a minute. We'll put her in your arms as soon as we can. You've had major surgery, and that's confusing." If I'd heard those words, even as Clara's birth moved out of my (completely illusory but still important to me) control, I think I would have had a better time afterward.

Sewn up, I was wheeled down the hall into the recovery ward. The nurse there was crazy and mean, insisting to me I would "definitely" get diabetes now because of my GD. Even in my drug-addled haze, I managed to argue with her about statistics and peer-reviewed studies.

Danny finally brought Clara in, and I tried to nurse.

Even though my milk wouldn't come in for another few days, I wanted her to latch on for the precious few drops of colostrum, aka "liquid gold," I had to offer. But between Willa, Stephanie, and my mother, no one could figure out how to get my huge nipple to stay in Clara's tiny mouth.

What did the medical professionals (again) not tell me? That Clara and I were both a little dopey from the meds. That she'd just completed the most traumatizing journey of her life. That maybe she didn't need to latch on that early, and that was no problem. That nursing presents specific challenges for women with naturally large breasts.

Finally, we were moved into our room. Note my use of the passive voice throughout. I "was wheeled." We "were moved." As when I'd had my miscarriages, I felt out of control, and looked, desperately, for some way to understand my experience. In the hospital bed, I still had my catheter and leg cuffs, and I was on a morphine drip. I felt beached.

For months of pregnancy and GD food restrictions, I'd planned my first post-baby meal. I was going to feast on prosciutto on a baguette with raw-milk cheese and hard cider. But the morphine and surgery left me without an appetite. Instead of my dream meal, I drank more miso soup, and I didn't even care. My remove, my lack of excitement or "happy tears" were, I now realize, problems. I put on a good show, and no one noticed. They were all so happy. I didn't want to bum them out.

A private room in our hospital cost eight hundred dollars a night (yeah, that's right). Not having shelled out the big bucks, Danny had to leave by ten that evening. "That was the worst," he always says. "It was the last moment in the world you should have been by yourself. My baby had been in this world for four hours. It was not okay."

He wasn't even allowed to sleep on the floor in the shared room. (A friend's husband did sleep on the floor next to his wife's bed at another top Manhattan hospital. It's the same place where Beyoncé delivered her baby in a luxury birthing suite. I assume Jay-Z got a bed.) Instead, Danny sacked out in Stephanie's basement, thirty blocks away. We sent Clara to the nursery.

After Danny left, I texted everyone I knew: *Baby is beautiful. Danny is completely enraptured.*

That last sentence breaks my heart. The truth was, I couldn't understand how Danny was already in love with this creature we didn't even know yet. I was used to fish-Clara, ultrasound Clara; I didn't know how to connect to real Clara.

If he'd been able to sleep over, Danny would have fetched our baby from the nursery three times that first night, rather than the nurse, wearing, of all things, scrubs patterned with *Día de Muertos* skeletons in kooky hospital-themed costumes. It was like the kid on the cereal box holding a cereal box with a kid on it holding a cereal box—but on morphine, with a side salad of macabre.

Before he left, Danny had asked that nurse to stay with me, or at least to make sure I could hold the baby.

When she brought Clara for the first of her night feeds, she asked, "Do I *really* have to stay?"

The distance between the Clara's Plexiglas bassinet and my arms' reach was too far and painful for me to stretch.

"I don't feel safe alone with her yet. What if I drop her?"

The nurse rolled her eyes.

"You won't drop her," she said.

"I guess you can go, then," I said. I watched her dancing-skeleton-covered back fade into the mist outside my door.

Clara gnawed my nipples for a few minutes, and then we both fell asleep, with her wedged somewhere between the side of the bed and my body.

Danny explained recently, "When I asked the nurse to watch you, I assumed because that was her job and I had asked her to, that she would do it. I'm a 'privileged' white man with a doctor father and information about how hospitals work. I think I deserve what I ask for, if it's reasonable. Imagine what would have happened if I didn't ask for help."

By the time Danny was allowed back into the hospital at seven the next morning, Dr. Bosch had already been to see me on her rounds. She told me I was recovering nicely. At least I think that's what she said. I was still on drugs.

For the next few days, as my body recovered, my mind drifted. Some of the nurses were wonderful, especially those on the day shift. Experienced, kind, they were willing to take a few minutes and help me try to get Clara to latch on, or to hold me while I tried to sit up by myself. But too many other nurses were deeply unhelpful and shaming.

For example, after surgery, my body forgot how to pee; it had been days since I'd activated my own bladder. When I told the nurse I was ready to try to use the bathroom, she handed me a plastic squeezy bottle, the kind chefs use to decorate plates with fancy sauces.

"What do I do with this?" I asked.

She gestured vaguely. "Squirt some warm water on your perianal area," she said. "That will signal your muscles to urinate."

"Can you, uh, help me?"

With visible irritation, she supported me as I hobbled to the toilet then sat down with major effort. She squirted me with surprisingly soothing warm water, and I peed with no problem.

The next time I had to go, I asked her for help again.

"You have to do this yourself!" she snapped at me, as if I had some sort of fetish.

I tried not to cry. Even though Dr. Bosch was widely admired at the hospital for her "good" scars, if I so much as hovered my hand near the six-inch incision above my shaved pubic hair line, I brushed the bristly hard ends of the plastic stitches. When I finally dared to look down, I felt ill—I was Frankenstein down there.

As with the surgery, it would have been relatively easy to make my hospital experience more positive. Moreover, these potential changes wouldn't apply solely to women who've had C-sections. Vaginal births also can involve all sorts of "normal" complications that require care and reassurance: prolapse, incontinence, and lacerations.

I wish a social worker had visited me in the hospital, to ask how I was feeling, mentally and physically, in the wake of this new birth and new way—to me—of giving birth. I wish a nurse had explained to me how excruciating it would be to move my bowels for the first time, how I might have to wait a week or more, and that it would be as painful (more, I'm sorry to say) than birth itself. I wish someone had given me the harmless and remarkably effective laxative MiraLAX, and told me to use it daily for the first few months, because the combination of new breast-feeding, changing hormones, sleep deprivation, and hemorrhoids confused the shit (literally) out of my body.

I wish a lactation consultant had visited me right away in the hospital, both to help Clara latch and also to explain that with my especially big bazongas, there were only a few comfortable nursing positions this early (no side-lying, no football hold). Instead, the only baby education I received in one of the best teaching hospitals in the country was the legally required "don't shake your baby" video on the in-room TV.

Jennifer Block is a journalist who's written about the issues surrounding our "maternal industrial complex." In a recent article in *Pacific Standard*, she writes, "Studies suggest that a warm-up begins in the days and even hours before labor, when the mother's brain, uterus, and mammary glands up the number of receptors for opioids and hormones such as oxytocin and prolactin." Many of us know oxytocin as the celebrated "love hormone" that drives bonding between mothers and their newborns, especially during letdown and lactation. It is also the chemical "push" for pushing, triggering contractions as well as beta-endorphins, "tweak[ing] a woman's state of consciousness (and her experience of fear and pain) during labor and flood[ing] the brain with a warm, fuzzy high following birth." These beta-endorphins "stimulate prolactin, which starts circulating during labor in preparation for the suckling newborn, who further stimulates its release."

This is only the tip of the iceberg (crown of the head?) of hormonal reactions between mother and baby. As Block explains, "The baby's body is an active participant in this complicated feedback loop, and the mother's and baby's systems play off of one another. In the throes of labor, for example, the fetus has a 'catecholamine surge' of adrenaline and non-adrenaline to shield its brain from trauma and prime the lungs to breathe."

What does the lack of these "natural" (which I put in quotes because everything that exists in nature is natural, including scheduled C-sections) hormones and reactions do? C-section moms have documented difficulties breast-feeding. They have a higher risk of postpartum depression and other psychological complications, as well as a higher likelihood of feeling detachment from their babies. I feel as if I'm in my own feedback loop here, constantly repeating *C-sections are bad, medicine is bad*, like a parody of a hippie midwife. But plenty of women have wonderful births on the complete menu of drugs, and many women who give birth without meds or interventions suffer from trauma or mental health issues after birth. The issue, as with so many women's health decisions, is information and reasonable choice.

We all agree too many American births occur in the operating room. Of the 32.7 percent of American women whose labor culminated in surgery in 2013, how many were "unnecessary"? According to a recent paper published by the American Congress of Obstetrics and Gynecology, more than half of C-sections are "called" due to slow or stalled labor, or abnormal or (the language here is important) "indeterminate" fetal heart rate.

This statistic begins to explain the frequency with which midwives advocate for reduced fetal monitoring. As much as technology has decreased maternal and fetal death rates, that technology also leads to raised medical anxiety (for lack of a better word), which in turn leads to more surgeries.

How do we reduce the number of C-sections that are not strictly necessary? According to recent (February 2014) jointly issued guidelines by the American College of Obstetrics and Gynecology and the Society for Maternal-Fetal Medicine, it is possible. Their recommendations include "allowing prolonged early phase labor, considering cervical dilation of 6 cm (instead of 4 cm) as the start of active phase labor, allowing more time for labor to progress in the active phase, allowing women to push for at least . . . three hours . . . [and] encouraging patients to avoid excessive weight gain during pregnancy."

In other words, if doctors would just do what the hippie midwives have been saying now for a generation: let the mother's body take the lead in this process. Step in when there is actual, rather than actuarial, risk. Educate patients about their options for "better" births before the contractions start (and stall).

Moreover, it shouldn't just be "informed" mothers who take hypnobirthing or natural birth classes, choose to hire doulas, or receive advice on how to avoid "eating for two." Process-oriented labor wouldn't be a rich ladies' game if insurance covered the costs of these economically, physically, and emotionally beneficial practices.

Though most of the women in the Mommy Group had C-sections, I'd willfully refused to apply the statistics to myself while anticipating Clara's birth. In Manhattan hospitals, the C-section rate is over 20 percent for babies of normal birth weight. I chose my OB practice vaguely based on their "natural birth" friendliness. To me, this meant unmedicated; I didn't ask Dr. Bosch's surgery rate.

Danny and I attended birth class at our local yoga studio. The teacher was a doula and labor and delivery nurse in training to be a midwife. We had an entire session on C-sections: what would happen, how the procedure would go. I thought I listened carefully.

"No, you didn't," Danny has always insisted. "I looked around the room and none of the pregnant women were listening. It was like you'd all shut down."

Michele the doula agrees. When I suggested to her that women need more information before birth about what they'll need after birth, she said, "Ladies don't let us [doulas] talk about after the birth. The birth is a big deal and should have a lot of support, but *afterward* throws you under the bus. I'll say, *Can we talk about the first six weeks of your baby being born? Let's talk about how much support you'll get.* In our postpartum package, we come and look at mothers and talk to them. We do dishes and pick up their dry cleaning and sit there while they breast-feed. We hold the baby while they shower. While we're washing the dishes, we check on the moms, and then it can be natural to say, *You seem like you're having a hard time. Here's a list of doctors.*"

While I was pregnant, I read *The Big Book of Birth* by childbirth educator Erica Lyon, carefully weighing my birth "choices." I was vividly affected by her commentary about the harm that an epidural would potentially do to my baby's brain. That is, I *thought* I remembered the quote until I actually went back and looked at the book. Lyons *didn't* report increased negative side effects for babies when an epidural is administered. The sentence that must have tipped me so firmly into the anti-med camp was this: "One thing to consider about medication in labor is they add more unknowns." Somehow I'd heard—enough to have it firmly in my brain, in contrast to all anecdotal experience among my friends— that epidurals and interventions were bad for me, bad for the baby, bad, bad, bad.

Dr. Bosch listened to my birth plan, like a "mother-friendly" doctor is supposed to do. I told her I wanted a natural birth, and she didn't counter my statement with the facts: that my gestational diabetes would affect my ability to control my birthing decisions. That being flagged from exercise for much of my pregnancy meant my pelvic floor muscles would be weak. That the need for pain relief is nothing to be ashamed of.

Mehera Bonner wrote in *Time* magazine in 2014, "Most people define a 'natural birth' as delivering a baby without the aid of any kind of medication. But maybe the definition of 'natural' needs to be broadened so that women don't feel like second-class citizens for requesting an epidural."

In her 2012 *Slate* article, "The Truth About Epidurals: Are They Really So Bad?" science writer Melinda Wenner Moyer explains that though they do slow labor, they also reduce exposure to stress hormones in newborns, reduce the likelihood of the use of instruments in birth, and, most crucially, do not raise the C-section risk. In fact, Moyer writes, "Based on all of this evidence—which, of course, is far from perfect—the American Congress of Obstetricians and Gynecologists published a position statement in 2006 concluding: 'the fear of unnecessary cesarean delivery should not influence the method of pain relief that women can choose during labor.'" I really, really wish I'd known.

. . . .

It was late in the afternoon on Thursday when the three of us finally came home from the hospital. I'd been away since early Sunday morning and a mother since Monday. My parents were back in Philly for a few days; they planned to return for the weekend. Dr. Bosch's post-C-section protocol was unusually strict: "No exertion at all for the next two weeks," she told me. "And you're house-bound except for trips to the pediatrician. I don't want to see you back here with popped stitches."

Fine with me. Exhausted, scared, and now in serious pain, I was unable to comfortably stand. I still didn't know what Clara's body looked like. From my hospital bed, I'd never seen her without a diaper. I decided these next two weeks were a medically prescribed "lying-in" period. I'd rest and finally get to know my child.

Over the previous month, Danny and I had transformed our comfortably bohemian habitat into a baby-friendly home. We bought a changing table at IKEA, set up a bookshelf next to our bed with toys and favorite Maurice Sendak books, and cleaned out two dresser drawers for Clara's tiny clothes.

We'd been back for about an hour before we remembered we didn't have a bed for her. My dear teacher and mentor, whose children were now grown, had insisted we take the wicker bassinet in which her babies had slept. I'd been excited and flattered by the gift, but once we brought it home, it so obviously predated infant safety regulations, I was convinced placing Clara in it would suffocate her. Now it sat in our bedroom, taking up space. The fancy convertible bassinet-to-crib we'd splurged on was still in pieces in its refrigerator-size box. We'd planned to put it together Sunday, but then my water broke.

My first thought was the Mommies, specifically Heidi down the block. "Call!" I said to Danny, panicked. "Maybe they have something." Clay was over three months old now and slept in a crib. Besides, we needed someone who knew what to do with a baby.

Five minutes later, Heidi's husband, Josh, was at our door, a collapsible (and built to code) bassinet tucked under his arm. After admiring Clara, he laid her on the ground, swaddled her almost as expertly as the nurses at the hospital, and placed her gently in the little bed.

"Now all you have to do is get through the night," he said.

Sometime in the early-morning hours, after we'd already woken up six or seventy times, Danny got out of bed to use the bathroom. Unaccustomed to our new bedroom setup (the tiny bookcase, cords for the night-light and humidifier, an upholstered chair near the bed for nursing), he tripped. I watched in horror as he flew through the air, hitting his head on the nursing chair on the way down, and falling flat on his back on the hardwood floor. For a moment, I imagined the tragic headline: "Mom Alone: Father Killed on Baby's First Night Home."

"Did I hurt her? *Did I hurt her?*" he screamed at me from the floor. Clara was in her bassinet six feet away, on the other side of the bed, sleeping like a . . . baby. I was laughing too hard to answer him. The next morning, there was dried blood on his forehead, and I felt terrible. But we'd gotten through the night.

Over the next few days, visitors came and went, but I didn't much notice their entrances or exits. I was in bed or on the couch, nursing, rocking, and staring at my baby. After she had Gus, Antonia told me, "It's like being on an acid trip that doesn't end." Her LSD comparison was the only description that made sense in those early days of parenthood. I was so tired that hallucinations seemed imminent; distance, time, and space, my sense of my own size and shape were distorted. Clara was a little self-contained Deadhead, concentrating on a single bead as if it were the Buddha, following her fingers like tracers past her face. But most of all, early parenthood was like a drug because when I was in it, I was sure, in direct contradiction to all evidence, that I was the only one who'd ever felt this way.

When I finally looked away from Clara long enough to glance at myself in the mirror, I saw—again, with the vicious clarity of hallucination—that I had become something else: a parent (I also saw gray hair, wrinkles, pimples, and a stomach that stayed the same whether I sucked it in or not). This is permanent, I realized, tracing the new lines on my face with a finger. As much as I loved Clara, I was heartbreakingly, cloth-rendingly sad. I sort of sat shiva for my past self for a while.

It's taken years of thinking, listening, and writing for me to realize why Clara's birth and the immediate postpartum period were so traumatic for me. I was probably already sick. I'd been through two miscarriages and a scary pregnancy; my hormones were unbalanced. I should have gotten therapy after the first miscarriage. All women should. It's a trauma, and traumas require help.

Danny and I didn't have enough support after Clara's birth. We should have hired a postpartum doula, should have asked my mom to come and stay for two weeks. We should have begged and borrowed enough money for me to take a real maternity leave: three months of bonding with my baby and (relative) ease. Of course, that also should have been legally mandated and supported, as it is in every other first-world country on the planet.

. . . .

It was more than four years later, and Antonia and I were at the annual benefit and silent auction for Clara's and Gus's preschool. Both kids were going off to different kindergartens in the fall, the first time since they were born that Antonia and I wouldn't have reason to see each other several times a week. Like most moms at a preschool benefit, we were drunk, and feeling good. Because I was in the process of finishing the edits for this book, and Antonia knew the story almost as well as I do, I was asking her some slurred questions.

Earlier that day I'd posted a request on Facebook for positive birth stories. My editor had reasonably pointed out that birth is not necessarily a traumatizing event, but I'd made it sound like torture. Over the course of that first day, I received more than fifty responses from friends and friends of friends to my query:

> It hurt like a bitch but I still loved it.
>
> As traumatic as my delivery was (exploratory surgery and appendectomy along with the twins) it was still the best day of my life!!! In fact—as soon as that epidural hit I was SOOOOO relieved from the enormous pain engulfing me.
>
> My oldest is turning 20 this summer, and my "baby" is 16. Yet, both birth experiences are as fresh to me as yesterday. If you currently have babies, you might think you'll grow hazy about the experience, but I certainly have not. My mom is 84 (pregnant 11 times, with 7 surviving children) and her descriptions are complete with clenched fists and squeezed-shut eyes and laughter/tears.

Reading these wonderful, heartwarming stories, worries about my own inadequacies flooded me. Each glowing tale of bearable

C-sections and beautifully painful vaginal births left me feeling like shit.

I wanted Antonia to reassure me that my negative perception of Clara's birth didn't mean something bad about me as a mother or person.

"Do I suck?" I asked her, with only a little edge of drunken whine. "Why did all of these women like their stupid births so much?"

Antonia swigged from of the tiny bottle of champagne we were sharing. "Birth is"—she stretched the next word out, a little slurred, in addition to her usual Australian pronunciation—"*e-le-ment-al*."

I took my own swig. "But even so, why is it that some people can take an elemental experience and make it sound so positive and I just . . . can't?"

"I don't know the answer to that," she said. "But I do know that *e-le-ment-al* experiences aren't negative or positive. They just are. Giving birth is one of those moments where you're close to death, and so people put their own range of emotions and feelings onto it."

"But why couldn't I just be *happy*?" I asked her again.

My dear friend took a long look at me. "You're happy *now*," she said. "That's what matters. And that's how you're going to make room for other people's experiences within your own."

"Birth happens how it happens," doula Michele said to me as she wound up our interview. "But it's really about the mending." She laced her fingers together to make a strong bond. "How you get from here to there. What happens afterward. The *mending*," she repeated.

Right. So, dear reader, dear pregnant mother-to-be or sleep-deprived new parent, make room for a range of experiences. Because beautiful, terrifying, unexpected, overwhelming, *el-e-ment-al* birth is just a taste of what's to come in beautiful, terrifying, unexpected, overwhelming, *el-e-ment-al* parenthood.

5. Lady Madonna

Baby at Your Breast

From Heidi

October 30, 2010

You're doing great! For the first week Clay was home, I was walking around sobbing and topless.

On our fifth day home, we couldn't wake Clara up in the morning.

"Come in right away," the pediatrician said over the phone.

In the cab, I reverted to my pregnancy sense of inevitable disaster, except a supercharged my-baby-is-going-to-die version. We'd known her such a short time, and now we were obviously going to lose her. I didn't know how I'd survive.

As soon as we set her down on the pediatrician's examining table, Clara started wailing her little head off.

"Look, she's fine," the nurse practitioner said. "She was just a little groggy. You have to feed her every four hours, whether she wakes up or not. And you should see a lactation consultant to make sure she's getting enough milk."

It *was* me, I decided, back to my familiar self-blame. From then on, I set my alarm to four-hour intervals, noting each feeding and dirty diaper on an app on my iPhone. Still, I worried. There was no way for me to tell how much she was eating. Her little mouth was moving when she latched on, but I couldn't tell by looking at her throat if she was gulping the milk down or hanging out like an unsuccessful groupie backstage at an Aerosmith show.

We called a lactation consultant, making an appointment for the next morning. However, before I saw her, the Mommy Group stepped in to rescue us all.

That afternoon, the Mommies came over for their first visit to Clara. The sound of them clomping and giggling up the stairs filled me with relief. When I'd checked into the hospital only a week earlier, it was ninety degrees—a climate-change fall heat wave. Now, in the first week of November, the weather was suddenly frigid. The babies were dressed in layers of fuzzy clothing from which their mothers carefully unspooled and unwrapped them. Isabella had been riding in a MOBY Wrap, strapped tight to Anna's chest, and Katie was in her car seat. Gus looked like a little white bear in his zip-up suit with ears.

"We're here!" Jane announced, unstrapping Katie. "But we almost killed this kid on the way up. Don't ever try to carry Clara in a car seat up those stairs unless she's buckled in. Where's a plate for cookies, or should we eat them from the box?"

The cookies were from Joyce Bakeshop, the delicious bakery around the corner that Danny and I had been boycotting for seven years because we got in a Seinfeldian fight with the owner. I craved those cookies every time I walked by the shop, and had told the Mommies I couldn't go in and buy them myself. They tasted like pure butter with sugar on top. Yum.

"Now hand over that baby," Antonia said. "What happened today? Why did you have to rush to the doctor?"

I burst into tears, telling them I'd thought Clara was going to die, and that I still couldn't tell if she was eating.

"Let's see her nurse!" they chorused. I bared my breasts and pressed Clara's little mouth to the closest nipple. She did exactly what she had for the last few days, sucking softly, blip of a nose pressed into my skin, eyes half-open.

"Don't let her fall asleep on the job!" Anna said.

"She's eating!" Jane said.

"Have some cookies! Build up your supply!" Antonia said.

"Once you get her weight gain on track," Jane said, "you can tell everyone to fuck off."

I sank back into the couch, feeling okay for the first time since I'd come home from the hospital.

Lactation consultant June Feinstein came to our house the next morning at seven, before the wake-up feed. I lay in bed, topless, as she removed Clara's diaper and stuck her on her portable fuzzy, sheepskin-padded scale. After nursing Clara on my right breast for five minutes, she then popped her off for a weight check.

"One ounce! You're doing great," June said. "Now the other side." Another ounce. Clara *was* eating enough.

"Don't try to pump yet," she added.

"But I have to!" I told her. "I need a freezer supply because I won't be able to go back to work otherwise, and I have to go back to work!"

She looked annoyed.

"Don't think about that right now," she said.

"Wow, that was the best two hundred fifty dollars I ever spent," Danny said after he walked June downstairs. "I feel totally reassured."

I made my mouth smile. Why had I needed a paid consultant for what was supposed to be the most natural activity in the world?

I wish I'd been easier on myself. Breast-feeding, as any new and lactating mother will tell you, is not intuitive. I have heard many women describe it as the hardest thing they've *ever* done. Nursing after major abdominal surgery, which a C-section most certainly is, is like learning how to skateboard in a parking lot full of broken glass. You're gonna get hurt.

In our first-world existence, we've lost many of the traditional practices and received wisdom that women have shared with each other for most of human history. In many cultures, women still spend a few weeks—often a month—lying in to recover from birth and establish nursing. Female relatives keep the new mother nourished and comfortable because they know how; most women spend almost the whole of their adult lives either pregnant or nursing.

We have lactation consultants.

Lactation consultant Freda Rosenfeld is known as the Breast Whisperer of Park Slope. She is the spiritual mother (and mentor) of the growing community of Brooklyn lactation experts, and an appointment with her is almost as de rigueur as an Ergobaby carrier. I'd heard about Freda, as everyone calls her, before I was even pregnant, when a friend told me I'd "have" to see her.

"Isn't breast-feeding supposed to just work?" I asked.

"That is ridiculous," she told me. "Trust me. When you need help, we'll call Freda."

When I needed her, I did call Freda. She was booked.

By the time I was writing about breast-feeding for this chapter, Freda had become a sort of superhero in my mind. Now I wanted to see the view from the other side of the breast-feeding looking glass. When I needed to go on a lactation consult ride-along, I called her.

On an extremely cold day in January 2015, I joined Freda

on a visit to Jennifer, mother of newborn twin boys. The babies were preemies, just home from long stays in the NICU. Jennifer was supplementing with formula but wanted to switch to exclusive breast-feeding for the health benefits, and she hadn't been able to figure out how to get the boys to tandem nurse (simultaneously).

When I arrived, Freda was holding both babies, cooing at them. With her dark hair and bright eyes, she looked as if she could have been my own mother or aunt. Jennifer was obviously exhausted, with circles under her eyes and milk stains on her T-shirt. But even amid the new-twins chaos, Freda's presence was reassuring.

Handing the boys back to their mama, she explained, "I want to concentrate on four things." Jennifer held one baby and rocked the other in a bouncy seat with her foot as she talked. "One, increase your milk. Two, get these guys to be better suckers. Three, put you all on a livable schedule. Four, increase their time at the breast for each feed."

This is what Mommies need, I wrote in my notebook. *Attention and care along with the lactation help.*

After inspecting both of their latches, she advised a visit to an ear, nose, and throat specialist for one of the boys' tongue-tie. "Tell her I sent you. She'll see you faster," she said. Then Freda hooked a Boppy nursing pillow around Jennifer's waist, positioning the twins for tandem feeding.

That's never gonna work, I thought to myself. Clara always just rolled off the Boppy, and so I'd relied on the more structured, cumbersome, and expensive My Breast Friend pillow.

Within thirty seconds, though, the babies were latched on and feeding like puppies. Jennifer was obviously shocked and overjoyed.

"Thank you, *thank you*," she kept repeating.

"Now, we'll meet again," Freda said. "I want to make sure these guys keep getting along well." We'd been there about an hour.

When we left the apartment, zipping up our parkas against the frigid cold, Freda was walking to another appointment.

The visit reminded me of the uniqueness of each mother and child's nursing relationship. Mom and baby both have to be physically capable of breast-feeding, which is not a given. There are so many problems that can affect nursing, especially early on, when everyone's new to the game. These can include latching issues and infant tongue-tie, and for the mother, pain or low supply.

The members of the Mommy Group had different levels of breast-feeding comfort and desire. Isabella had a very hard time latching in public. Was it because Anna was distracted and grief-stricken? Was nursing particularly difficult for this child? Anna used what she dubbed a "Frankennipple"—a little clear plastic shield that fit over her breast, providing a smooth and easier surface for Isabella to latch on. Even so, they had to be alone, in a darkened quiet room, to get any real "work" done.

"It's as if she's telling me to stay home," Anna said when we met up at the Teat Lounge when Issie was a month old. "But I need to get out!"

Jane's daughter Katie, if you recall, was born underweight, and she stayed that way for quite a while. Jane blamed herself for Katie's feeding issues. She was still in the hospital, with Katie in the NICU, when "the whole world became about nursing."

As for me, when the newness and emergency of early feeding finally abated, Clara ended up taking to the breast like a champion. As my stitches healed, we stopped supplementing with formula (until I got postpartum anxiety, but that would be months later). Still, I was more housebound than I'd anticipated. "Oh, you should try to get out," people would say. "Fresh air and a walk—great for you and the baby."

Taking that advice was easier said than done. For the next six months, every time I wanted to get out, I had to dress myself and Clara in the many required layers (including nursing bra and easy-access top for me), bump the Snap-N-Go stroller, car seat, diaper bag, and baby down two flights of stairs, snap the car seat onto the Snap-N-Go, and finally buckle Clara into the seat (usually I'd have to take her out at least once to add a layer or, God forbid, change a diaper). Not to mention, remembering my purse, keys, water bottle, and snack (because in those early nursing days, a sudden hunger pang made me feel worse than morning sickness). If Clara had stayed asleep through all this, it was almost guaranteed that she'd wake up at this point, which meant she'd want to eat.

On Mommy Group Mondays, we'd all get to the Teat Lounge between 1:00 and 2:00 p.m., even if we'd planned to meet at noon. Anyone whose baby wasn't nursing at that moment would get the others food and drink, while the rest of us sat around, shirts open, babies noisily sucking. Nursing a new baby isn't a passive activity. Newborns do a lot of grunting and falling off the nipple when they feed. They roll their eyes back in their heads and snuffle their noses and fall asleep and spit up.

Once together, we'd check out each other's . . . techniques. Each of us had her own modesty requirements. Antonia could nurse with Gus in the carrier (an elegant Mei Tai Baby with a Japanese print), an accomplishment we all admired. Melissa was the queen of the open cardigan that draped with extra fabric. Antonia sported a leopard-print nursing bra, a punk touch I would have mimicked had that bra come in my size. Anna let it all hang out, literally and figuratively. Issie wouldn't nurse without the Franken-nipple shield, so out in the world, Anna looked more than naked, almost obscene, with her dental-dam-like accessory stuck on her bare boob, pinching it into the shape Issie's mouth needed to latch. Renée was the only one of us who used a Hooter Hider, one of those drapes that snap around the mother's neck, patterned with a Lily Pulitzer—esque print.

I think I nursed with a receiving blanket tucked over my shoulder, once. It seemed as if I was suffocating Clara, and she worked her little head out anyway. When the cover slipped off, I figured, What's the point? My boobs were too big to successfully cover. I was not like the exquisite wood-carved medieval German Madonna with elegant teacup bosoms that I'd often admired at the Metropolitan Museum. No, I was full-on High Baroque, Rubens-eat-your-heart-out. If I didn't smother Clara with an enormous tit each time I fed her, we were ahead of the game.

There are two schools of thought on the issue of when to feed the baby: nursing on demand or feeding according to a schedule. Some books and experts advocate nursing on demand for as long as the parent can stand it. Others advise feeding every three hours and letting babies cry it out until their bellies adjust to the rules. (There are lucky parents whose little ones "decide" on a civilized meal and snack schedule. I have never met one of these babies, but I have also never met a Komodo dragon.)

Clara and I were nurse-on-demand gals. By the time she was a few months old, I took it as a challenge to nurse anytime, anywhere. In front of my father or my father-in-law? Whatevs. We're a hippie family, and Danny's dad is a doctor. In the snow-covered park, while wearing a parka? As long as Clara was wearing a hat, all cool. At brunch in a Manhattan restaurant? In the back row of the Big Apple Circus? Yes and yes.

I was lucky with nursing. Breast size isn't supposed to make a difference in milk production, but it sure seemed to help in my case. Where other women could store a coffee creamer, I had the dairy case at Whole Foods. Before pregnancy, I wore a 32 G bra, and at the height of my lactation, the boobs overflowed a K cup. After hauling such knockers around for decades, they were getting the workout they were made for. (Finding nursing bras that didn't make me look like the "adult female" illustration from the seventies hippie classic book *Gnomes* was a task.) Let me advise all the pregnant and new mommies out there: a few weeks after your milk comes in, find a specialty bra shop, buy the best and most attractive regular bras you can find, and have them altered to become nursing bras. Your self-esteem and your lifted and shapely bosoms will thank you.

Early nursing is only the first part of the breast-feeding "journey." Back when I was pregnant, I'd excitedly registered for an expensive portable electric breast pump (which are now covered by insurance, at least in New York state), and I knew who I wanted to buy me that pump: my good feminist aunts Barbara and Cheryl. Barb went to medical school when her kids were little; Cheryl was an attorney in the City Solicitor's office in Philadelphia when she had my cousin Lily. It seemed appropriate that they would provide the means both for me to get back to work and to bring Danny into full co-parenting mode. They were cool with it and bought the pump but didn't feel as passionate about the gift as I thought they would. This may have been because the idea of extracting milk from your breast in the workplace is relatively new; the high-powered yet portable electric machines didn't exist until the nineties.

Before giving birth, I calculated that if I pumped twice a day from the moment my milk came in, I'd be able to build up enough freezer supply to enable Danny, my conveniently insomniac husband, to take half (exactly half—equal!) of the night feeds. Egalitarian parenting, thanks to modern technology.

Perusing Amazon.com reviews, I discovered a few bestselling choices: the Medela Pump-In-Style or the Ameda Purely Yours (whoever came up with these names doubled in the douche-dubbing department at Annoying Lady Products International Inc.). Both came with a convenient black nylon tote or backpack (I kept thinking they were designed to look like the hideous black nylon Prada backpacks that had been the height of fashion back when I first moved to New York), and were "dual-action," allowing the nursing mother to express milk from both breasts at the same time. Imagine the time saved! I chose the Ameda; its reviews mentioned fewer nipple blisters. (Sorry, I know the phrase *nipple blisters* is one that requires a bit of a breath.) I thought I'd hook myself up, get a whole bunch of milk, and we'd all be pumping-in-style twenty-four hours a day.

When I received the pump, I stared at the white and shiny photo on the box with hope. This was going to be my all-access pass: to earning my own income, to Danny's successful co-parenting, and to the chance that I'd be able to go out by myself for more than a two-hour sojourn to the local coffee shop.

But even unwrapping the thing daunted me. There seemed to be thousands of tubes, flanges, diaphragms, and valves for the pump itself; bottles, nipples, lids, bags, and ice packs for milk storage. Though we had approximately one square foot of unaccounted-for space in the kitchen, all of these parts would need to be cleaned, sanitized, and stored. We bought a bunch of Tupperware and a special basket for the dishwasher, a drying rack for the countertop, and extras of all the parts.

When I finally set out to use the pump, a few weeks after June the lactation consultant's visit, I felt optimistic and feminist as I set up the apparatus, inserted the tubing in the valve and jamming my nipple into a funnel-shaped flange. I turned the thing on, waiting for geysers of milk to issue from my milk glands (I had no idea I had several on each nipple), and experienced . . . the feeling of my breasts being sucked down a tube, while an almost invisible thread of moisture issued from each one. Googling revealed I needed bigger flanges, so Danny was off to the local baby supply store. Now each breast issued a thin trickle, and the sensation was less painful than just weird. Twenty minutes later, I had an almost full bottle of yellow-tinged breast milk (thank God it wasn't pink—pink means blood, and if you see that, call a lactation consultant ASAP and give your poor boobies a rest). That bottle represented barely one feed for Clara. How often would I need to pump to keep up with her needs?

You have to get one of those hands-free pumping bras, Antonia wrote to me. Back to Amazon, where the top choices were the Simple Wishes and Free Expression models, both of which resembled strapless jogging bras with cutouts for the pump's funnel-shaped nipple flanges. Once hooked up, would I look like the overjoyed white workin' lady on the packaging, typing emails while my milk coolly exited my body?

Antonia had a freezer exploding with pumped milk and months of timely answered emails (not) to justify her love of the hands-free bra, but with my pendulous breasts, I was out of luck. I might have "simply wished" to watch *Mad Men*, but instead I was cleaning up the milk that had "free expressed" all over my couch.

Once I started pumping regularly (one breast at a time), I noticed something strange. The pump talked; it told me what to do and how to do it. The Mommies had warned me about this. Jane and Anna both heard their pumps murmuring, "Whip it," I heard "Push it" and "You go." When I turned the knob to high, the pump became more frantic, yelling at me to "Come on, come on!" Shocker: pumping and the "ideal" of exclusive breast-feeding can become its own maternal stressor.

So, yes, the electric breast pump is a miracle. For many women, it's also an albatross and an uncomfortable joke, especially in the workplace. On the otherwise hilarious TV show *The Office*, there was a recurring gag about a new mom who insists on pumping milk at her desk. The guys at Dunder Mifflin stare at her boobs, copping a glance if not a feel. Every time I watch it (which is a lot, because Danny has it on a constant insomnia loop), I always feel sorry for that mom. Her feminist ire that she can't pump in full view, and her insistence that her lactating breasts are not sexual, makes me sad. Sure, most women wouldn't *want* to pump at their desks, in full view of colleagues, but the legal reality is that a lot of workplaces view this "right" as more akin to peeing than to eating a yogurt.

Renée wrote to the group about her workplace pumping issues. Back at her job as a hospital administrator, she developed clogged milk ducts. *With Charlie, I would massage the clog out, because I was home,* Renée wrote to us. *I can't sit at my desk massaging my breast at work, though.*

Clogged ducts create hard lumps in the breast (never a good thing, obviously), and they *hurt.* You have to either get the baby to suck the clog out, or pump it out. "Position baby's head on the opposite side of the clogged duct," say the websites. When I first felt the rather sharp pain of a clogged duct, I tried to figure out how to position Clara, as if her head was the moving second hand on a clock. I couldn't hold her upside-down to nurse, which seemed to be the correctly opposite direction. The stakes were real. If left untreated, a clogged duct can lead to mastitis, a full-on infection that can only be treated with antibiotics.

Heidi pumped four times a day for months. Clay stopped nursing in public when he was about six months old, but Heidi still wanted to give him as much breast milk as possible. She admits now she may have been a little obsessive. "I don't want to say I was sadomasochistic pumping that much," she said at a recent Mommy Group dinner. "It kept me connected to Clay. I set aside time at work every day, and I would look at pictures of him and think about him. I was doing this good thing." She laughed and shrugged her shoulders. None of us could figure out, in reflection, if the pumping was more for Clay's benefit or her own.

Back when we were pregnant, we'd discussed how we'd attach photos of our babies to the pumps, because that's what the books said to do. Really, though, as the mothers of children less than six months old, children with sitters in a whole other borough, a train and a bridge or tunnel away, children who (God forbid something happened, most of us had been in New York on 9/11) might be separated from us for who knows how long, how could we go for more than a minute without thinking of our babies?

Even with all the problems, all the Mommies pumped, every night. Because the pumps existed, we pumped. We worked, therefore we pumped. I must add that pumps have gotten more efficient and less bulky even in the few years since the Mommy Group's babies' births. There will eventually be more options, and they'll be easier. But the problem of pumping—the why and import of this bizarre task—will not cease.

. . . .

The phrase *breast is best* is all too familiar to most of us, and, yes, it's true—a lot of the time. Women who are physically, logistically, and emotionally able to nurse their children should do so—*if it continues to work for them*. However, many really healthy women either don't produce milk, don't want to breast-feed, find the schedule physically incapacitating, don't get the support they need from partners or family, feel unpleasant psychological triggers when nursing, or have to work at jobs that don't allow for comfortable pumping. In these and many other cases, supplementing with or exclusively using formula is a godsend. Women should allow themselves to turn the breast-is-best volume down, especially if it's negatively impacting their relationship with their babies.

No one likes to talk about how breast-feeding can become almost a leisure-class pastime, especially if you're spending forty to seventy dollars each on nursing bras, two hundred dollars for that lactation consultant appointment, and whatever insurance doesn't cover for your pump. Working-class women are also less likely than white-collar women to work at jobs with maternity leave and designated pumping rooms.

The statistically proven benefits of breast-feeding have much to do with skin-to-skin contact, with mommy and baby gazing into each other's eyes, and synching their breathing. It is obviously possible to receive those benefits with formula feeding.

My ease with breast-feeding allowed me to nurse for more than two and a half years, much longer than I would have anticipated. And—spoiler alert—during and after my postpartum mental illness, nursing seemed like the *only* thing I could do in the mothering department with any level of competence. So I guess I was lucky, sort of.

. . . .

Melissa was the first of the Mommy Group to wean, when Sofia was nine months old. Melissa never liked breast-feeding much, feeling self-conscious and uncomfortable. Still, when she told us, I was shocked. It hadn't even occurred to me at that point that I could wean, let alone that I would want to. I hope I managed to keep my side-eye to myself, because I now know my judgment was *not* okay.

"Why did you wean?" I finally asked Melissa recently, figuring she'd have a PC explanation like that she and Sofia had other ways of bonding. Instead, she giggled.

"I wanted to go on vacation without her and have sex with my husband!"

We were at Joyce Bakeshop, that same local patisserie/coffee shop where Danny and I finally ended our boycott. Melissa had just dropped Sof off at her preschool a couple of doors down, and we were drinking cappuccinos and eating baked goods. Decadent for a weekday morning, but we were going to go deep; we needed pastries.

She continued, after a bite of muffin. "I hated pumping, and we were already doing some breast milk and formula together. Patrick and I really wanted to have that weekend alone." She sounded defiant. "It was purely based on my own convenience. I know you're supposed to nurse for a year, but that was never my goal. I figured if I did it for six months, I'm feeling pretty good. And I made it past that!"

"Sofia suffered *sooooo* much from your decision," I said. Sofia is—well, it seems impolite to call such a pretty girl with blond curls a bruiser—tough. That girl kicks a soccer ball like she *means* it. I made sure my comment was delivered with obvious sarcasm.

"I know, right? She's so unhealthy," Melissa said, matching my tone. It was good to talk so frankly with her. I'd always felt a little self-conscious about my own long lactation.

Now I was trying to explain this to Melissa, because I'd always felt guilty about our different timetables. "Having so much anxiety—it felt like the only thing I was doing well," I told her. "I felt like I missed her babyhood in a lot of other ways."

"It was the opposite for me," she said. Another mark against one-size-fits-all mothering.

By their babies' first birthdays, all the other Mommy Group members were weaning. Jane was the last holdout along with me, but even she pulled the plug (as it were) at thirteen months when their pediatrician thought Katie would gain better on a wider range of foods. The mommy blogs, general culture, even my pediatrician aunt agreed. Once a child is old enough to ask for it, isn't nursing a little weird? Apparently, not for me.

A seminal moment in our nursing relationship came when Clara was a little less than a year old. She was talking a bit: "Dada" and the occasional "Hi!" One night, we were alone on the couch, getting ready to nurse. As she approached my bare breast she growled, "Mmmm, good." I started laughing so much I almost dropped her. With a review like that, I never wanted to wean.

Clara was eating solids—hummus, yogurt, cheese, pears, apples—and gnawing on dried mango. Like all toddlers, she went mad for Cheerios and Veggie Booty. But she always chose "nuk" (her word) first.

The moms made fun of me, gently. "Don't worry, you have a few years until sleepovers start," Renée said. "She'll probably be off by then." Antonia tagged me in a photo to our Facebook group of a cunningly crocheted baby beanie that looked like a breast, with a big hot-pink nipple.

Very funny, I responded, looking at the computer screen over my nursing child's head.

When Clara was just over a year, we were visiting Philadelphia, having dinner with my pediatrician aunt Barbara. I casually mentioned that the baby should still be getting most of her calories from breast milk.

Barbara was horrified. "No," she said. "That is *not* correct."

I pretended I was joking. "She loves solid food! I was about to feed her some hand-pureed kale, but I lost it!" Clara did manage to gum down enough yogurt and hummus in front of Barb that I didn't look like a complete liar, but as soon as my aunt left, I pulled out my boob and let Clara eat her real dinner. Barbara's words stayed with me, however. She was right. A one-year-old should be getting most of her nutrition from solid food.

According to lactation consultant (and Clara's godmother) Stacy Greene, "Kids' caloric needs are actually higher per kilogram of weight than adults'. Babies peak out on their intake of breast milk and formula at around seven months—and thirty-two ounces. Introduce vegetables and meat early, because those are tastes that will be harder to get kids to like later. At a year, though, the goal should be about sixteen ounces a day of milk, and three meals and two snacks of solid food."

At this point, "solid" can actually mean a variety of textures. While most parents still rely on purees as their baby's first foods, even very young eaters can handle real food cut into tiny pieces. According to the baby-led weaning method, kids eat as they choose, sucking on whole pork chops or pears if they reach for them.

Stacy told me, "Once they can chew, a 'meal' could be half a sandwich or some pasta, along with vegetables and fruit. A snack would be a piece of fruit or plain yogurt. Offer milk *after* the solid food." She laughed, knowing how challenging such a rigid format would be in practice. "You should aim for balanced meals, but what's really important is to form the habit of sitting down for three meals a day. As they get older and exert their will, that can be harder, so start when they're young. At the beginning, solids aren't providing very much nutrition. It's about the practice."

She added that my aunt was probably concerned because by the time they're a year old, kids are *capable* of drinking eight ounces of milk three or four times a day. However, filling their bellies with liquid not only offers too little nutritional variety but can block iron absorption and lead to anemia. (Due to this potential iron deficiency, many pediatricians automatically advise iron supplements for young children.)

I felt guilty as Stacy and I talked, because I couldn't recall if Clara had *truly* been getting most of her nutrition from breast milk, or if I just joked about it. Maybe I couldn't even tell? As with adults, children's portions are fist-size, and one-year-olds have very small fists.

When I finally weaned Clara, it was surprisingly easy. I was able to tell her it was going to be the last time, we went to the toy store together and bought a special doll, forever named "Nuk Dollie." That night, we sat down on the couch, and I opened my shirt for her as I'd done so many thousands of times since she was born. She latched on as she always had, closing her eyes, enjoying not simply the "nuk," but me, I was sure, my smell and touch, and the feeling of us being connected in that animal way. Tears rolled down my face, but Clara didn't notice. She pulled off for the last time, and Danny put her down for bed. After snuggling the new dollie in her crib all night, she didn't ask for my breast again, ever. We were done.

6. When Something's Wrong

Jane, Katie, and the Lesson of the Changing Table

From Jane

November 28, 2010

We had a physical therapist and occupational therapist evaluate Katie through Early Intervention yesterday and they confirmed she has high muscle tone in her upper and lower body. I couldn't help but cry during the evaluation, and on and off since. The good news is that this seems to be motor related, not cognitive. The bad news is that cerebral palsy is the concern with hypertonia in infants, and we won't know for some time. Apparently, Katie is going to teach me to be patient.

We were at a Mommy Group meeting in Antonia's apartment in early winter. We'd already had lunch, tea, and cupcakes and were starting on the beer. The living room was like an animal burrow from a Beatrix Potter book, safe and warm.

We'd gotten to the fun part of the after-lunch chat. Who was actually having sex, and how was it?

"I don't know about you guys, but things do *not* feel the same down there," Antonia said. "No one tells you when you do natural childbirth, how . . . rearranged you get."

Those of us who'd had C-sections winced. "Guess that's the only benefit of surgery," Melissa said.

I stayed silent. At three months old, Clara was the youngest baby. Danny and I had tried to have sex exactly once. It didn't go well, and left us sad and confused. Was this all we would be now? Parents?

I was about to ask the crucial question—did it hurt so much for everyone?—when Jane interrupted the juicy talk to get a diaper from her stroller in the hall.

"Wait, don't say anything good," she hollered, leaving five-month-old Katie lying on the changing table a few feet from where we sat in the living room.

"Do you want one of us to hold her?" Melissa called after her.

"Nah. She won't roll off."

We all looked at each other. It was one of the basic rules: Don't Leave Baby Alone on the Changing Table for a Second.

Jane turned around, registering our shocked expressions. "What? Your babies would flip off?"

"Yeah," we all said.

"Fuck," she said. "It isn't all in my head."

Katie's fists had always been clenched, and she'd always seemed tense, like a baby Type A lawyer. She always looked surprised, with wide eyes and pursed lips. Katie also had trouble gaining weight, remaining perpetually below the bottom of the chart. Still, she was a bright, alert girl, sleeping well, making eye contact, clutching her mama with tight little howler monkey fists.

Later, Jane explained how confusing those first months with

Katie were for her. "One of the harder things about having a kid with a mild delay is that you're concerned, but you don't always get external confirmation of that concern."

Jane and her husband, Carl, had been together for nine years. When she got pregnant, she was working at a big public high school in Brooklyn, and feeling as if she'd landed in her dream career. After bumping through various fields in her twenties, she finally realized that hands-on work with troubled adolescents fulfilled the needs of her own disrupted childhood. Carl is an architect, rising but still junior at a big-name firm. It was a prestigious job, but wouldn't be lucrative for years.

Jane got pregnant easily, but then miscarried. She recovered quickly, conceiving again within a few months. By the time she realized the pregnancy would stick, she'd decided she wanted to experience motherhood without professional pressure, even though that would mean quitting her current job to stay home with the new baby for a full school year. She hoped she'd be able to find an equally satisfying position again, but figured the New York Department of Education was hardly a low-turnover employer. Something great would be there when she needed it. In the meantime, on one income it would be a tight squeeze but worth it.

Jane had been worried that something was wrong with Katie since the day of her challenging birth: the C-section, when Jane was awake enough to hear the residents discussing how to insert her uterus back into her body. Then Katie spent her first five days in the NICU with jaundice.

When Katie was a week old, Jane and Carl took her to the pediatrician for her weigh-in. She wasn't gaining.

The doctor stuck his finger in the baby's mouth. "She's got high tone in her jaw," he said.

Jane knew the term from her training in early child development. "That meant high muscle tone—very tight," she recalled three years later, tightening the muscles of her own face to demonstrate. The doctor also thought Katie seemed to have high tone in her clavicle and upper chest. All of this was causing her suck to be too strong, which was why nursing was difficult. "That was the first time I was a little bit scared," Jane recalled. "But it was also the beginning of me deciding, *I'm going to try to understand this as much as I can.* Still, it was a shitty feeling. It wasn't joyous."

Carl had an unusually long parental leave of four weeks. Once he went back to work at his firm, Jane felt terribly alienated. Breast-feeding was going better, but after working full-time her whole adult life, living on the third floor of a walk-up with a nursing infant was alienating, to say the least.

"I was the first one of us to cry in front of everyone," she reminded me. "Katie was like three weeks old. It was so hot, and I couldn't keep it together anymore. Remember?"

I didn't remember, I told her, because I wasn't at that particular meeting. It was August, I was still pregnant, and Danny wouldn't let me walk that far (about a mile into Park Slope) in the blistering heat and humidity. I'd found out they were all hanging out later, and I'd been worried that my new group was already picking teams without me.

"Sorry. We all needed to eat chocolate croissants and drink iced coffee!" Jane said, laughing. "Anyway, it's not like you didn't get to see me cry a lot more later on."

Jane's own doctor told her Katie was simply high-strung. "Wonder where she gets *that* from," he said, and Jane felt too shamed to press the matter further.

Still, she worried. Enough that when she was home in Portland for a visit and a friend offered her a session with her own osteopath, she went for it. Osteopathy is an alternative medical treatment in which practitioners use their hands to make adjustments on patients' bodies. Some people believe osteopathy to be a powerful, yet noninvasive, form of medical treatment; others regard it as new-age quackery. Jane was somewhere in between, but she was willing to try it for Katie.

"The osteopath definitely noticed the tension that I was talking about," Jane explained. "It was nice to have confirmation of it. But then she correlated it to birth trauma, and said, 'Don't be surprised if you see her reenacting her birth, such as getting stuck in tunnels.'" Here we both cracked up. "When is she in a tunnel? Maybe she meant turtlenecks? The bullshit monitor was going off in my head, but then I could tell that after she did the adjustment, Katie was looser."

As we chatted, we were sitting in the spare bedroom (a futon on the floor of a side room) in the house Jane and Carl had bought a few months earlier in the Sunset Park section of Brooklyn. It's a three-story with a rental apartment on the top floor, and a fixer-upper for sure. But there's also a huge yard where Jane can garden and Katie can play. After moving in, Jane finally felt some version of settled.

During our conversation, then four-year-old Katie barged in every few minutes, asking for juice or a snuggle. Carl made crepes that morning, offering me one, warm from the pan and sticky with

Park Slope Food Coop jam. Even at the center of this idyllic picture, Jane cried during our interview.

She asked her pediatrician for a referral for Katie to be evaluated at their six-month appointment. Katie's weight was still below the bottom of the chart, a sign that something was off.

"Not meeting milestones is always very difficult," Dr. T. J. Gold told me in a phone call. Dr. Gold is not my pediatrician aunt (that's Dr. Barbara Gold), but she is Clara's pediatrician, as well as (probably more important) the lead physician at the Park Slope branch of Tribeca Pediatrics. In practice since 2008, Dr. Gold has referred many children to the New York State Early Intervention Program, a free therapeutic program for children with disabilities.

Many people don't realize how common such diagnoses are. According to an article published in *Pediatrics* in 2011, one in six children in the United States was diagnosed with a developmental disability in 2006–2008; these disabilities include "autism, attention deficit hyperactivity disorder," as well as other developmental delays.

I asked Dr. Gold how she differentiates between a child with a potential problem and one who is not "quite" on schedule.

"It's tough to identify a delay before six months because babies change so much between two and six months, and delays can be plus or minus a month," she explained. "I become more critical at the six-month appointment."

How does she express concern to vulnerable parents? "I don't sugarcoat, but I am straightforward. Parents look ahead and think that their child's problem will be insurmountable. Early Intervention is an incredibly useful tool. [Ideally,] by the time the child gets to kindergarten, the delay has become a nonissue."

What if the problem is bigger? Dr. Gold answered carefully: "When it's something more significant, that's a more difficult conversation. I try to enroll the parent in wanting to be an advocate for their child. Then we can take *some* of the emotion out of it."

The process for evaluating an infant starts with a home visit by whichever types of therapists seem warranted. Both physical and occupational therapists came to Jane and Carl's apartment.

"At that age, the evaluation is big picture," Jane explained. "Your kid is delayed, but they don't define it as anything. The evaluator said it was a motor disability. *I* pushed and asked about cerebral palsy, and she said, 'We can't rule that out.'"

Katie qualified for services: two sessions of physical therapy (PT) per week for gross motor skills, and one session of occupational therapy (OT) for fine motor skills.

"Then once you get your evaluation, it's weird to have therapists come to your house," Jane remembered. "You've just woken up, you smell like breast milk, there's a knock on the door, and it's your child's physical therapist. Our life revolved around these PT sessions for a long time, and they were so intimate."

Jane and Carl took Katie to a pediatric neurologist. "We were worried because she was curling her toes, as well as showing some other issues," Jane told me. "He said, 'Oh, she's what we used to call clumsy!' I wondered, 'Am I being that stereotypical mother worrier?'"

In addition to her motor delay, Katie had some sensory challenges—she was especially sensitive to noise and motion. Jane said, "We did this music class. In retrospect I can imagine that for little six-month-old Katie, that was probably incredibly overwhelming."

Though Katie's delays were relatively mild, Jane still had to learn early on the lesson that all parents of kids with special needs have to learn: how to be Katie's advocate, above all else.

This meant fighting for the maximum services, with someone whom Jane frankly called "a bureaucrat in a crappy office in downtown Brooklyn. I'd be there telling the gory details of my birth story to this stranger, explaining what my kid couldn't do."

Later on, fighting meant realizing and admitting that the part-time nanny she'd spent weeks finding was not the right fit. "She kept Katie out all day in the stroller. She went to the library, and the zoo, she took her over to other people's houses for playdates. She was a veteran nanny, and was telling me Katie was okay. I *knew* it wasn't best for Katie to be stuck in a stroller all day. She needed to engage her body in a comfortable place, like our house. Katie's work starting at eight months when we got services—and what is still her work—has been the task of learning how to move her body. Now I can say to her, *What do you think you need to practice at PT? Swinging?* It's *hard* for her to coordinate pumping her legs. She has to have someone explain the movements: *Keep your eyes on the horizon, pick a focal point.* But then, soon as her PT teaches her those little tricks, she's able to access movement."

Jane hired our friend Stacy as a sitter on my recommendation. Stacy was just starting graduate school to become a dietician with a specialty in early childhood as well as a lactation consultant. She needed money and loved hanging out with Clara and me when she could; I found her presence to be a balm. So did Jane.

"Things started to change after Stacy started coming over," Jane told me. "Now there was an adult I really liked in the house with me."

. . . .

Parenting a child with disabilities is extremely alienating. Often, parents feel as if they can't take a spare moment away from their child; remediation and therapies are constant and crucial in the early years, when brains and bodies are most malleable. It's hard to choose to take care of yourself when your kid needs so much. And when your child is ill, you don't want to be around "shiny, happy" moms and babies.

After our friend Stephanie had her son James twelve weeks early, she was unprepared for almost everything about their homecoming.

"When you have a preemie, you have no time," she told me. "There are so many therapies, and they happen at home. James had *twelve* half-hour PT, OT, speech, and play therapy sessions each week, and we also had a nutritionist come for an hour a week."

She continued, explaining that mothers of typically developing children have different concerns than mothers of children with special needs—another point of alienation.

"Sleep training is important, but if your child isn't eating, you're worried about him not meeting his milestones on a whole other level," she explained. "And I felt very insecure about my knowledge of my own child. Every therapist who came in was an expert in child development, and I wasn't. That had started in the NICU. I wasn't allowed to hold my baby for two weeks. Even then, I had to get the nurses' permission, and I needed them to move the wires and make sure he was okay. For four months, I never bathed my baby or changed a diaper!"

James came home with an oxygen tank and a respiratory

monitor that went off throughout the night. "We were scared as hell," Stephanie explained. "When we didn't have any nurses, he didn't seem safe anymore."

Now James is in a school for kids with developmental issues. I asked Stephanie if that's made a difference for them in terms of community, finally.

"Well, it's not a community school," she said. "The children come from all five boroughs of New York. Even if we schedule playdates, we have to travel to them." When they do go to their local playground, "people don't know that James has special needs because he's not visibly disabled, so I feel a lot of judgment in public, even with close friends. People don't understand that he can't do 'better' sometimes. He hasn't learned how yet. But he *will*."

Parents of kids with disabilities need community even more than those with "typical" children do. Unfortunately, they're the last people in any position to organize one, especially in the baby stage. Perhaps, in this case, looking for an organized or facilitated group could be an answer.

Becca is an old high school classmate of mine. I noticed she'd posted photos of her tiny premature newborn on Facebook. That's not quite right: I first noticed her posting photos of her baby, who looked about the size of a "normal" newborn, but she'd been captioning the posts with "three months adjusted age!" It turned out she'd had a "very unexpected" C-section at twenty-nine weeks' gestation, just as she was beginning to build community through childbirth and prenatal yoga classes.

When I wrote to her to ask if she'd received any specific support for preemie parents, she responded that no, there'd been no in-hospital group support. Even after her baby was home, the specific issues around having a preemie—"trying to navigate pumping every two hours, bottle-feeding a baby who would stop breathing during her bottle, and fear of all germs"—made it difficult for her to relate to other mothers. When she finally did find a regular mommy group, she "ended up feeling envious of moms with 'normal' deliveries and pregnancies." Finally, she tried a paid group moderated by a therapist. "We didn't focus as much on our babies as we did on our lives, which made me feel like my experience was a bit more universal," she said.

Virtual mommy groups can be very helpful. Ella is a social worker living in Phoenix, Arizona, expecting her second child. At the end of her first trimester, after her nuchal fold test and blood work, she'd received the news that her son tested potentially positive for the chromosomal markers of Down syndrome.

Already predisposed toward finding a community of mothers (after she had her daughter, in her early twenties, in Portland, Oregon, she founded her own mommy group), Ella went straight from the doctor's office to her computer. "I got on Facebook and I started searching for other mothers with the same issues," she said. Over the months of her pregnancy, she was able to "meet" many women and families, from all over the globe. The virtual community has been especially helpful in her finding other families in her exact situation, with older "typical" siblings. Her hope is that these burgeoning friendships will support both her and her children for years to come.

Danny's first cousin Sam and his wife, Tiffany, have also benefited from online organizing with their child with disabilities, though in a different context. Their middle child, Jack, is severely autistic. At thirteen, Jack speaks a few words and is unable to control his emotional reactions.

Sam and Tiffany's lives are consumed with helping Jack make what may seem like tiny breakthroughs. For them, those signs of progress—he says his beloved uncle Josh's name, he sleeps through a few nights in a row—are huge. Each moment of connection and contact shows them his potential for growth and change.

When Jack was around six years old, Sam needed an outlet to help him deal with the frustration and sadness he felt around parenting this child. He decided to raise money for autism research by running marathons, but not just one or two. Sam ran a marathon every week, zigzagging across the country to every race he could find. He called the project Operation Jack, and figured he'd stop at the year mark.

"I wanted to take a chance and do *something*," he says now— and he has. Operation Jack has raised over $300,000, and serves as a platform for other autism organizations to raise their own funds.

"Now we're 'autism people,'" Sam explained. "We help steer other parents in the right direction, and we have a huge network online." When Jack was having an extremely difficult time at his school in Colorado, where the family had relocated for Sam's work, they were advised by members of this network to move to Pennsylvania for better services. They took that advice, and found a community waiting for them. None of this organizing has "cured" Jack, but it's made the family healthier and happier in general. Which is what we all want, right?

. . . .

Because Danny and I were conscious that autism has some genetic predisposition, we were especially aware during our early pediatric appointments as Dr. Gold checked for developmental delays. As dictated by the Centers for Disease Control and Prevention's checklist of developmental milestones for six-month-olds, Dr. Gold noted if Clara responded to her own name, to other people's emotions, copied sounds, "liked to play with others, especially her parents," and whether or not she seemed happy. The CDC's guidelines explain that social skills at the six-month point "should" include a child's "know[ing] familiar faces and begin[ning] to know if someone is a stranger" and that she "likes "to look at [her]self in the mirror."

Dr. Gold never specified what she was doing when she asked us these questions in what another mother friend described as a "neutral" tone of voice. We knew. According to the CDC, "Research has found that ASD [Autism spectrum Disorder] can sometimes be detected at 18 months or younger. By age two, a diagnosis by an experienced professional can be considered reliable." The American Academy of Pediatrics "recommends that all children be screened for developmental delays and disabilities during regular well-child doctor visits at 9 months, 18 months [and] 24 or 30 months."

The pediatric practice of screening young children for delays is relatively new, and not without controversies and confusions. There are debates over the specific language or even the definition of "delay." For example, walking is developmentally appropriate between nine and eighteen months. It's the same with speech. Even if a child doesn't "hit his marks" exactly, it doesn't necessarily mean he has a disability. It doesn't mean he doesn't, either.

Jane told me, "The worst thing that people said was, *I don't see what you're talking about. Your child's great. Whatever bad thing you're thinking about her isn't true.* It made me feel like I *wanted* something to be wrong with my kid. As if my response was going to be, *No, she's not great.* When in fact it was, *I want to help her struggles.* That message was undermining."

With modern medical and technological developments, there are more kids with disabilities than ever before. Which means there are also more parents (and aunts, uncles, grandparents, and friends) who know the particularly fierce love such children give and engender.

"It was the most difficult for the first two years, when we were *so sad* that we weren't happier," my friend Craig Teicher said to me. Craig and his wife, Brenda Shaughnessy, are poets and parents to seven-year-old Cal and four-year-old Simone. While Simone is neurologically "typical," Cal has severe cerebral palsy. As I've watched their family grow and change, through birthdays and moves and health crises, they've shown me the true strength and joy of parental love.

"The worst fear for us was at the beginning," Craig continued. "Once we knew who Cal was, we didn't [spend our lives sitting] there staring over an abyss of fear, like we did in the first two years. After that, when he did something funny, we laughed. If he was sad, we were sad. And if he didn't communicate the way others do, we decoded it, and that became the adventure of parenting this child."

Now that Katie is almost age five, it's hard to tell that she ever had a problem. She still receives physical therapy and (perhaps as a result of so much practice) seems to understand how her body works better than most kids her age. Jane will never quite get over that feeling, though, of worrying about her child.

After a few years, Jane finally returned to a position at a New York City public school—the local one in her neighborhood, where Katie will attend kindergarten.

"I don't know if it's my dream job, but I just want to make sure she's okay for a few more years. Is that crazy?"

"No, it's being a mom," I said.

7. Back to Work

Breast Pump or Tote Bag?

From Heidi

December 10, 2010

I'm feeling so guilty about sending Clay to daycare—the early morning! the germs! the lack of mommy attention! Did I mention that my mother-in- law is staying on our couch to "ease my transition" back to work? For two hours in the night, it was a crying baby, a tired and cranky husband, and a mother-in-law.

From Antonia

December 10, 2010

You have to believe and know that you are NOT depriving Clay of anything by going back to work, that a healthy baby-work balance is GOOD for you and so GOOD for him (not to mention good for the household economics and equilibrium generally) and that you WILL BOTH adjust.

Down the block, Heidi nervously went back to work after her maternity leave. Clay was now almost five months old. As a school administrator, she'd managed to arrange an extra two (unpaid) months with him before going back, as well as finagling Wednesdays off in exchange for longer days the rest of the week. She was the first of the Mommies to return to full-time employment, the first to enroll her child in daycare. We were all watching her and Clay carefully.

While most of did not want (nor could afford) to stay home full-time, we also didn't want the nine-to-five (or, New York–style, nine-to-eight) full-time-job grind. According to the Park Slope Parents 2013 Nanny Survey, a full-time nanny costs an average of $15 an hour. Shares, which are very popular, are cheaper, around $20 an hour for two kids. Daycare—the only group option available for children under the age of two—averages around $12.50 an hour. Oh, to live in France, we'd sigh, where we'd have long parental leaves, subsidized childcare, and affordable raw-milk cheese.

As I've mentioned, I returned to tutoring students when Clara was five weeks old. Though I only went three afternoons a week, I was shaky and exhausted, racing home by seven, in time for Clara to cluster-feed for the next eight, twelve, or sixteen hours. While I was out, she'd be with her daddy or our lovely kooky babysitter Michele (the same Michele who later became a doula), but I was *sure*—rationally or not—she'd rather be with Mama.

While I was working, I'd space out about the simplest details. "Don't you find it ironic that *you're* supposed to be organizing *me*?" one of my longtime students said with a teenage smirk, after I left my Metrocard and ATM card at home for the second time that week. Thank God, I was working with families who already knew me well, and for moms who remembered what this was like. No way would I have made it at a real job. And forget my own writing. There'd been no space for *that* since the beginning of my third trimester, when I found myself obsessively researching organic crib sheets online when I was supposed to be finishing my novel.

Jane, too, was trying to get back to some version of her professional life. She applied for a part-time social worker gig at a local school but obsessed over every aspect of the process, from what to wear to the interview to whether or not she was up to the responsibilities to what she should ask for in salary.

In many ways, for all the Mommies, nothing seemed less "right" than going back to work after our babies. It wasn't that we didn't like our jobs any longer. We'd been professionals for more than a decade; we chose these careers, pursuing them through graduate school and slogging up from entry level. Our professional selves had been who we were before giving birth. We wanted to want to return to the "us" we'd been before, those competent, professional women. But it was impossible. No amount of work *or* time spent with our children was enough, to any of us.

Before Clara, I imagined I'd relish the return to my professional life. Instead, working at five weeks postpartum felt like a violation. I had no choice; I was a freelancer in a country with no subsidized maternity leave. Danny and I both had to work nights, weekends, whenever and however we could get the gigs. Always in debt, we relied on the kindness of our families, especially when it came to Clara. We were, we are, lucky to have relatives who chip in as generously as they can with time and money. Otherwise, we'd need to make different choices.

Commuting to my tutoring gigs on the subway, I felt as vulnerable as when I was heavily pregnant. People were still giving me seats, as if they could tell by looking at my exhausted, puffy face and body that I'd been up half the night nursing.

I'd sit with my students, ostensibly working but wondering

whether Clara had napped . . . drunk her bottle . . . Would Danny send a photo? Did Clara miss me? How would I even know?

I trusted the sitters, and (of course) Danny, knowing that it was good for Clara to have care from difference sources. Yet, I felt guilty leaving her. At least I was making money, right? Right?

From Elizabeth

January 30, 2011

Clara is now on her fourth day in a row with a sitter. Danny has mostly been home, but working nonstop for a deadline (literally—he informed me this morning he fell asleep in his desk chair at three last night). The catch? He is writing this piece FOR FREE!!! Which is something that would have been relatively normal and moderately frustrating pre-baby, but now has made BOTH of us insane. I thought the extra tutoring I was doing today would bump us up in terms of cash, but between the increased sitter costs and the fact that one of my students forgot he was doing the lighting for a school play this week, I am just breaking even.

So, yes. Heidi was going back to work full-time, and she was nervous as hell. The daycare they'd chosen looked great; it was cheaper than a nanny, and they were on a two-teacher budget.

The plan was that Josh would do the school drop-offs and then go to his own job as a primary school music teacher, trying to sneak in some practice time on his saxophone during his free periods. Heidi would pump milk in her office four times a day, her peekaboo window blocked with construction paper. By the time she arrived home, Clay would be at his witching hour, that nightmarish time in the evening when babies process their days by crying their bloody heads off.

On the first day of Heidi's return to work, Danny and I got

a frantic phone call. "My sister is watching Clay, Con Ed is digging up the street outside our apartment, and the power went out. Can she bring over all of my pumped breast milk and put it in your freezer?"

A few minutes later, the sister arrived with a bulging tote bag. It didn't seem like enough to justify Heidi's months attached to the infernal pump.

I didn't see Heidi herself for a few weeks, until one Monday when I was on my way to the usual Mommy Group hang. It was freezing out, but I was sweaty, breathing heavy from my baby and baby gear–laden schlep down our steps. Heidi was pushing Clay past in his stroller. Both of them were teary.

"Hey!" I said, happy to see them. "Isn't it a school day for you guys?"

"I was at work, but then the daycare called and told me he had diarrhea. This is the second time he's gone home sick in two weeks. Carl and I don't even have any days off left, because we used them all up on our leaves . . ."

I pushed Clara through our gate and patted Heidi on the shoulder. She continued, voice cracking. "How can you even *tell* if a four-month-old baby has diarrhea? When I went to pick him up, she yelled at me and told me I should feed him differently. All he eats is breast milk!"

Wiping her nose with her hand, she checked on Clay, now sound asleep under a pile of blankets. "The worst part is that when I walked into the school, the babies were all strapped into bouncy chairs, wailing, and I couldn't tell if that was like a particular moment of the day when they're all in bouncy chairs, or if that's the whole day. I don't know how we're going to afford it, but I'm going to start interviewing nannies."

Recently, Heidi recalled that day we ran into each other, adding details I hadn't known back then.

"He was only in daycare for two weeks!" she said. "He was hysterical every day. They kept calling me. He was having what I now think was stress-induced diarrhea! I went back to work on a Monday. I had to pick him up Monday. I think I had to pick him up Tuesday. They said he couldn't come back without a pediatrician's note. They were like, 'Oh, he still takes two naps a day?' And I said, 'He's six months old!' "

On the day she and I ran into each other, the owner of the daycare had "expelled" Clay. "Maybe you should wait until he's more ready for school," she'd said.

Heidi continued, "That night, at home, I started throwing up. I kept saying, 'I can't go back to work.' Josh was on and off the phone with my parents all night. My mom wound up offering to pay for a nanny to get us through the school year, and I instantly stopped vomiting."

What does this story teach us, other than that Clay seems to have inherited his mother's penchant for stress-induced intestinal distress? Daycare doesn't work for every child. Having the money—or having family with the money—to throw at the problem helps, big time. Especially in this country.

For most working parents, daycare isn't *a* choice, it's the *only* choice. Accepting that Heidi and Clay's experience was not ideal or typical, I talked to an old friend, Amanda. Her two daughters, now eight and three, have experienced the full range of care options: daycare, preschool, and a nanny.

Amanda is a high school English teacher. She lives in Manhattan, but teaches full-time in Westchester County, about an hour's drive from her house. Her husband is a chef, so their family works on the shift system. Amanda gets up with Rosie, their eldest, around six, leaving the house by six thirty to make it to both of their schools (traffic allowing) in time for her first class at eight. Dad is usually home from his restaurant by midnight, and wakes with three-year-old Maya, waiting to leave for work until the nanny arrives around seven thirty.

When they only had one child, the schedule was easier.

"We couldn't afford a nanny," she told me, "and we needed childcare close to where I worked."

This is a good point. Many families feel better with daycares close to their workplaces rather than their homes. That way, if their small child is ill, it's easier to do a pickup. Many parents feel more secure when baby is a short drive or single stop away on the subway, rather than a potentially long and anxious commute.

The daycare Amanda found for Rosie was an in-home setup, run by Miryam, an Iranian immigrant who'd already raised her own children.

"My coworker recommended it to me. When her daughter took her first steps at daycare, Miryam got as choked up as she did. She loved these kids."

Initially, the fact that neither Miryam nor her assistants were native English speakers gave Amanda pause. She explains that, "I found—and this was the amazing surprise of daycare—that her personality, which was big-hearted, her intelligence, and my trust in her, ended up being the most important factors. The language piece could come later." The kids napped for two hours every afternoon in Pack 'n Plays set up in the living room. Lunch might not have been of the highest quality (Amanda eventually started sending Rosie in with her own nitrate-free organic hot dogs), but everyone ate.

The "school" consisted of nine kids ranging from six weeks

to three years. Amanda is sure this age split helped Rosie mature and develop social skills beyond her age. "She learned to wait her turn, to share, to understand when someone else's needs were more pressing than her own. She would have to wait until someone had time to change her diaper or give her a snack."

On the "con" side, Amanda felt that communication could be challenging. Her coworkers whose kids were at other daycares received a daily sheet saying how much each kid slept, ate, pooped, and so on. "I went and looked at different facilities," Amanda said, "and was even on the verge of making a change. But I was so attached to these caregivers."

I asked if it bothered her to be missing milestones. To be fair, this is a problem for all working parents, not only those who choose daycare. "For sure I felt sad about that, but because of my school schedule, I could pick up around three. Rosie and I had time together in the car driving there and back. I still felt present on a daily basis. Exhausted, but present."

When Rosie made the transition from daycare to preschool, she cried and had some separation issues but adjusted quickly enough. "That was very anxiety producing," Amanda said. "I had to get to school on time. I couldn't stay to linger on the sidelines while she got acclimated."

Baby number two added complications. There wasn't time for Amanda to double her school drop-offs, so she broke down and hired a nanny for Maya. "It's turned out to be a blessing, because I can ask Margaret to stay for full days, so that I can get other work done," she said. "For our family right now, the combination is successful." She paused. "I want to say for the record how much I *like* the professional and intellectual demands of working. I don't feel as if I'm missing much with my daughters' development; I still spend many hours a day with them. And most important, they're happy and independent."

Amanda's approach in choosing the best care for her family at different times in their lives is a good model for all families.

Back on the job, Heidi developed a de facto mommy group of two with Marcy, a fellow teacher at her school.

"Believe it or not, we were the first women in the history of the school to take maternity leave, and then come back right away to teach after having children! Everyone else chose to quit," she said. The friendship began when they were both pregnant, with babies due about a month apart. "We have all these photos of each other posing belly-to-belly." While on maternity leave, they talked on the phone throughout the day. Marcy started back at work a month before Heidi, and helped her navigate her challenging work-life balance.

When Heidi was distraught over Clay's difficulties in daycare, Marcy would tell her, "Everybody should be glad we're here. All you have to do is pump and cry right now." They pumped together twice a day, bringing each other lunches and snacks.

Because working-mother culture was so new to their school, they created their own standards. "At first, people acted as if the breast milk was hazardous waste. We would put the milk bottles into brown paper bags; then we starting leaving it in the nurse's office."

The school's director of facilities is a courtly but decidedly old-school gentleman named Dominic. Heidi laughed as she told me a story. "One day Dom came to my office and said, 'This new lady who's starting is gonna have to do the thing you did with, uh, the machine and the milk.' I had no idea what he was talking about!"

Coincidentally, Heidi and Marcy both got pregnant with their second children in sync as well. By this time they'd received promotions and their jobs were more challenging. "Our pumping sessions turned into meetings," Heidi explained. "At first we'd be working by ourselves, then we started talking to other people on the phone in their offices. But by the time we were a few months in, we were inviting other people in while we were pumping."

"We had no qualms about it," Heidi continued. "And we created this culture where other women felt free to confide in us about their own lives." She mentioned one coworker, Maria, who often sat in on these meetings while she was also pregnant. After taking a year off, Maria will return to the school this fall. Score one for creating a culture of working motherhood.

"Being a working parent is all about adjusting your expectations," Heidi said. "I'm a huge fan of *Lean In*, and I always think of this passage where Sheryl Sandberg agonizes over the fact that she and her husband don't get home until six to have dinner with their kids. But he was happy they had dinner with the kids every night." (Sandberg's husband, Dave Goldberg, passed away very suddenly in the spring of 2015, making this passage and their co-parenting relationship especially poignant.)

Still, so many working mothers don't feel entitled to ask for such parity—even if their partners would want it.

"I was complaining about Josh to a friend at work," she continued. "When he comes home, he goes and stretches for ten minutes, then he takes a shower, and he comes in and eats something. I'm still in my work clothes and already on the floor playing with

Play-Doh. My friend was like, 'What I'm hearing is Josh takes really good care of himself!'"

Heidi hasn't stopped feeling conflicted about the amount of time she works. "I have this thought: *What if something happened to one of them. Would I feel okay about how much time I spend with them?* Which is a morbid way to live your life," she said. "I mean, I know they're both *fine. I'm* the one who struggles with it."

The conflict for working parents doesn't need to be this stark. In Katrina Alcorn's excellent book *Maxed Out: American Moms on the Brink*, she lays down the issues: we live in a country where working parents don't receive the help and respect they deserve—and which would also make them more reliable and productive employees. Alcorn developed a panic disorder when she returned to her own high-level tech job when she had her second child. After a full year of recovery, she decided to devote her professional energy to helping other women understand how to work and raise their families.

"All too often," Alcorn writes, "employers look at the years we stay home with young children as a black mark, wasted time." As an alternative, she proposes a sort of "GI Bill for moms," arguing that with relatively minor government subsidies and incentives, women (and men) would be able to make a slower return to full-time work, maximizing their own energy, earning, and leadership potential in the process.

Alcorn cites numerous studies and articles, as well as her own research. Some key facts: 62 percent of working mothers would prefer to work part-time; less than 50 percent of working mothers stay home for three months; American workers are at "epidemic" levels of stress. The solution is relatively easy to figure out, if difficult to accomplish. If employers care (and they should, for economic reasons if nothing else) about losing women workers to motherhood, they must provide more opportunities for part-time work, job sharing, and reduced hours—without cutting access to benefits or eliminating the opportunities for eventual promotion. With flex-time policies in place, working mothers would be able to keep their jobs *and* feel happy in them.

And, *pace* Sheryl Sandberg: women with power must lean in *and* out. That is, think about the people you employ to care for your own children. Nannies and childcare workers are also working women. Give benefits if possible, as well as paid sick days and vacation; make their jobs as secure and flexible as you want your own to be.

A recent *New York Times* article that made the rounds with the women in my social circle seemed to reveal the great secret. The title almost said it all: "How Some Men Fake an 80-Hour Workweek, and Why It Matters." The article went on to detail how some employees at a global consulting firm "passed" as workaholics. The author, Neil Irwin, writes, "They made an effort to line up clients who were local, reducing the need for travel. When they skipped work to spend time with their children or spouse, they didn't call attention to it. One team on which several members had small children agreed among themselves to cover for one another so that everyone could have more flexible hours." The gender of the vast majority of the employees who faked it to make it? Male.

Heidi brought this study up as both inspiration and caution. "Children require *more* workplace flexibility as they get older," she said. "And women have to create it for themselves."

An example immediately came to my mind. All the Mommy Group kids entered kindergarten in the fall of 2015. In Brooklyn, we have "school choice," which means that most of us toured many schools. These tours inevitably took place in the mornings, and each lasted about two hours. Between Danny and me, we attended twenty—an average number. That's a full workweek, spread out from October through February.

"At first, I asked my boss for the morning off and told her I had to look at kindergartens," Heidi explained. "Then I realized I didn't owe her an explanation. I'm great at my job, and I'd make up the time. So I started saying, 'I'll be in by this afternoon.' You know what? No one even noticed."

I'm not envious of Heidi's job. It's extremely challenging, requiring incredible patience as well as long hours and phenomenal social skills. I am jealous of the *context* of her job: full-time, with oversight commensurate with seniority. When I had to visit our local zoned school, the one in which Clara would be automatically enrolled if she didn't get into one of the nineteen other schools we applied to, the tour coincided with the one day my boss at my new college teaching job could come in to observe me. I had to take the tour, and so wasn't observed, a crucial component for my continued employment.

Ironically, *my* boss was unable to schedule another date to visit my class because she was about to begin her own maternity leave. When she rehired me to teach another term anyway, I thought, *Thank you, working mom solidarity*. I really don't need to mention that this sort of favor is the kind men have given each other in the workplace for generations. Sometimes a bulky breast pump is more useful than a hammer for smashing that glass ceiling.

8. Community Building

In Which We Finally Realize These Babies Are Here to Stay

From Elizabeth

December 12, 2010

Yesterday was really fun! Thanks, Melissa, for hosting. I can't believe the babies played, rather than lying around like a bunch of fish. It was way more relaxed not to have to deal with bitchy waitresses/bartendresses/other people. Now that many of us are going back to work, we'd like to plan a night out? Heidi, how'd it go yesterday with back to work and daycare???

"Where's our lasagna now?" This became Danny's *cri de coeur* as we approached Clara's three-month birthday and the end of the "fourth trimester." We still needed help, he thought. Feeling good for the first time in over a year, I was more confident.

I could fit into my favorite dark-green, straight-leg, no-stretch jeans (I don't fit into them anymore, though. What happened?). They were tight over my belly, but I could button them, walk, and sit on the subway on the way to work. When people told me I looked great, I believed them. My C-section scar only hurt sometimes.

We no longer obsessively worried if Clara didn't make a sound for an hour or more at night. We were all sleeping, not eight straight hours, but enough. On Christmas Day, visiting my family in Philadelphia, Danny and I watched all of *Marathon Man* (Jews on Christmas; we do our best) with my dad, as my mother prepared Hanukkah dinner for the rest of the family. Clara shocked me by nursing and dozing through the whole movie, like a little baby was supposed to do.

"Is it safe?" the Nazi doctor kept asking Dustin Hoffman, cranking his teeth with pliers, and we squealed and giggled in horror. Clara sucked, *glug, glug, glug.* I could get used to this mommy thing if there were even occasional easy days like this.

That night, my family—aunts and uncles, my grandfather and his lady friend—came over, lit the menorah, and ate latkes. Mostly, everyone admired the baby. It had been a whole month since they last saw her on Thanksgiving, and she required another full examination.

We had a good night. Pediatrician Aunt Barbara approved of whatever it was we were doing to keep Clara gaining weight and making eye contact; my aunt Cheryl brought five bulging bags of baby clothes that had been marked down 75 percent at her favorite designer-clothes-for-less chain. At ninety-three, my grandfather was so happy just to be there, to see this daughter of his granddaughter, named after his beloved late wife. My dad played the cello for Clara that morning, the same Bach suite he'd set words to for me when I was little. Between the cello and Pop-Pop Lenny's declaring Clara a *shayna punim*, I was done. My emotional cup overflowed.

A day later, the East Coast was blanketed with what the newscasters insisted on dubbing Snowpocalypse. *Our block isn't plowed! Don't try to come home!* Heidi emailed me. *You'll freak out!*

(Exclamation points Heidi's own.) We stayed on in our hotel for a "snow rate," going stir-crazy enough that I took to wandering the halls with a glass of wine in my hand à la *The Shining*, but pushing a stroller.

Even so, we were cozy and happy in our little hotel room. On the first night there, we gave Clara her first real tub bath. Not that we hadn't washed her in two months (although, in the first couple of weeks, I think we were too overwhelmed to do even that), but we'd been giving her sponge baths, too scared to submerge her in that much water. The hotel tub was so clean and well lit that we got over our fear. Clara had other plans, screaming as if she'd been boiled when we lowered her into the tepid water. On night two, I climbed into the tub first, and then Danny handed Clara to me. It was like the warm, watery birth I'd wanted. Clara kicked her legs, snuggled into my body, and even nursed—heaven. Family bath became a nightly ritual once we finally made it home to Brooklyn. It was healing. Every night I reclaimed Clara, bringing her back to my own body.

"This is it," I agreed with Danny. "We are no longer in crisis."

My friend Chris picked up Danny, Clara, and me at Penn Station when we finally made it home after Snowpocalypse. The drive took two hours, half of that time spent going two blocks down our own street. There was no way we could walk with the drifts still covering cars, the streets virtually unplowed, and the sidewalks only sporadically shoveled.

I'd known Chris for almost two decades. We'd been roommates for years, both in college and beyond. He'd come out of the closet to me only hours after he'd told his parents; I'd promptly introduced him to Randy, his boyfriend ever since. We'd all traveled to Australia together for his sister Susanne's wedding; it was their house I'd run to on the morning of 9/11, and he and Randy had traveled to Los Angeles for Danny's and my engagement party. Of course he was the guy who would rescue us from Snowpocalypse.

The problem was when there wasn't a natural disaster or some other crisis. I wanted him to come over when the streets weren't impassible, to sit and watch a movie with me while Clara nursed or rolled around on the floor, to be the uncle Clara didn't have. When we got together now, I felt as if he only talked about restaurants I wouldn't get to check out or movies I wasn't going to see—which pissed me off. Couldn't he see how hard this was? I didn't want to hear about the fun I was missing; I already felt like I was losing brain cells. For his part, he's told me he felt forgotten. I'd been his confidante, the person he could always call with a question or joke. Now I didn't pick up the phone—or remember to ask how he was doing.

Our conflict came to a head, at least for me, one night in January. It was the day of Clara's three-month appointment at the pediatrician's. She'd gotten two shots and her first oral polio booster. I'd been terrified she would cry, but our doctor was so adept, she hardly whimpered. (I'd had to look away, and then sit down with my head between my knees. Danny held the baby.) Clara seemed fine when I left to tutor on the Upper East Side, with only a turquoise Band-Aid to cover the pinprick of a bump on her fat little leg.

Chris's sister Susanne was visiting from Australia and she wanted to meet the baby, so Danny and I made our first "big" plans since Clara's birth. Chris had arranged a dinner at a seafood place in Williamsburg that he liked—a neighborhood far away enough that we'd have to hire a car to get there. Danny and I had gone out to eat a few times in three months, but only within our new-parent five-block-radius comfort zone. Still, I was determined to see Sue and to have a night out.

I was tutoring when Danny called, Clara wailing in the background.

"I can't get her to stop!" Danny said. He sounded as if he was about to cry himself. "I guess she's cranky from the vaccine."

My tutee's mom heard Clara crying through the phone in another room. "Do you need to go home?" she asked me. "That sounds serious."

"No, no, it's fine," I said. I was determined to both finish the lesson and keep my plans, but I felt my stomach churn and my breasts ache. When I was finally finished, the hour's subway ride to Brooklyn never felt so long.

By the time I got home, Clara had stopped crying, but she started up again as soon as she smelled me, and then latched on like a limpet. Her weight was soft and warm in my arms, and her little body needed all of me. A long meal, and cocktails, in a loud and boisterous restaurant, with a big table of people eager to chat and catch up? Cracking crabshells one-handed while nursing? No way, not tonight. Danny called and canceled our plans while I cried too, with frustration. I'd really, really wanted to be that mom who could do it all. But I wasn't.

Chris came by in the car to see if maybe he and Susanne could come up, meet the baby, and say hi.

"Please tell them to go away," I said. I was too exhausted to pull on my bra and shirt, to talk about anything but that my heart felt as if it was going to lurch out of my body when I heard my little girl crying over the phone.

Danny went downstairs to tell them he was sorry, but we

couldn't figure out how to go out that night. We weren't the groovy, easy-traveling parents I'd imagined we could be. I didn't want to see anyone else, even people I loved, when I was in this state.

I didn't think Chris understood. What seemed like his disinterest in and resentment of Clara made me wonder if we'd reached the end of our friendship. He seemed angry, but he was hurt. As the months went by, that became our new relationship. Hurt and angry, back and forth.

When I told the Mommies the story—the crying over the phone, the vaccines, the inability to go for a "fun" night out—they were predictably and collectively soothing.

"Williamsburg?" Renée said. "At night? We had friends who gave us these baby-sized noise-canceling headphones at my shower, so we'd be able to 'go out to shows' with Emme. I mean, really."

"Gus ran a fever and cried for three days after his shots," Antonia added. "You can't go out with that going on. This is parenthood. You have a little tiny baby. People still should be coming to you. And you went to *work* already today."

It was true. My rules had changed. But I didn't know how to explain that to Chris. Which meant I didn't know how to include him in my new life.

It wasn't until recently, after Chris read the initial manuscript of this book, that he was able to articulate to me what was really going on with him back then. "I wasn't being callous," he told me, and I could hear the discomfort in his voice.

"No, no, of course not. I know you were sad I wasn't present for you . . ." I began, ready to mea culpa my way out of the awkward conversation.

"When you had Clara, it hit me harder than I expected—that

I wasn't going to choose to have this, and that even if it was my choice, it was still very difficult." He paused to clear his throat, and then continued. "I was mourning the child I was never going to have."

I remembered: he'd told me that at the time, that he and Randy had decided, once and for all, not to pursue starting their own family. Absorbed as I was with the overwhelming minutiae of motherhood, I hadn't taken him seriously. Not because he's gay, but because in all the years we'd known each other, he'd never expressed a desire for fatherhood. I didn't catch that the finality of my crossing that parental Rubicon confirmed it for him: he wasn't going to do this.

I go into these details not because I want to rehash what was one of the most painful conflicts of my early parenthood but because so many women feel similar conflicts with their "kid-free by choice" friends. Having a child is still the default setting of contemporary adulthood. Not becoming a parent is its own brave choice, and one that deserves respect and discussion. If Chris and I, two highly verbal people with a long history of mutual confidences and confessions, couldn't find a way to tell each other how sad our diverging paths made us, then who could?

The answer, as with so much about friendships, is: just try. If you're a new mother wondering why all your childless friends are out to lunch, ask them how they're feeling. Sure, it might seem like overkill when you have sore nipples and have slept only in two-hour increments for the last six months, but honor your friends' paths as well. You might end up with a better—and not simply a different—perspective.

By three months old, Clara could hold her head up; she could almost roll over.

We hung a swing from the kitchen door frame, and she bounced and bounced.

I kept buying her hats: striped, with ears, tying them under her chin.

"In Denmark, they leave the babies outside to nap!" Heidi told me.

All I knew was I needed to get out. Even if the only regular place I had to go was Mommy Group.

Our meetings became less casual. Antonia had the moms over for lunch, making chicken adobo in the slow cooker. The next time I had them over I prepared chicken paprikash. Strong flavors for women who needed them. We all ate like wolves, like bandits. That winter, we needed to keep our strength up.

We met at Melissa's house for the first time in January. She made us delicious vegetable soup from scratch and a salad with pomegranate seeds. We were all impressed. I'd rarely stepped into my kitchen since my morning sickness in early pregnancy. After lunch, we ate cupcakes and drank wine while the babies tried to roll on her Persian rug. Her place looked ready for a photo shoot about hip Brooklyn parenting: a huge loft space furnished with a tasteful combination of classic midcentury modern pieces and quirky accents. No threatening piles of paper (like at my house or Heidi's), and no drifts of cat hair (like at Jane's). Melissa's husband, Patrick, was coming home that night to cook dinner for his wife (unlike at Anna's).

When Melissa and I met, I thought she was a little remote, or . . . something. Maybe it was that she was pretty in an intimidatingly sporty/artsy way, with Day-Glo sneakers and good jewelry Patrick bought her for birthdays and anniversaries (the jewelry made me conclude they must have a great sex life).

Before Clara was born, Melissa had confessed to all of us one day in Prospect Park that she'd gone on medication for postpartum anxiety. I hadn't heard of the disorder. It was fall—the new, post-climate-change version. The leaves weren't completely off the trees yet, but it was unseasonably warm, and we were wearing light jackets. The babies were all in their Snap-N-Go strollers and car seats, except Sofia, who lay in her swank Bugaboo like a princess on a stack of mattresses.

"I just went on an antidepressant," Melissa said. Her face didn't betray much emotion to match her words: no tears. "I was so anxious I couldn't get myself out of the house." I imagined Sofia in her Bugaboo and Melissa pushing her round and round their loft, like a wind-up circus bear on a tin track.

Nodding, I empathized but distanced myself. Maybe Melissa needed medication before even having Sofia. Poor woman. Feeling that bad must suck.

When we gathered at her house in January I only vaguely remembered she'd had any difficulties. I was too busy obsessing over her "grown-up kitchen" with a professional range, real wood cabinets, and a stainless steel fridge with a special freezer drawer. Danny and I would never have those things. Our rental has cabinets our landlord picked out at Home Depot fifteen years ago. Our fridge is so loud it sounds as if someone is mowing the lawn in our kitchen.

Sofia and Clara had the same "baby gym," the optimistic name for a cloth play mat with toys that dangle over your little one's head. Ours was a gift from Danny's parents. I requested it specifically because it was a little out of our financial reach: the fancy Skip Hop Barnyard Fun model, all cotton, and no plastic crap. After a couple of days in our house, the mat was gray around the edges, but Sofia's mat was snowy white. Because Melissa washed it. In a washing machine. In her house.

Danny dragged our dirty clothes to the Laundromat a block away for fluff-and-fold service when we couldn't stand the pileup anymore. When he brought it home, the clean laundry sat on the floor until I got up the energy to put it away.

That night, after our lunch, and still woozy from the afternoon's libations and cupcakes, I told Danny we needed to wash our mat.

"We can do that?" he asked. I burst into tears.

My jealousy of Melissa confused me. First-world problems, I told myself sternly, as I continued obsessing over her granite kitchen countertops, her doorman, her elevator. Danny and I had more than enough, I repeated to myself. We'd made the right choices for us. But I lost perspective when I came home to unpaid bills, a husband exhausted from working three jobs and composing at night, and the worry that our beautiful baby would eventually need to wear something other than a hand-me-down onesie, not to mention acquire an education.

I felt as if I was always failing in some crucial way. Antonia would arrive at Mommy Group with Gus strapped to her body in her carrier, limp and sweetly sleeping. I'd try to carry Clara in the Ergo, walk twenty feet, and my back would start killing me. Not being able to use a carrier made me feel incompetent. Why?

As the weeks went on, I became more jealous of everything and everyone, even the Mommy Group members, my new friends. Melissa's house was nicer; Jane's husband, Carl, had a better job than Danny; Jane had the energy to cook and clean. Renée lived in Park Slope, a more desirable neighborhood than ours, with a better school district, and they'd already done this baby thing before, so they knew their stuff.

I was even—sometimes—a little jealous of Anna, now in the midst of a fling with a younger guy. Sex, attachment-free, with no kid in the next room. Sure, she told me she came home from his house and cried her eyes out, but I ignored that. Looking back, I can see we were struggling, all making the same middle-of-the-night decisions, the same sacrifices. So what if one of us had more orgasms or unstained countertops? Realizing how beautifully the Mommies met me in my current emotional place, I vowed to stop with the jealousy. We were all in this together.

"We didn't have mothers' groups back when you were a baby," my mother said to me when Clara was a few months old. "I mean, I guess some people did, but it seemed so fifties. Like for housewives in Levittown."

I heard this as disparagement. She never needed anything like my group; I must be weak for requiring such support.

"You had Yetta," I reminded her. "You had Aunt Barbara. You didn't have a C-section. You had live-in *help*." It was true: my father's mother lived ten minutes away throughout my childhood, as did my aunt, uncle, and cousins. My mother was twenty-eight when she had me; my conception and birth had been easy on her physically and mentally. She'd loved breast-feeding, but then stopped when I indicated I was no longer interested, at around thirteen months. She and my father had lived in a crazy huge run-down house with dirt-cheap rent. For childcare, when my grandmother wasn't available, they had a series of art students who babysat me in exchange for room and board.

My mom was listening. I could tell, because she didn't say anything else.

As the months went on, she started to ask every Monday, "Did you see your mommy group today? I guess I do wish I'd had something like that."

One day she called me, very excited. "You have to talk to my friend Laura," she said. "She *did* have a mommy group, in the early eighties in Philly, and it meant *everything* to her!"

I dutifully wrote to Laura. She responded with her group's story. Unlike most mommy groups I've heard of, they provided each other with childcare—a nice twist.

> We were a group of about eight neighborhood women with children of varying ages. I joined when my son was two. When it was your turn to host you planned an activity, such as a craft, a healthy snack, and free play time for about ten children. The other Moms met at someone else's house for coffee. Play group for the kids and group therapy for the Moms! When I moved to the neighborhood I knew no one, had a husband who traveled all the time and I missed my family and friends in New York. My baby suffered from the worst colic, I was seriously sleep deprived, and a nervous wreck. I never thought I would have another child. Honestly, there would not have been a Mary [her daughter] had I not known these women. The group lasted continuously for at least ten years, until the kids grew up, and more of us went to work. A few years ago, we had a reunion. Those children have always had a special bond, even as adults.

As I wrote this book, I put out a call for mommy groups via email and social media, and was thrilled to receive so many and varied responses. As I've talked to, and even visited, these groups, I've realized how powerful community is for new mothers. We all need it, and many women will go to great lengths to find it.

Margarita, founder of Astoria Moms Meetup Group, was one of the first to contact me. Astoria is in Queens, about forty minutes from Park Slope by car. Traditionally a Greek neighborhood, Astoria has become a sort of second "brownstone Brooklyn" for families. The houses tend to be postwar, but they have large front and backyards, the neighborhood schools are good, and the community is truly diverse (and the Greek food is incredible).

These days, it's hard to imagine that Astoria—a neighborhood where the median home sale price is more than $700,000, and that boasts almost as many kid-oriented businesses and activities as Brooklyn does—was ever less than "child friendly." When Margarita's older daughter was born in 2005, the neighborhood still felt "closed" for those mothers not from the motherland. Though full of families, there were few *specific* resources such as classes, play spaces, or community events for young children and their parents. Margarita decided to create the community she craved.

Using Meetup.com to organize, her first event was a lunch. About twenty mothers came. Before she knew it, more than two hundred people subscribed to the list. "I feel like when you have a baby," she told me in a phone call, "you have a window of openness to meet and start this new life in a group. And you feel good if there's impact beyond yourself."

Claire is another original member of the Astoria Moms. Born in Essex, a London suburb, she moved to New York City without connections to other women planning families. After her son was born, she started attending the meetings Margarita helped organize via Meetup.com.

They became obsessed with building the group, their own world of experts. When they went to playgrounds or restaurants, "and saw that terrified new mommy looking kind of lost, we'd ask if she'd heard about the mom's group." They even made business cards.

For Claire, the effort required to build community was unexpected. "A lot of people I grew up with never left East London or Essex. They're still within a stone's throw of the houses they grew up in. There was never a need for a moms group because it was already an established community."

Mocha Moms is a mommy group founded to address the needs of an established but geographically wide community. According to its website, "A Mocha Mom is a woman of color who has modified or eliminated her employment in order to devote more time to the care and nurturing of her family. It is also anyone who supports the mission of supporting at-home mothers of color." Founded in 1997 by four mothers in Maryland, the goal was always to create a national organization. Now it boasts more than one hundred chapters and is a registered nonprofit corporation, devoted to both mothers' needs as well as active community service.

Eisa is the co-chair of the Brooklyn chapter. She joined a few months after having her son. They hold weekly meetings during the day for moms to come together and talk about everything from breast-feeding to schools, to "micro-aggressions our kids and us might be facing," Eisa explained. "One of my favorite things is that it's a mixed age group of kids. Since my son could sit on my lap, he would watch the big kids run back and forth. Now that he's a big kid, he's wonderful with the younger ones." It's become an extended family.

Sometimes the week's meeting has a thematic focus that goes well beyond how to use a baby carrier. In the fall of 2014, as the issue of police brutality against African American young men (finally) captured national media attention, the group was able to host "a private conversation with two members of the NYPD, moderated by a Mocha who is a former Kings County (Brooklyn) Prosecutor."

The organization also has regional and national meetings and conventions. Eisa even visited the White House for a Mocha Moms policy summit. "I didn't meet Michelle," she said, with only a touch of disappointment, "but it was still an amazing experience."

Keep in mind: sometimes a mommy group is not the right fit for you. Krissy lives in Raleigh, North Carolina. Her kids are older now—well out of elementary school—but when she was pregnant with her fifth (!) child, she knew she needed a community.

"The first one I was in for about six months," she told me, "but it was superficial." She was eighteen when she had her first kid, and she married her husband soon after. "I left the group because of the first Obama election in 2008. The group emails were full of Obama bashing. I am very liberal, and there was no acceptance of how I felt. When Obama won they all posted on the communal message board that the country's gone to hell."

That was bad enough, but when she asked them to be more respectful of other points of view, one of the other moms flamed her, writing that she "and her bastard child were going to hell." Krissy didn't let the experience set her back (if you have five kids, determination is the name of the game, I would imagine). She got back on Meetup.com that night, and found the group she's in now, appropriately called the Hip Mamas and Papas. " 'Open-minded' was in their description," she said. "I was welcomed immediately."

In other words, if the group isn't working, if you're not finding what you're looking for, then get the hell out. Otherwise, you risk not finding community at all.

. . . .

In my search for various mommy group styles, I found myself doing modified push-ups on the concrete floor of the Sports Basement sporting goods store in a strip mall in San Jose, California. I was there, with no small level of trepidation, to attend Baby Back boot camp.

San Jose is a little too far to be a San Francisco suburb—the drive is about an hour with no traffic. It's in the heartland of Silicon Valley, a mix of new money and "normal." There aren't coffee shops and playgrounds every fifty feet. Mothers who want community have to organize in other ways.

I was at Baby Back through the wife of a friend of Danny's. Sarah is a labor and delivery nurse. After she had her first child, she found herself looking for activities. She bought a Groupon for the four-times-a-week class when Violet was around six months old. At first she was in it for the fitness. Then the classes became something more: her community, her child's playgroup, and her circle of support. They also turned her baby into a portable free weight, as children attend Baby Back's classes along with their moms.

I'd attended a few boot camp classes in Brooklyn, but still wrecked from postpartum blues and Clara's birth, I never quite got into them. Actually, that is a total lie: the classes were too tough for me, I was intimidated, and I already had the Mommy Group. When I started exercising again, I didn't want a class; I wanted some alone time with headphones and the gym's Bravo subscription.

In general, I think of Northern Californians as "outdoorsy types." They hike for fun, maybe even rock climb. The cavernous Sports Basement's inventory did nothing to dispel my fears: heavy on the windbreakers and crampons and light on the cross-training gear. This was going to be hard-core, and I was scared.

At 9:25, the ladies began to arrive for the 9:30 class. I was expecting everyone to be superskinny and fit. Instead, I was pleased to see a "normal" range of mommy bodies. My four-years-after-baby-and-I-still-have-a-gut figure was okay. The strollers were bigger than at a similar Brooklyn gathering: double-wide joggers, and not an umbrella in the mix (car culture means bigger strollers). The class held twelve women, each with one or two babies or toddlers in attendance. Emma, the instructor, was inspiring, if you want to look banging in a skort (I do, actually—kill me now). Her four-year-old daughter co-led the class in a purple tutu and ladybug rain boots.

We started with a short run, maybe five minutes. By the end, I regretted scoffing at the other women's bodies. I was at the back of the pack, lungs burning. The hour continued with (if I had actually been able to complete the circuits) three hundred jumping jacks, forty burpees, and God knows how many push-ups. Throughout, the mommies were happy to chat, but I was breathing too hard to ask them questions about community building.

Sarah was the group leader. First there and back on the run, she crunched her abs while her three-month-old son, Asher, spit up milk on her chest. If that had been me three months postpartum, I would not have finished the set.

After class was (finally) over, I headed to a coffee shop on the other side of the mini-mall with Sarah and Nia, another mommy from the group. Nia's kids—three-year-old James and eighteen-month-old Sadie—were still in their PJs (Spider-Man- and Christmas-themed, specifically) and would only let us talk after a bribe of BBQ chips, which made me feel a lot less maternally intimidated than Sarah's abs of steel and working-out-through-spit-up routine.

With her first child (aka Spidey), Nia hired a nanny, returning to work as a corporate litigator when he was five weeks old. Then baby number two came along, and she decided to quit, for a while at least. Now Bryn was seventeen months, and Nia was starting to feel as if she was getting it together. Sipping on a cup of water, she explained the difference between staying at home and litigation. "It was the best thing and the worst thing that ever happened to me. My whole life was what I did. When that was taken away, I didn't know who I was anymore. Learning to sit still and play with toys—I'm only now coming to a place where I'm okay with that."

Joining Baby Back added structure and support to her day. She met mothers who were not going to judge her for wanting to be strong, ambitious—and dissatisfied.

Nia didn't feel supported among other mommy groups in the area. "Some groups take motherhood to the extreme. And if you're not the type who is at home, making your own organic baby food, hand-sewing your own baby clothes out of organic hemp, and you know, like, volunteering for Habitat for Humanity with your kid in your front pack, you're failing as a mom."

Sarah agreed, vigorously, nursing Elias under a Hooter Hider (In my PC Brooklyn, free-the-boobs way, I'd always made fun of Hooter Hiders, but Sarah was such a badass in general, she made it look cool).

Nia continued, "With this group, there's the 'I barely got out of the house, I'm fifteen minutes late, my kid's in pajamas, but guess what, I'm here.' And we all go, 'You're here!'"

When I arrived back at Sarah and Noah's house, a *Frozen* play-date was in full swing. Clara was Kristoff, bowing to the primacy of Violet's Elsa costume. She didn't want to leave, but we were driving to LA to visit Danny's family—and for me to meet more mommy groups.

"I don't feel like every mom is capable of being honest about her experience," another group organizer, Kate, told me. She and six other neighbor families have met weekly for six years at the plastic picnic table in her front yard (in winter they move inside, because it's Minneapolis, and they're not crazy). Though they'd lived on the same block for many years, it wasn't until they all had small children that they moved beyond chit-chat. One "random night, we were out front clinging to each other. We had so much emotion and desperation," she explained, laughing ruefully at the memory. After bringing out the "worst food ever"—cheese cubes and hot dogs, plus beer for the grown-ups—all the mommies perked up. What did they all need from each other with such urgency? Connection and honesty.

"My qualifier with any new mom that I meet," Kate told me, "is I want to be able to swear in front of them, and they have to be able to say something honest within the first few times I meet them. The kind of mom who says everything's great, I can't be friends with her. If you see a mom in your neighborhood and your community, you have to be able to say I am having a horrible day, and my kids are driving me nuts."

The Minneapolis mommies organized sufficiently to have a babysitting co-op until their kids were school age. Kate still vows that her fellow mommies saved her bacon, adding, "When you leave the hospital they should assign you a mommy group. Every mom I know has this huge struggle. I compare it to being married. The big secret is marriage is tough, and it's the same with parenting." Well, yeah.

. . . .

In my fantasy world, mommy groups would be a codified part of the New Parent Experience. It's possible. Lauren Beem is a mommy who now lives in Connecticut. When she heard about this book through a friend of a friend, she was eager to talk to me about the group she joined in Australia when her older child was born.

She and her husband moved to Brisbane, a city in Queensland, when she was five months pregnant. She didn't know anyone there, and especially not any young families. But Australia's thoughtful and mother-friendly maternity policies helped her more than she could have ever imagined.

"When you have a baby in Australia, you stay in hospital for five days," she explained. "They're pro-breast-feeding. They want to make sure you have that set up."

Pediatricians are not as crucial a component of those first early months of parenthood as in the States. Instead of our "well child" visits, new mothers are referred to Child Health, a government-funded program, receiving home visits from midwives at two and four weeks postpartum. These midwives provide assistance with breast-feeding, weigh the baby, and generally check on whether the new family is doing well.

"I kept wanting the midwife to come back because I was having a hard time with feeding," Lauren explained. Luckily for her, Brisbane was like a big village. Throughout Australia, baby nurses visit local pharmacies on set days; new moms line up to get their babies weighed. Both the visiting midwives and the nurses refer women to mothers' groups, which are also highly organized and state subsidized.

Everyone in Lauren's group had babies born in the same week, and the meetings were facilitated by a baby nurse or a midwife for the first six weeks. "All the groups have some structure, like an organizing topic each week," Lauren explained, "but then everyone goes off on tangents." By the end of the six weeks, "you've got friends, and if you want to keep going, you do."

What would it take to create such a system in the US? Hmmm, let's crunch those numbers.

To start: Aussie mothers get eighteen weeks of paid maternity leave and the option to take an additional twelve unpaid. By contrast, the United States only guarantees twelve weeks of unpaid leave for full-time workers in companies with fifty or more employees. Hmmm . . .

Susan Fox is the founder of Park Slope Parents (PSP), the Yahoo Listserv that in a decade has grown into a family resource of more than five thousand members, dedicated to "supporting parenting life in Brooklyn . . . by providing a way to exchange information about parenting issues and living in an urban environment" (aka, the email account filler of parents across brownstone Brooklyn). I think Susan Fox is a rock star. She has a PhD in interpersonal communications and wrote her thesis (way back in the nineties) on online communities. She's a doctor of the internet! This experience proved invaluable when her first daughter was born three days after September 11, 2001.

PSP started as a sort of craigslist for the cast-off baby gear Fox kept finding along curbs in Park Slope. Then a separate list for advice was added. As the Listserv grew, "there were calls for things like, well, can we have a list for older kids and younger kids?" Fox explained to me in an interview. "We didn't want to do that because then somebody who would say, 'Oh! Five years ago, I did this, and it worked. This is how I got my kid to brush their teeth.' "

Whatever parenting question a member might have—say, how to install an infant car seat in a Subaru station wagon (I'm not naming any names, but I may have posted that question at forty weeks pregnant)—receives many answers. Over the last four years, not only did postings on PSP lead to my mommy group and my writing group but also to Clara's crib mattress, Exersaucer, and much of her clothing. We've been able to pass on her toddler bed and get recommendations on winter coats (for me) and a local pulmonologist (for Danny).

Most of all, though, I've read PSP's emails daily for the last four years because of the variety of posts and comments. Someone is looking for the best fresh mozzarella in the neighborhood and someone else wants to know what to do if her baby has an undescended testicle. Heidi received C-section information on PSP when she was still pregnant with Clay, and Antonia buys bags of brand-new boys' clothing every few months from a PSP connection (Gus and Verne look *sharp*).

As the overseer of a group that automatically generates mommy groups based on members' children's birth years and months, Fox has a lot to say about parental organizing—including the reality checks that they can offer worried new parents. She explained, "[As a society,] we have fewer children, and therefore a higher stake in raising fewer children. We spend so much time and energy trying to make life perfect for our kids. We, the parents, need a community too."

PSP and the Mommy Group gave me the freedom to say that motherhood is not this pretty picture. Fox agreed with me, but added, "After I had my second daughter, I would see other people with two kids, and I'd say, *Isn't it hard?* They'd say, *No.* I wanted to be mad at them, but . . ." For her, a mommy group offers perspective at the most myopic point in a woman's existence.

One of the keys, Fox stressed, is making sure groups allow members to feel like individuals. "In my online group," she explained, "we had probably twenty-five people. There were the people who went back to work. There were the cry-it-out and the attachment parents." But those differences weren't the issue. "But more people can diffuse the sense of responsibility. There is a magic number. If you find that sweet spot, you can get that real connection."

One of the difficulties of mommy groups is that they most easily and obviously serve middle-class women with enough time to organize and attend. Sadly, it is the women who probably most need a mommy group who would have the hardest time organizing one: poor women, immigrants, and young mothers.

These days, our friend Stacy works as a lactation consultant and dietician at the WIC program at Coney Island Hospital in Brooklyn. In spite of Coney Island's reputation as a fun yet sordid boardwalk community, it's also one of the poorest neighborhoods in New York. The hospital serves a cross-section of the local community: African American and Latino families who've lived in the area for generations, as well as recent immigrants from former Soviet countries.

As I've mentioned before, WIC is a nutrition program for poor women and children. Members receive vouchers to buy specific food and, especially, formula (this is ironic, as WIC now has a stated breast-feeding initiative). Almost all of the WIC offices offer "Loving Support," a peer counseling program, to organize members, including in group situations.

As a lactation consultant, Stacy hopes to organize mommy groups at her location. There are challenges. "My clients aren't online," she explained. "There's a big population that speaks Uzbek, and another population that speaks Russian, so there's obviously a language issue. There's an office in Brownsville [another neighborhood in Brooklyn] that's been doing afternoon teas for their moms, which are very well attended. I'd love to build up to that."

I would add: when women organize, when we codify our groups, à la Mocha Moms or Park Slope Parents, we will be able to advocate and agitate for the institutional changes and power we seek—as mothers.

I always wondered if my mommy group would have worked if Anna's marital crisis hadn't brought us together. After speaking with so many women about their groups, I'm sure we would have.

9. Postpartum Anxiety

I'm Dancing as Fast as I Can

From Elizabeth

February 20, 2011

I've been diagnosed with postpartum anxiety. I'm on a bunch of meds, so I have to pump and dump. Clara's great through all of this, though she's been upset when I can't feed her. Your support means so much to me! I'm hoping to get stabilized on meds quickly, but in the meantime, this is really scary and sad.

We'd made it through the dreaded fourth trimester. From here, the books said, things would get easier. I looked forward to attending parties, readings, and concerts. The new, post-baby version of my beloved internal life could begin. I would write while Clara napped and read when she nursed. Easy peasy pudding pie.

The moms tried to warn me that it wouldn't feel much better, but I didn't want to listen. Heidi was juggling a part-time nanny, her sister, and visiting parents for childcare. When Stephan took Isabella, Anna was too depressed to leave the house. Renée was busy. Between both kids and Benji's business travel, she'd become an email-only Mommy Group member. Jane was overwhelmed with Katie's occupational and physical therapy appointments. Antonia was obsessed with Gus's sleep schedule. Melissa was available, but I was still a little self-conscious around her.

I felt silly mentioning it, but I wondered if something was wrong with me. I was tired. Commuting on the subway rendered me nauseous and dizzy. The effort of bumping Clara down the stoop for a stroll in the winter sunshine was insurmountable. I planned our Mommy Group's first-ever-night-out-without-babies, but then worried too much to show up. What if I didn't get enough sleep? What if I was too tired to work the next day? We relied on the money I earned. What if Clara needed me that night, and Danny couldn't get her to stop crying, and they were both scared and alone without me? Better not to go, even though I'd been looking forward to it for a month.

My fantasy of writing proved as elusive as my "natural" birth plan. Clara started howling as soon as I opened my computer. I'd pop her in what our evil baby book called the "mechanical mommy" swing, she'd conk out, and I'd frantically type for twenty minutes until she howled again. The sound of the swing became the rhythm of my writing.

At night, when Clara woke in her bassinet beside me to nurse, I couldn't get back to sleep, lying in bed, heart thumping, fearful heat rippling my skin. Danny might have been a chronic insomniac, but I was the one buzzing and awake.

In February, Danny had to go to upstate New York for two nights on a work trip. He'd teach a seminar and enjoy a performance of a piece he'd been commissioned to write for the occasion. The snowy drive to Syracuse was eight hours each way. He was paid one thousand dollars for the whole deal, and we'd already cashed the check and spent the money.

Though I was worried about his trip, I kept telling myself it was only two nights. Renée's and Melissa's husbands traveled often, and for longer stints. My dad toured for a *month* with the Pennsylvania Ballet when I was Clara's age, and my mom had been fine. I wanted to prove I was strong like them, like a good mother should be.

The first night of Danny's trip, I prepared for the worst but hoped for the best. Clara was generally a good sleeper. But on that endless night, it was as if she knew something was off, waking more times than since her newborn nights. Instead of falling asleep myself between feedings, I lay sweating in bed, reading all of *Bridget Jones's Diary* (the most soothing book I could think of), counting down from a thousand in the hope I'd hypnotize myself into a few minutes of rest.

The next morning, I was so tired I was ill. My arms vibrated when I held Clara. As I walked to get coffee and a scone, passing faces grimaced and swelled into malevolence. Car alarms, sirens, and unexpected footfalls made me jump.

Thank God, I had childcare for the day.

When Danny called to see how we were doing, I didn't want him to know, but I'm a bad liar.

"Do you need me to come home after my concert tonight?"

I couldn't imagine sleeping any better knowing he was driving on icy roads.

"No, sweetie. I'll be fine."

I'd heard of postpartum depression, of course. Brooke Shields had it. Danny and I had even discussed it, along with all the other "what-ifs" of pregnancy and early parenthood. I'm not, characteristically, a depressed person, and thought I was an unlikely candidate for PPD. I'd been in therapy good old psychoanalysis for more than ten years, finally "finishing" soon after Danny and I married. My happy ending. I was resolved. Right?

Then, after Clara's birth, I cried—a lot. Everyone told me it was normal, but I wasn't sure. I filled out online questionnaires for postpartum depression, but I didn't fit the diagnosis (Danny, worried about me, did them too, with the same result). So I focused on recovering from surgery and my challenging pregnancy. Successful breast-feeding, getting back to work, acupuncture, long walks in the park, good food . . . These were all supposed to help my mood, to reassure me that having a baby would, eventually, become part of my life story, part of me. I was sleep deprived, but Danny and I are both good on little sleep. I was handling this. Clara was perfect. What did I have to complain about?

I knew several of the other Mommies were on meds. Anna called a doctor the day after Stephan left. Who wouldn't? Jane, too, had more than typical "baby blues." She told us she was taking Zoloft, but explained she'd been on and off medication since she was a teenager. Then there was Melissa and her panic, but I hadn't really understood that.

I've always been an anxious person. Several times in my life (particularly after a bad drug trip early in college and a terrible breakup in my twenties) I even experienced panic attacks. My therapist worked through the causes with me, never suggesting medication. And maybe because of that experience, I thought people who went on psych drugs were weak. I mean, unless they were really sick—suicidal or bipolar or something. Everything else, I suspected, could be worked out with talk therapy and a glass of wine.

On that horrible day after my sleepless night, I realized what I was experiencing was not normal, and I was not myself. A switch had flipped in my brain. I didn't want medication; I *needed* it. But what exactly was wrong with me?

I spent hours online, but I found little about postpartum mental health problems other than depression. Then I came across the website Postpartum Progress.

To this day, when you go onto Postpartum Progress's home page, these are the first words that come up: *The Symptoms of Postpartum Depression and Anxiety (in Plain Mama English).*

When I saw the word *anxiety*, I actually traced the letters with my finger, reading them on the screen as if they were in a reference book. The site continued: "You may have postpartum anxiety or postpartum OCD if you have had a baby within the last 12 months and are experiencing some of these symptoms . . ." The list described, well, my current emotional and physiological states: panic, racing heart, insomnia, fear of being an incapable mother, fear of being alone with my own baby, and on and on. Usually I love doing well on tests, but acing this one didn't feel like an accomplishment.

Melissa was the first person I called. Now I was grateful she'd been honest about her own panic and anxiety. Out of town on a "dirty weekend" in Miami with Patrick (the one for which she'd weaned Sofia, now home in Brooklyn with Pat's mom), Melissa got back to me right away.

"Get meds, for sure," she said. "I'm sorry I'm not home, or I'd take Clara for a bit."

Anna was my next call. "I'd come over, but Isabella's asleep and I'm by myself here. I'll send you the name of my psychiatrist, though. He's good."

Thank God Antonia was free. "Give me half an hour," she said. "I'll bring hot food."

When I heard her ringing my doorbell, I was so relieved I started shaking as hard as I had when my epidural hit.

Anna's psychiatrist fit me in within twenty-four hours, first diagnosing me with "moderate to severe" postpartum anxiety over the phone and prescribing me Ativan for anxiety, Ambien for the insomnia, and the SSRI Zoloft as a stabilizer. Soon I felt bound by pills. Zoloft takes a few weeks to kick in; in the meantime, symptoms can worsen. And Zoloft's serotonin bump can cause anxiety. More jumpiness required even more pills. Gas, brake, gas, brake. I was like Hunter S. Thompson, except I wasn't having fun (or getting any writing done).

"This will take a while, and that's okay," Danny told me, as did Ellen, my new, wonderful therapist, my parents, and Clara's pediatrician.

We developed a sad routine. In the mornings, if Danny had to go to work and I was too nervous (or too sedated) to manage Clara on my own, we brought in the babysitters, an ever-expanding cast of girls from Blue Marble, the ice cream and coffee shop around the corner. Those girls saved my bacon.

During the day, I hovered between panic attacks. Sometimes I made it out of the house, even to work. On other days, I'd run home after walking a few blocks, weeping and apologizing to Danny and Clara, and gulp down a pill. Then I'd go to bed and cry more, until the medicine put me to sleep.

Postpartum anxiety often includes "intrusive thoughts" of harm coming to the baby, but that wasn't my problem. I was obsessed that harm might come to *me*, which would mean I would fail Clara, Danny, and everyone and everything that had ever mattered to me.

Then there was breast-feeding. When I took an anti-anxiety pill, I couldn't feed Clara for four hours, but I had so much milk I'd have to pump and dump. If I held her when she was hungry and I couldn't nurse, she clawed at my chest, scrunching up her face and screaming until her daddy appeared with a bottle. In those moments, I felt like the worst mother in the world.

At the end of every endless day, Danny took Clara out of my arms after her last feeding and nestled her down in a bassinet in his office. She slept peacefully there, swaddled tight, surrounded by his piano, scores, and books. When we were ready to go to bed ourselves, I dutifully took my Ambien and Ativan. Danny walked into our room, snuggled with me for a while until my medication kicked in, and then headed out for the couch and the night shift. We all reunited in the morning when he brought Clara into bed with me to nurse again.

The new system was expensive, in various ways: my lost hours of work, extra childcare, therapy costs. As with my miscarriages, we were open and honest about what was going on. A few friends dropped out, as if my fritzed emotional frequency was too much to handle. After Danny told his department chair about our extreme circumstances, the guy decided he needed tough love or something, reducing Danny's course load (and therefore his salary) for the next semester.

The Mommy Group did not indulge in such bullshit.

"I hate it when people pretend all you need is a hot bath and a night out with your husband!" Jane said to me when I called her one night, weeping. "You are dealing with a major chemical imbalance. A chocolate croissant is not going to fix this." She paused. "But it will help."

From Elizabeth

March 21, 2011

Can we meet near me today? My anxiety meds make me a little sleepy and dopey. I want to see you guys, but need to get home easily.

From Melissa
March 21, 2011
Sure—whatever you need.

My parents also came through even better than I could have imagined, traveling to Brooklyn from Philadelphia every other weekend (and helping us with cash for extra babysitting during the week). Before this, when they'd held Clara, I couldn't tell if they were comfortable with her. Their last intense contact with such a small baby had been me, some thirty-seven long years before.

Perhaps now that my need was an established fact, Momo and Lala (names they spent much of Clara's gestation refining) took over. My mother stocked the freezer with soups and quiches; my father sang Clara made-up songs in the loudest possible voice, delighting her in spite of our repeated admonishments for him to calm down.

Amazingly, my illness seemed to affect Clara not at all, other than to make her even more social. While many babies screamed if anyone but their mamas tried to hold them, our girl chuckled and blew spit bubbles for her father, grandparents, and our cast of babysitters.

Clara grew, learning to roll and sit up, singing what we were sure was the tune to "Itsy Bitsy Spider" when she was six months old. If the village was raising her, they were doing a damn fine job. And if sometimes I felt a little left out, I reminded myself, "I'm still Mommy. Letting other people love her is the best parenting I can do."

I missed my old life, especially the easy intimacy with Danny. Though he reassured me repeatedly that he still loved me through all of this, in my current messy state I couldn't imagine why or how.

"You had our baby," he said, holding me as I wept, night after night. "You're taking one for the team. How could I not love you more after this?" I heard his words, but they didn't quite penetrate. I was still too raw.

In one of my early sessions with Ellen, my therapist, I recounted the story of Clara's birth and how I'd yelled "Is that my baby? She needs me!" "In my heart, I didn't believe my own words," I told Ellen, sobbing. "When they finally put her on my chest, she was clean and swaddled in a blanket; she could have been anyone's baby."

Even as I spoke, I wondered what was wrong with me, recounting the first moments of my beautiful perfect daughter's life as anything other than magical.

Ellen let me cry. When she finally spoke, it wasn't from a cool, professionally reserved point of view. "This is not right," she said. "Our system failed you. You may have needed a C-section, but you deserved a better experience, and it wouldn't have been difficult to give you one."

"What about once the birth was over?" I asked. "Isn't it my job to be a mother without alarm, without issues?"

"No," Ellen said. "It is your job to love your child and take care of her. Which is exactly what you're doing by coming here."

The Mommies were the ones who finally convinced me that she and Danny were right.

One day, when I was feeling particularly weird and shaky, Renée met me in the park. She didn't ask me anything, but let me talk when I needed to. Her quiet calm felt reassuring and almost maternal. Another morning, Anna ordered me out of the house: "Sometimes you have to push through the cobwebs and get in the sunshine."

Their gentle support, in bulk, was so powerful for me. She was right. Day by day, and sometimes hour by hour, I started to feel better. However, like childbirth itself, postpartum mental illness forever changed me.

It had also changed my marriage. I wasn't ready to think about that yet.

I've joined several PPD groups on Facebook, thinking I would "pay it forward" by sharing my experience, and maybe learn something about the reality of this illness for other women at the same time. I can still barely read posts without feeling triggered. One young woman—nineteen years old, I think—kept writing in: "When do the intrusive thoughts stop? What is the difference between a psychiatrist and a psychologist? My boyfriend told me I was a bitch last night because I'm never happy." Her baby was six weeks old. I googled psychiatrists in her area in rural Ohio, but there were none within an hour's drive. Farther away, there were a few, but no one listed PPD as a specialty.

Who was going to tell this poor girl it was safe to breast-feed on Zoloft, one of the most common questions posted on these boards? Who was going to tell her that while her body adjusted to the SSRI she wouldn't feel better immediately? That her anxiety might actually increase?

There is simply not enough help. My PPD didn't start until four months in, well past my standard six-week follow-up OB appointment. What if I hadn't known doctors, didn't have insurance or a husband who was emotionally and physically able to help or parents who were willing to drop everything and give (not lend—give) us the money we needed for childcare? What if I weren't an educated grown-up with the life experience to know I was sick but probably curable? What if I were most women in this country, in this world? What kind of statistic would I—and Clara—have become?

Often, a child's pediatrician is the person who catches that a mother is not doing well, but pediatricians are not formally trained or instructed to follow up. If they do, it's strictly voluntary. Our pediatrician, Dr. Gold, makes it her business to help her baby patients' mothers.

"In an ideal scenario, there would be several moments to help mothers," she told me in a phone interview. "Before that six-week OB visit, mothers should receive information on the different types of postpartum mental illness, and there should be a check-in earlier with a nurse, if not a doctor. Next, there should be an organized network of physicians and practitioners for referrals. I scramble to get moms help—especially to find doctors who take insurance. Finally, postpartum is not part of pediatric training. It should be added in to the pediatric residency."

Instead of steady follow-up, most women get communal or anecdotal knowledge, passed down. "It hit at around three months—when my hair started falling out," Melissa told me. Most women experience hair loss at around three months postpartum. It signals normal decreasing estrogen levels after pregnancy, and estrogen level is tied, for many women, with mood.

By the time a baby is six months old, if the mother is exclusively breast-feeding, she's producing about thirty ounces of milk a day (almost a quart!). It's well known that nursing mothers require more calories than even pregnant women (about five hundred extra a day for a single baby), but what is the hormonal and emotional expenditure of peak breast-feeding? If hair is falling out, what else is going on with the body? No one would tell an injured NBA forward in playoff season that all he needed to do to train was take a daily multivitamin and eat enough leafy veggies. It would be a given that such physical expenditure warrants a precise training and nutritional program. Why shouldn't new mothers get the same consideration as professional athletes?

"Increasing healthy life behaviors is also helpful, like getting enough sleep, eating healthier foods, taking the time for walking, and so on," the official Perinatal Screening Tool for Obstetrician-Gynecologists advises doctors to tell patients in their "Perinatal Depression Script." Ah yes, walking. Brilliant. Why didn't I think of that?

Between 10 and 15 percent of women experience postpartum mental illness. That constitutes an *epidemic* of women with depression, anxiety, insomnia, obsessive-compulsive disorder, mania, and (in rare cases) psychosis. These issues can occur anytime in the first year postpartum to qualify under the diagnostic rubric of "PPD." Doctors know the stats, but they don't generally screen women past that six-week postpartum visit, even though it is common medical knowledge that major hormonal changes don't stop at six weeks.

In the past, these women, like Margaret, Jane, and me, might have ended up institutionalized, alcoholic, or worse (electroshock therapy, even lobotomy, were not unheard-of treatments).

In Adrienne LaFrance's 2015 *Atlantic* article "What Happens to a Woman's Brain When She Becomes a Mother," she explains, "Becoming a parent looks . . . a lot like falling in love. At the brain level, the networks that become especially sensitized are those that involve vigilance and social salience—the amygdala—as well as dopamine networks that incentivize prioritizing the infant."

Everyone told me I would fall in love at first sight with my baby, but I have always been anxious when falling in love. My friends can recall, with still-fresh irritation, how many pro-and-con lists I needed to make when Danny and I were first dating.

Even though I was sure he was the guy I wanted, I couldn't help second-guessing myself.

Poor Clara was no exception. LaFrance continues: "Perhaps . . . motherhood really is like secret space in a woman's brain, waiting to be discovered . . . [T]he act of simply caring for one's baby forges new neural pathways—undiscovered rooms in the parental brain."

What if *my* brain takes longer to forge my neural pathways? Maybe in my postpartum illness, I lost my way, temporarily, to those "undiscovered rooms"?

Imagine a world in which we actually walked into motherhood with the idea that it would be psychologically discombobulating. That even if you're not one of the "one in ten," the hormonal and life changes would affect you profoundly. What if, as part of our leaving package at the hospital, new families received (in addition to the free formula samples and tiny keepsake hats) referrals to excellent, professionally run group therapy?

When I put my call out for mommy groups, Amy, a friend of a friend in Sonoma, California, was one of my first email responders. She was bouncy and enthusiastic in our initial emails. "Come and meet my gang!" she wrote. We corresponded jovially for a couple of months, until I told her I was coming to San Francisco for a family trip in January and would love to get together. Then I began to get the sense that she was less enthusiastic than she'd initially seemed. "It's a therapy group," she wrote. "We're pretty intense."

"Bring it on," I wrote back. "I can drive up for a visit."

Sonoma is a famously gorgeous community about an hour north of San Francisco. As I pulled off the freeway, mist still draped the streets at noon, half-hiding cute little Arts and Crafts houses; birds sang in the trees. It was a delicious high contrast from the brutal East Coast winter I'd left behind.

Amy's house was picture-perfect West Coast. The living room—lived in, but neither particularly messy nor neat—was painted a calming slate-blue, and there were sweet little framed embroidered bird hangings on the wall. Her four-year-old son was home sick with an earache, wrapped in a blankie on the couch, and watching *Daniel Tiger*.

Korin, another member of the group, was already waiting for me at the sunny kitchen table, placed in a bay window looking out on an orange tree, heavy with fruit. Amy laid out a selection of treats from a local bakery (as with every piece of food produced in the Bay Area, they were delectable) and poured hot, strong coffee into pottery mugs.

Amy is skinny and intense. Korin, heavyset, with red hair pulled back into a ponytail, seemed anxious.

Amy's little girl sat at the table with us, chomping on a biscuit.

"*This* is what I think of as normalcy," I wrote in my notebook.

Amy explained her mother would be along shortly to take the kids. "But I can give you some background now," she added. Their group has been meeting for several years. Because it's a therapy group rather than a conventional mommy group, their meetings aim to create an atmosphere where dissent and disagreement are not only acceptable, but used as a way for the members to go deeper.

Amy explained, "It's a safe place to be able to say . . . horrible things to another mother, like [I disapprove of Korin putting her three kids in daycare, so I say to her] *I think you're abandoning your children*. That's not meant for Korin exactly. It's me talking from my own unresolved past. I *want* to be the evolved woman who supports everyone's choices, but inside, I feel so abandoned that I am not there yet. The purpose of the group is to be able to set aside the lens that you see [other mothers] through and connect."

She interrupted herself as her mother, a typical, active-grandma type in a tracksuit, arrived and gathered up the kids. "Thanks, Mom, a couple hours is perfect." Turning back to us, she explained the pastries. "So this is a morning glory muffin. We also have a cranberry muffin, chocolate croissant, a maple pecan scone, and a buttermilk biscuit. Please, help yourself." I selected a scone. Amy continued, "Having children has become my life's work. It's cracked me open. And that's through the therapy."

Korin added, "Before I gave birth, I did a lot of therapy . . ." She paused, and I could tell she was about to say something big. "I'm a rape survivor, and I wanted to make sure that the birthing process didn't get screwed up." Amy and I were both silent, waiting, giving Korin the room and space to speak. "I didn't want to have flashbacks at the birth. But I never prepared myself for [how] my kids' experiences would trigger thoughts of all the things that I went through. As my daughter becomes the age at which it happened to me, *she* triggers me. She's five."

She paused. Amy added, "In the group we all talk about how we're starving for deep friendship. Korin and I both have had life experiences . . . that keep people at a distance."

I waited for her to compose herself.

"My wonderful, sweet mother, whom you just met, was raped, repeatedly, by her father. The only reason I even know that is it came out when my stepbrother sexually abused me."

Korin and I were both silent, listening.

"You can't protect your own child when you're not healing your own wounds. But the defenses we have keep us closed off and not able to connect with other women."

As Amy paused, Korin picked up the thread: "We're all work-ing on ourselves, and yet we have each other. If you were in a group of other moms outside of that structure, people [might] break off because they have different ways of looking at things."

Reaching for a muffin as I finished my scone, I could only nod. I'm an adult; I've known many women with sexual abuse or assault in their histories. But this was not a Take Back the Night speak-out, and these people weren't my longtime friends. Amy and Korin's candor to a relative stranger—and a writer at that—moved me profoundly.

Korin added, "If I can be open and honest, and that helps some-one else think, 'Maybe it wouldn't be bad if I went and got my anx-iety checked out,' well, then I've done something."

Amy said, "There's not a forum or a venue where people can share [the prevalence of postpartum depression]. When you have a group you find out how many more people are experiencing it."

I would add: the more women know how many others are depressed, or anxious, having intrusive thoughts, or wondering whether they made a mistake having this child whom they don't know how to care for, let alone love . . . Well, when you meet those women, and you're honest with each other, and help each other . . . it's one of the best things.

I have debated whether to mention my drive to Sonoma, or, rather, that driving, period, was a postpartum-anxiety rite of passage for me. There is not much call for driving in Brooklyn; Danny and I don't own a car. When we do need to drive somewhere—to Philly to visit my family, to our yearly Jersey Shore beach trip, or when visiting LA—Danny's always behind the wheel. He's a West

Coaster, and an excellent, unflappable driver. I, on the other hand, drove for a couple of years in high school and have rarely practiced the skill since. Early in our relationship, we drove cross-country from Los Angeles to Miami. I've mentioned before that in our two-week journey, I was chauffeur for a mere twenty minutes one morning in Texas because Danny was having an allergy attack.

Since having Clara, I hadn't driven at all. I was scared: of driving, of the responsibility for my family, of the panic attack I worried I might have. But when Danny, Clara, and I left for this trip to California, I told Danny I wanted to drive.

"Really?" He looked doubtful.

"I have people I want to interview. I need to be more independent."

Until I actually sat behind the wheel of the rented Hyundai and drove from the San Francisco airport to our rental in Pacific Heights, I wasn't sure I'd be able to do it.

Four-year-old Clara was shocked.

"You can drive, Mommy?" she asked from her perch in her backseat car seat.

"We'll see, baby," I said, starting the engine.

When I set out a few mornings later for Sonoma, I was prepared. Soy cappuccino in the cup holder, GPS directions, and a *Serial* podcast on my phone. And I did it. No panic, not even much stress. It was one of those moments (and anyone who's had a debilitating mental or physical illness knows what I mean) when I felt, *Oh, this is normal. I can be normal.*

I got back to our apartment rental late in the afternoon, exhausted and keyed up from the interview, and having navigated the freeway, hills, and the Bay Area's notorious rush-hour traffic.

"Mommy!" Clara ran to me as soon as I walked in the door. "I'm so *proud* of you driving."

I thought of Amy, Korin, and all the other women who'd generously shared with me about their struggles. Four years, countless bottles of Zoloft, and hundreds of therapy sessions later, I'd done it. Take that, postpartum anxiety. My little girl is proud of me.

10. Crying It Out

Antonia Gets Some Sleep; the Experts Sit on Some Tacks

From Antonia

March 20, 2011

Gus is not sleeping. It's my fault. Motherhood is a long string of opportunities to fail. At night I hear Gus cry, nudge Dillon to wake up, and he says, Right, I'll get to it, and falls back asleep. If Gus suddenly slept ten-hour stretches, I'd STILL wake. It is possible to get PTSD from having a baby?

From Renée

March 30, 2011

It has been documented that otherwise normal, non-psychotic individuals can have a break with reality and even hallucinate when sleep deprived.

Spring finally broke, with crocuses poking their little heads through the filthy remnants of Snowpocalypse (though traces of the storm would remain until May). Gus was almost eight months old, and still would not, could not sleep through the night. Antonia was losing her ever-loving mind.

One Monday afternoon in April, Melissa, Antonia, and I were on our way to Renée's house, gnawing on mini pizzas from Joyce

Bakeshop, strolling the babies under the budding spring trees on Eighth Avenue in Park Slope. Charlie was in school, so Renée had finally been able to invite us over for some toddler-tantrum-free fun.

"Guess I'm not a vegetarian anymore. This pizza seems to have bacon on it," Antonia said, wiping her mouth with one hand while pushing the Baby Jogger with the other. "Whatever, I'm so tired, I don't care. Gus, will you *please* stop kicking!" Blowing his best ten-month-old spit bubbles of glee, Gus pounded his feet harder. Antonia sighed. "This is what *seven* wake-ups in the night looks like. We took away his swaddle and his pacifier this week."

"You're kidding? Still?" Melissa asked. Sofia was happily stretched in her stroller, chewing on Sophie the giraffe and nuzzling her blankie.

I leaned over Gus's stroller. "Little boy, chill out. Your mommy's having a nervous breakdown." He chortled again, drool shooting out of his mouth with enough velocity that a strand landed on my nose.

"Welcome to my world," Antonia said. "Dillon and I aren't speaking." Her chin began to quiver. "I read an article in the *Times* about a mother who went to a hotel for a night to get some sleep. Not that we can afford it. I guess I could go to that Best Western near the Brooklyn Battery Tunnel, with the transvestite hookers."

"Why take away Gus's sleep props," I asked her, "if he sleeps better with them?" Clara was four months younger and curled right up when she saw her swaddle. The prospect of taking her blanket and its instant Pavlovian calming properties seemed like a pointlessly cruel idea—to all of us.

Antonia's accent grew more pronounced with her rising agitation. "He's not a newborn anymore. He needs to sleep with fewer props. The Baby Whisperer says so!"

Oh.

"But then he's up constantly. I'm losing my mind!"

We nodded in sympathy.

"I'm sorry. I'm in a bad mood because I haven't had a chance to shower in three days."

It's a true cliché that sleep dominates the first year of parenthood. The little worms are up, they're down, and parents are responsible for making them transition to a human—or mammalian, diurnal—schedule. Infant sleep problems (and the ensuing adult sleep deprivation) can lead to a very unhappy mommy and daddy. Contemporary parents are not *allowed* to be tired. And why is that? Say it with me: we go back to work within a few weeks or months of birth, live far away from family who could help with the baby at night, and read in magazines about getting back in the groove sexually before the baby can sleep through the night.

Antonia's son, Augustus, looked and acted straight out of a British children's story about a beautiful elf child: mouth and apple cheeks in a perpetual puckish grin, his front tooth already chipped in a playground accident by the time he was ten months old. His laugh was a bubbling chortle, his soprano screams uniquely piercing, his first baby-talk syllables were charmingly accented: "booook" and "doig."

He also was a lousy sleeper from birth, waking up through the night, his crib a few feet from his parents' bed. Every night. All night.

Dillon had been wanting to just let Gus cry and so escape from the Baby Sleep Disturbance Tyranny. But he wasn't the one with the milk, and Antonia wouldn't let him forget it. Who was right?

Soft-hearted Mommy or pragmatic (and, according to Antonia, stubborn) Daddy?

They lived in a one-bedroom apartment with an ancient dog; Gus's crib was separated from their bed by a paper Chinese screen. Every evening, Antonia and Dillon argued about bedtime technique while Gus screamed his head off. Then Dillon headed to the couch for the night, and Antonia stayed up in the bedroom with the baby.

Before our fateful walk to Renée's, Antonia wrote frequent middle-of-the-night missives to the Mommies:

> November 9, 2010
> Just tanked up on strong, black tea.

> November 11, 2010
> Gus slept well last night! I only got up twice! I feel like a new woman!

> November 22, 2010
> Gus' longest sleeps are 4–6 hours.

In her desperation, Antonia also read every book by every sleep guru on the market, taking each as her guru in turn. First, she swore by *The Happiest Baby on the Block*, by Harvey Karp. This bestseller has cover blurbs from Michelle Pfeiffer and Larry David; it must be good. Dr. Karp's "Five S's" have become such received wisdom, they're practically folklore. The theory is that infants need to return to womblike conditions in order to feel secure enough to sleep through the night. Danny and I—as well as all the other members of the Mommy Group, except for Renée, who knew better from bitter experience—also read *The Happiest Baby on the Block*. In fact, the *HBOTB* (not to be confused, children of the nineties, with NKOTB) is so popular that I will list all five S's here.

The Five S's

1) Swaddling: The nurses at the hospital swaddle newborns, who then look so cute and happy in their little stripe-edge blankets. Danny and I diligently registered for soft muslin blankets with froggie and duckie prints ($35 for a pack of three). But swaddling Clara with them was like trying to mummify a live duck. On Antonia's advice, we then bought swaddles with Velcro fasteners, trussing Clara into such a tight package that she looked like a baby spliff. Every night, Danny raised her to his lips and pretended to smoke her, to mutual hilarity. Clara was so happy in her Velcro swaddles that we kept her in them every night for most of her first year. At first, Antonia swore by swaddling.

2) Side/stomach position: Putting a baby on his or her stomach to sleep goes against every pediatrician's recommendation that you should never ever put a baby on his or her stomach, due the risk of Sudden Infant Death Syndrome. However, holding babies on their sides can work like magic. The thing is, you have to keep holding them there so they don't flop onto the dreaded stomach. Karp even cautions, "When a baby is in a stomach down position do not leave them even for a moment." In spite of dire warnings, and Heidi's natural anxiety, at four months her mom put Clay down for a nap on his belly. He

slept for seven hours straight and was a stomach sleeper forever more.

3) Shushing sounds: "These imitate the continual whooshing
sound made by the blood flowing through arteries near the
womb," Karp writes, recommending running a vacuum
cleaner in Baby's room. On our third night home with Clara,
desperate for her to stop crying, we ran the Dustbuster next
to her head—and it worked! Until it ran out of batteries, and
her crying amped up as its motor ran down. Melissa swore by
the Sleep Sheep, a soft toy lamb that makes a whooshing noise
for twenty minutes. Sofia went down for her nap every time
Melissa snuggled her up with that damn sheep. We bought
one as well (I was desperate enough that I actually went out
in a blizzard to purchase it), but Clara woke up the instant the
sound timed out. In the end, we got a white-noise machine for
the bedroom. Less cute, but more effective.

4) Swinging: Karp writes, "Newborns are used to the swinging
motions within their mother's womb, so entering the gravity
driven world of the outside is like a sailor adapting to land
after nine months at sea." Gus slept best in his Fisher-Price
Papasan My Little Lamb Swing (its full name must be used
at all times, like "Calvin Coolidge" or "Clark Kent"), at max
speed and max swing. We also purchased the Fisher-Price
Papasan My Little Lamb Swing from Amazon in the middle
of the night. It arrived like a messenger owl from *Harry Potter*
at eleven on a Saturday night, in a box bigger than me. Stacy
and her husband, Jayson, were over, and Danny and Jayson
insisted on putting it together immediately. Assembled, it

dominated our small living room. After loading it with six
C batteries and turning it on, the swing emitted a cranking
creaking noise that sounded like an asthmatic mechanical
donkey.

"I am not putting my baby in that thing," I said, clutching
a screaming Clara—she'd been up most nights for a week.

"We have to try it!" Danny insisted.

"Don't you want to see it in action?" Jayson added (he
was proud of his handyman efforts). "Come *on*."

I couldn't watch as Danny strapped our tiny baby into the
fluffy lamb-head-shaped pillow seat. It looked gruesome.
He turned it on: *hee-haw, hee-haw*, it wheezed.

Clara regarded us for a minute, stretching her fingers in
the air experimentally. Then she closed her eyes and fell fast
asleep. For hours.

5) Sucking: The logic of this one seems obvious. If you can
   get your baby to take a pacifier, do it. Nipple confusion is
   a myth! Otherwise, your baby can just chomp on your tits
   twenty-four hours a day (can you tell Clara never took a
   pacifier?).

But Karp's wisdom eventually ran out, and Antonia turned to her
next bible, Elizabeth Pantley's *The No-Cry Sleep Solution: Gentle
Ways to Help Your Baby Sleep Through the Night*. That one didn't
last long.

Finally, strung out, she read *Secrets of the Baby Whisperer: How
to Calm, Connect, and Communicate with Your Baby* by Tracy Hogg
and Melinda Blaue, and swore it was *the* answer.

From Antonia

December 5, 2010

I have put Gus on the four hour E.A.S.Y routine from the *Baby Whisperer*, and it has been nothing short of miraculous. My non-napper has been taking two-hour naps twice a day and is down to one night feed! It's a hideous acronym: Eat, Activity, Sleep, which leaves time for You = E.A.S.Y. When they get to four months, they are supposed to go on a four-hour cycle—30 mins to eat, 1.5 hours to play, two hours to sleep, repeated twice in the day. We still have some issues to work out—he's waking up one other time in the night, so Dillon soothes him back to sleep. He still needs his swaddle, pacifier, white noise machine, and sleep positioners.

We were suspicious.

"1.5 hours of play?" Jane wrote. "Where does watching Mom drink coffee fit into the schedule?"

A couple of days later, Antonia admitted, "I was a little too evangelical about the Baby Whisperer. Gus regressed on Monday."

Why do new mothers become so obsessed with experts? Recall, Antonia was the person who told me that new parenthood was like being on an acid trip. And, like people on acid, we needed guides. In our sleep-addled, hazy states, almost anyone with a "system" looked like the messiah.

After Clara was born, I asked everyone I knew for the "best" book on parenting.

"What about Dr. Spock?" my mother asked. "We used him for everything."

Dr. Benjamin Spock's *Baby and Child Care* was first published in 1946, and went on to rule the parenting roost for the next fifty years, selling more than 50 million copies. Spock's advice to parents ran in direct contrast to the instructions parents had received for the previous, oh, millennium. His lengthy obituary in the *New York Times* in 1998 (he died at the age of ninety-four) explained his importance:

> *In the opening chapter of the book, first published in hardcover in 1946 with the title* The Common Sense Book of Baby and Child Care, *Dr. Spock counseled his readers not to "take too seriously all that the neighbors say." "Don't be afraid to trust your own common sense," he wrote. "What good mothers and fathers instinctively feel like doing for their babies is usually best."*
>
> *Such relaxed advice, given in the easy, practical, reassuring way that he had with parents, was light-years from the stern dictums of earlier standard works, like the 1928 book* Psychological Care of Infant and Child *by Dr. John B. Watson. "Never, never kiss your child," Dr. Watson commanded. "Never hold it in your lap. Never rock its carriage."*
>
> *Dr. T. Berry Brazelton of the Harvard Medical School, another noted pediatrician-author, once said of Dr. Spock: "Before he came along, advice to parents was very didactic. He opened the whole area of empowered parenting. He gave parents choices and encouraged them to think things out for themselves."*

Even so, I told my mother, "I think Dr. Spock's out. We ordered this other one on Amazon. *The Baby Book* by Dr. Sears."

Dr. Sears did teach us . . . something. We didn't yet know that parenting books (often pitched to white, educated, middle-class mommies like me) prey on fears. If we read this one book, or subscribe to this one school of thought, we'll be the best mothers, the ones who have it all together, who bring home the nitrate-free bacon, fry it up in the pan, and never once complain about who didn't wash the bottle parts before they turned into a stinky mess on the countertop.

At first, I admit, I dug *The Baby Book*. It advocated "Attachment Parenting," (AP) which seemed to support exclusive breast-feeding, co-sleeping (in the family bed), and Mom (or Dad, but usually Mom) wearing the little munchkin in a sling or carrier until he or she was old enough to buy cigarettes.

I already planned to breast-feed Clara exclusively, wear her as much as possible, and put her down in a bassinet—and later a small crib—next to my side of the bed. Then I reached Sears's recommendation that we buy a bigger mattress, allowing the whole family to sleep together. He also emphasized the dangers of Mommy working outside the home, writing, "Have you considered borrowing the extra income while your child is an infant and returning to work later to repay it?" Reading further, I learned that letting a baby cry is responsible for increased stress levels (in the infant, not the parent), which in turn will "create a distance" between you and your and baby, keeping you "from becoming an expert in your child."

Who *was* this guy?

Dr. William Sears is the father (in several senses—the man has eight children, several of whom are also pediatricians) of the Attachment Parenting movement. *The Baby Book*, first published in 1992, is in print in eighteen languages, and has sold more than 1.5 million copies. He's also the author of a book that doesn't make it onto his official bio: *The Complete Book of Christian Parenting and Childcare*, which advocates "fearing God" and suggests that parents *"pray for wisdom to know whether spanking in general is the proper way to deal with your child's offenses"* (emphasis his).

The phrase "attachment parenting" sounded innocuous to me at first. Then I realized it was like when I checked the box for "alternative music" on my college dorm preferences survey and ended up with a Morrissey fanatic as a roommate. With both *alternative* and *attachment*, I didn't know the adjectives were genres until it was too late.

In May 2012, when the Mommy Group babies were around one and a half, *Time* magazine's cover featured a hot blond mom breast-feeding her . . . three-year-old boy. The photo caused a hullabaloo. For many Americans, the sight of a mother suckling a kid who could walk, talk, and possibly even fix himself a sandwich was obscene. For others, particularly parents who'd heard of Dr. Sears and AP, the cover was less shocking.

The article, written by *Time* staffer Kate Pickert, started out innocuously, but then went for what I thought was the jugular: "The practicalities of attachment parenting ask a great deal of mothers. . . . It's not a big leap from there to an inference that can send anxious moms into guilt-induced panic: that any time away from their baby will have lifelong negative consequences."

The story spawned as many in-print responses as there were working-mom journalists to vent their ire. One of the least invective-filled and most informative was in *The Atlantic*, by journalist Jennie Rothenberg Gritz. She started by informing readers that Dr. Sears was not actually the OG of AP. That title is rightfully shared by post–WWII psychologists Mary Ainsworth and John Bowlby. Gritz wrote, "In their research, groundbreaking for its time, [they] found that a mother's attention does make a difference . . . [E]arly attachment allowed children to grow up confident and secure."

202 ELIZABETH ISADORA GOLD

Sears's admonitions to take out bank loans or ban the electric swing (aka the "mechanical mommy") were not part of the original AP plan. Gritz continued, "Babies thrive emotionally because of the overall quality of the care they've experienced, not because of specific techniques."

Say it with me: *"Babies thrive emotionally because of the overall quality of care."* Or, as a wise friend told me when I was still pregnant and worrying over whatever detail of whatever off-gassing crib finish was going to kill Clara and make her hate me: "People go to therapy for twenty years to be able to even say the words 'I might not really love my mother.' You would have to do something unthinkable to get to that point."

Danny insisted on throwing *The Baby Book* away sometime in the fog of our first month as parents. "We do not need someone making us feel guilty for not ever taking Clara off our bodies," he said. "You don't need that."

But back to Antonia, eating bacon and crying. Melissa and I wanted to convince her to step away from the experts.

"Or," Melissa finally said—and I knew how strong her feelings must have been to overcome her usual reticence about giving advice—"you could try crying it out."

A long silence. Melissa shot me a look, as if wondering if she'd gone too far.

Melissa and I had both been practicing cry it out (CIO) for months, since our kids had been three or four months old, the earliest time doctors advise for sleep training. Neither of us felt we had a choice. When the plane is going down, the adult is supposed to put on the oxygen mask first. Postpartum anxiety is a full-blown emergency, so Mama sleeping through the night is a whole oxygen tank's worth of sanity. These days, Clara only woke up once in the night for a bottle (or so Danny told me). Sofia was the same. While our families did CIO the earliest, the other mommies had eventually all given in. Only Antonia resisted.

Now she looked at Melissa and me, her nose running, tears rolling down her cheeks. "I can't bear hearing him cry," she whispered.

"Yes, but can you bear this?" I asked. "You're losing your mind!"

"It's over fast," Melissa giggled nervously. "Turn up the TV. Put on headphones—or earplugs!"

"I can't start it tonight, though. He has a cold," Antonia said.

Melissa and I exchanged a triumphant look. We were both relieved to finally give someone else parenting advice. Postpartum made us feel incompetent, and here we were, talking like experts. Sure, at letting our babies cry, but whatever.

Many new parents hear the phrase *cry it out* and instantly picture an *A Child Called It* scenario with a wailing baby, cold and alone in a dark room. First delineated by Dr. Richard Ferber, the practice is actually much more nuanced than detractors imply. Ferber is the director of the Center for Pediatric Sleep Disorders at Children's Hospital in Boston; he teaches at Harvard. He doesn't advocate sticking children in their cribs and leaving them alone with no comfort until morning—because he's not crazy or abusive. Instead, he prescribes "gradual extinction," or letting babies cry for slowly increasing intervals. The idea is that when a child knows his parent is nearby, he eventually learns to soothe himself to sleep.

Dr. Sears claims that crying it out causes a baby's nervous system to "degenerate" and for that child to experience "panic and anxiety." For overtired parents, it's easy to believe the worst of something that actually might feel the best—for you.

Take Heidi's story:

> From Heidi
>
> November 22, 2010
>
> I'm looking for support/ideas about reducing nighttime feedings. The pediatrician said that given Clay's size (he's a chunker) and age (almost four months), he only needs to eat every six to eight hours at night. He usually has one long stretch of sleep, but then is up and wanting to eat every few hours. When I tried to soothe and not feed him, he latched onto my FACE!

With no magical solution forthcoming, and her back-to-work deadline looming, Heidi decided to try the Ferber method then. Clay cried for hours. It wasn't working! She took a drastic step, calling Dr. Ferber's office herself with a question or two.

As she recalled the conversation over drinks, she couldn't stop laughing. "Ferber's nurse called me back and asked, 'What is the problem?' I told her we were putting Clay to bed at seven, but then he screamed until ten thirty. She paused and said, 'Why don't you try starting the bedtime process at ten-fifteen?' "

It worked.

But back, once again, to Antonia.

After our advice-filled walk to Renée's, the Mommies got an email from Antonia two days later:

> WHY . . . didn't I do this months ago? After all my talk about how I wouldn't let Gus Cry It Out when he had a cold, it turned out I couldn't do another night. He cried for about forty

minutes, woke up a second time at two, I fed him, and then
slept until six-fifteen. Last night he cried for about six minutes,
woke again at midnight, cried for about eight minutes, woke
again at three, and I fed him. Tonight, total cold turkey.

I was convinced it was no coincidence that she and Dillon found
a new two-bedroom apartment not long after. They were finally
rested enough to actually agree on something. Unfortunately, it
was pretty far out into outer Brooklyn, a subway ride away from
what little support Antonia had: us. In New York, it *always* ends up
being about real estate.

11. Happy Birthday to Us

School's Out for Summer

From Antonia

June 14, 2011

Hi from Bondi Beach, where Gus and I have been enjoying the surf and sand. He's sleeping OK-ish—some nights straight through, other nights broken. Teething like mad, putting all kinds of unsuitable things in his mouth, and showing signs of walking imminently.

From Elizabeth

July 14, 2011

On the locomotion front, Clara is crawling!

From Melissa

August 13, 2011

I am at the playground right now and there are a bunch of sexy dads. Come on over!

That whole summer is dreamy in my memory, as if through an old movie camera, all supersaturated colors and quick vignettes. My body was finally relaxing into my medication. The Mommies corresponded from beaches, lakes, and the Land Down Under. The changes were coming fast as the babies pushed over the year line.

Inspired by their change of venues, encouraged by the presence of grandparents, they learned to crawl, walk, and eat avocado.

When we were in town, and free, we hung out more than ever, lazily picnicking at "our spot" in the park—a shady patch of grass across the path from the littles-friendly Tot Lot, where our now official toddlers could play. One afternoon, Anna coaxed Isabella to drag herself up and down a hill for a slice of Oscar Meyer ham. Clara wasn't crawling at the beginning of the summer, but we could tell she wanted to when she raised her diapered butt into down dog pose, swaying back and forth on her ridiculously chubby legs.

Anna's practice slowed down for the summer, and she set up an almost daily open house in her less-than-air-conditioned living room. It was hilarious. She had two upstairs neighbor girls and a friend's daughter who wanted to be "mother's helpers." Ranging in age from seven to ten, they were *almost* old enough to watch the babies if one of us needed to pee or fix a snack. Still, they sat quietly while we talked our usual Mommy Group talk—bleeding and breast milk and men problems.

One day I filmed the proceedings with my phone. Anna is wearing a white sundress, sitting on the floor to play "Michael Row the Boat Ashore" on her guitar. The big girls sway and sing, and the babies clap their hands.

When we grew bored with hanging out inside, we meandered to the Third Street Playground in Prospect Park, as if on a day camp field trip, albeit one with a wide age split. The "big" girls were always grabbing the babies around their middles, making them cry, and then wondering why. It was idyllic, if you believe (as I do) in the gospel of seventies-era *Sesame Street* and city living as utopia.

Danny, Clara, and I became regulars at Vanderbilt Playground, less than a block from our house. Antonia, Melissa, and Heidi met us there most days with their babes. Sofia and Gus were fierce, each a head taller than my short girl. Sitting in the little shade the playground offered, we watched in astonishment as Gus ran on all fours on his knuckles like a baby baboon, straight into the sprinkler full of big kids. Sofia pushed a walker through the chaos, over bumps and pebbles, almost down stairs, as Clara tried to follow close behind, dragging herself on her diapered butt. Clara also hung on to the dripping sprinkler, which was shaped like a gloved Mickey Mouse hand, pulling herself up, drinking water from the (filthy) fingers. Watching Clara and Clay squeak down the baby slide together in June, I felt true joy for the first time in months.

They were ragamuffins, our kids, filthy with fountain water and playground dirt, streaked with sweat. And we were the moms, finally, who had our shit together, standing on the playground in a chatty cluster, drinking wine from plastic cups in the park, laughing and letting the kids try to stand and fall, spraying on sunscreen and retying hats, rolling balls to hapless hands. It was finally fun. We imagined a future in which our kids would be muddy and bossy and loyal to one another.

Before I had a kid, I always thought of children's birthday parties as a drag. Why did my friends with children even invite me? Screaming children running around, balloon strings threatening to garrote me, the birthday child crying into his or her fallen cupcake. I'd ostentatiously rattle my bottle of Advil at some point in the proceedings. But that summer, as each of the babes turned one, I changed my mind. I *loved* these first-birthday parties. We celebrated with picnics in the park for Gus and Clay and an elegant brunch for Melissa (I mean Sofia). There was always prosecco, and space for the babies to roll around relatively unattended, and . . . Well, pretty much all I needed that summer was bubbly and a blanket.

When I'd first gotten sick, in the spring, I didn't know if my parents' regular visits would continue when I started to feel better. My grandparents Yetta and Len had been the most important people in my life, after my own parents, and I knew my folks had fantasized about playing the same roles for Clara. But Philly was not a five-minute drive away. Now they were collecting Amtrak Guest Rewards and figuring out hotel deals, visiting every two weeks. They were part of our crowd, excitedly telling me how they'd hung out with Antonia at the swings at Vanderbilt Playground, or ended up eating ice cream next to Heidi and Clay at Blue Marble.

The Mommy Group had been meeting at least once a week for a year. We knew whose husband was uncomfortable with the baby seeing him naked (Jane's), who wanted to go back to her career more than she wanted to have another kid (Melissa), who planned to breast-feed until her baby was three (me). When it came to our histories, though, and what we had in common beyond the babies, we'd only scratched the surface. Now we began to become real friends. It was sophomore year.

When the Mommies asked how I was doing, I began telling them about my work, in addition to Clara's latest cute move or my worries about withdrawing from my medication. The next time Danny had a concert, Renée and Benji came to the show, hiring a babysitter and everything. We sat together in the audience and hung out backstage afterward, like old friends.

I didn't *need* to know that Jane worked on Obama's campaign or that Melissa also couldn't wait to see the Balthus show at the Met, but it was exciting to figure out what we had in common beyond our children and the crisis of the first year. That summer, I embraced these new relationships and situations, seeing the hidden upsides of parenthood, beyond the obvious one of having a baby.

Jane and I grew close first. We both grew up in hippie households. Her family was more spartan and political than mine, less druggy and boho, but we understood each other in the way I've often found with other children of the counterculture. And we shared certain sensibilities—making rather than buying Halloween costumes and birthday cakes, belonging to the Park Slope Food Coop without complaining about its arcane rules or excess of soy products, singing "If I Had a Hammer" to our baby girls.

On Jane's birthday, she invited me out with her "other" (prior to baby) friends. Walking up Seventh Avenue in Park Slope, I realized I hadn't gotten her a present. The bookstore was still open, but I had no idea what she would like. Did she even read fiction? Worried about being late to meet her and Carl, I bought *Hunting the Wild Thistle*, a book about foraging for edible weeds because Jane . . . liked to eat organic food.

A few hours later, tipsily tearing open the wrapping paper at the bar, she shot me a puzzled look.

"It looks interesting, and there's a pretty woodcut on the cover!" I said.

"Well, thank you. I love you." (A year later, on her next birthday, when I gave her a critically lauded novel about growing up on a commune, she winked at me. "I did read the other book from last year, you know, every single weirdo page.")

Our husbands also got along, chatting about music and books

(Carl was obsessed with Kristin Hersh from Throwing Muses, and Danny lent him her memoir). Best of all, though, was watching Katie and Clara form their own "friendship," even if for now that was limited to rolling around on the floor together or occasionally pulling themselves up side by side on a couch or coffee table.

Thanks to regular physical and occupational therapy, Katie's hands finally unclenched, though Jane still had to adjust her knees and ankles out of their natural splayed position every time she sat up. However, Katie was slow to crawl, and, as the rest of the babes turned one and started walking, she stayed grounded on all fours.

"The doctor says she's still in normal range," Jane would say quickly when we saw got together and Katie still didn't seem interested in walking. "Don't gasp like that when she falls down!" she told me when I raced to help her. "She's learning."

"Of course," I'd answer, hoping to myself that Clara, almost four months younger than Katie, wouldn't walk first. I didn't want my friend to feel bad.

Melissa and I also grew closer. We spent so many hours watching Sofia, who *was* an early walker—and strong—push Clara around in a little cart on the playground. Melissa and I were both trying to get back to our lives as artists, her to painting and me to writing.

"I don't know how to set aside the time," she confessed to me as we monitored the girls, "especially without a studio of my own. I'm thinking of renting space, though! Sof—be careful, sweetie. That's bumpy." As it wasn't clear that the children exactly understood English yet, I wasn't sure her warning would keep her daughter from tipping mine onto her head.

"You don't want to work in your house?" I asked as we both ran over to rescue our children. Sofia had pushed Clara into a weedy corner and didn't know how to back out. Clara didn't mind, but all I could think about were the many kids I'd seen peeing on those weeds.

"I can't concentrate there anymore," she said.

"Yeah, me neither," I said. "But I can't remember when I *could* concentrate."

There was so much catching up to do. When Danny's teaching year ended in June, he and I looked at each other and realized we'd made it through the long, hard winter. We'd learned how to parent Clara and take care of me in a major health crisis. I was on a steady dose of meds and could now spend long stretches of time alone with Clara, and by myself. I didn't need any Ativan during the day anymore, and I'd been at the same solid dose of Zoloft for two months.

Now we were like a real family, not two incompetents in a frenzied game of House. On the playground, we pushed Clara in a swing, padding her with a blanket to keep her from falling out. I only dared a few inches up and back, but Danny would push her higher and faster, and she'd squeal and giggle with the wind and the motion.

We took the subway to the Metropolitan Museum, Clara (miraculously asleep) in the stroller while we actually looked at art together. We drove to Philadelphia to visit my grandfather Lenny and dressed Clara in a tiny Phillies shirt and white shorts. She looked like Pop-Pop Lenny back when he used to hang out by the Park Towne Apartments pool when I was a kid.

July brought a week at the Jersey Shore with my folks. Clara learned to crawl there, while my father assessed every possible threat to her safety. Bamboo bar stools! A glass-topped coffee table! High tide! When Clara dipped her little toes in the ocean, she withdrew, screaming. The sand also freaked her out. She'd just gotten used to moving on solid ground, and now there was this unstable grainy . . . stuff.

My parents took Clara in the mornings while Danny and I slept in late—together—in a room where we could hear the ocean. We celebrated my birthday that week, and Danny brought me a rose and a cupcake on the bus from Brooklyn. We went out for a seafood feast at one of the last old restaurants in Atlantic City, where Italian ladies with cocktail rings on their gnarled hands reached out and grabbed Clara's generous thighs. "What a baby!" they said. "God bless." We agreed.

In August, we flew to Los Angeles to visit Danny's family. Baby's first plane trip was fine. We stayed at a friend's house in Venice, where jasmine bloomed in the backyard, and Clara met her great grandparents at their Orange County nursing home.

When we got home to Brooklyn, Clara was talking, saying "Hi!" to everyone who passed, before continuing in her baby Gaelic. It was all real. Clara was real.

And then, finally, I was really writing again. Amazing: I sat on the sofa with my computer, and, as in days of old, I put one word in front of another. I'd been working on a novel for a couple of years when I got pregnant. When I look back on the daily manuscript backups I sent myself, there is a clear gap: 8/13/10 (about a month into my third trimester) to 6/23/11, a few days after my tutoring school year ended.

"I'm better, don't you think?" I asked Danny one afternoon, after I'd written for an hour. "Maybe you can even start sleeping in bed again?"

We'd slept in the same room on vacation, but at home he was back on the couch, taking the baby night shift in case Clara woke.

He was prioritizing my health and Clara's well-being, which was the right thing to do. Right?

I was scared to ask, but I wondered if he *wanted* to be on the couch. Was this his way of distancing himself from my problems and me? I missed us, the couple who we were before all of this started. Not that I would change having Clara for the world, but Danny and I were having trouble regaining our spark. I hoped it wasn't permanent.

A few weeks before Labor Day, I called *New York* magazine's top-rated temporary-wall installer (yes, such a thing does exist). We'd always planned to divide our bedroom in half, once Clara grew old enough to need her own space. But Danny and I needed to get our bedroom back, together, now. Which meant moving her out of Danny's office and into her own room. In a few days, we'd all be starting our first full year back to work and teaching, without pregnancy or a brand-new baby. It was time.

When the wall went up, we papered Clara's side with a map of the world, propped a Maurice Sendak print on her dresser, and lined her bookshelf with stuffed animals and toys. Our side got a coat of satiny turquoise paint, and I hung our windows with shades I made out of blue-and-gold African cotton. That very night, Danny and I lay in our bed together in our own room for the first time in months.

"Shouldn't we be having wild sex or something?" I asked. "It seems like a strange idea after all this time."

"What if we wake the baby?" he said.

"Yeah, what if we wake the baby?" I repeated.

We paused, and then reached for each other in the dark. We woke the baby; she went back to sleep soon enough.

. . . .

Then it was September. The leaves hung heavy on the late-summer trees, and the Mommies kept meeting at the park, lingering at the playground in the early twilight. Anna threw a birthday blowout for Isabella: an old-timey hoedown at a bar in Red Hook. All of her friends brought their instruments; kids were rolling and running over the room's splintered floors. She baked what seemed like hundreds of banana (Issie's favorite flavor) cupcakes. It was a joyous, righteous celebration of everything she'd accomplished that year, and of the people who'd helped her get there. Stephan was *not* in attendance. She'd made it through such a dark season; she needed Carnival.

Clara's birthday was coming up fast. As soon as Danny and I had found out my due date was at the end of October, we'd started planning Halloween birthday parties. We're both suckers for Halloween; not sexy ghoul–style but real, old-fashioned getting-sick-on-candy, homemade-costume, *Día de Muertos* fun (except when used as patterning for hospital scrubs). Trick-or-treaters besiege our block every year, and our neighbors put on their witch hats and set out smoke machines and fake tombstones. People who can't imagine October thirty-first in the big city haven't been to Brooklyn.

When I was pregnant, before Clara's first Halloween, we'd made big plans to sit on our stoop with our costumed newborn baby, handing out candy, introducing our new addition. Instead, Danny and my dad gave out small bags of fun-size candy bars and then came back upstairs to me, still bedridden after my surgery, only three days home from the hospital.

This year, though, would be a different story. We'd made it through the fourth trimester, postpartum anxiety, first words, and now first steps. We wanted a big party.

Clara Yetta

a.k.a.: Babygirl, The Stuff, The Bean,
Monkeybutt, Wildebeest, Shrimp Scampi

Is 1 Year Old!

Snacks, libations, and cake will be served.

Halloween garb encouraged (especially for babies).

Danny and I have a history of differing approaches to social events. My ideal gathering is a dinner party for close friends. Danny likes to invite everyone he's ever met to every event. I wanted to invite thirty people to our wedding, dreaming of a City Hall ceremony. Danny's invite list topped three hundred. We compromised: 140 people, at a delicious tapas restaurant in Philly. My dress was short; he didn't wear a tie. The guests included hip-hop musicians, writers, many cellists, and slightly more Jewish relatives. Because we refused to make a seating chart, everyone table-hopped and hung out with each other. There was a ton of food, cava, sangria, and heart-shaped pot brownies—and I didn't want it to end. After our wedding, I became a convert to Danny's social planning.

So, Clara's first birthday. My immediate instinct was for a small, home party, but Danny convinced me we needed size. We decided to hold it at Soda, a bar a block away from our apartment. In my pre-Danny days, I'd met online matches there for first dates of cider and burgers. There was a side room off the bar, not by any means toddler-proofed, but large enough for the mass of people we wanted to invite.

Before sending the invite, I surrendered to party-planning detail-obsession. A few weeks before the event, I tried to make Danny drive us two hours upstate to the Storm King Art Center to take photos for the invite. Our Zipcar developed mechanical problems before we were even out of the Bronx, and we ended up in Sleepy Hollow, where I insisted we would find a locale macabre enough for the birthday-invite photo.

With no headless horsemen to be found, pushing Clara's stroller on the shoulder of a highway as she wailed, Danny came up with a new rule: "Never say we're going to have 'family fun'!"

Eventually, we found a candy store where I staged photos of Clara holding Dracula and Frankenstein-themed PEZ dispensers. More like she stuck them in her mouth, and I quickly had to remove and dispose of the choking hazard.

Clara's costume was the next order of birthday business. Danny wanted her to be a blueberry. I had other ideas (actually, one: gnome), but Danny's vision was fierce. He didn't know that I'd had homemade Halloween costumes every year of my life until middle school, when I started wearing vintage dresses and going out dancing with my friends instead of trick-or-treating. Yetta and my mother always made my costumes together, using an old sheet to make a witch or princess dress, dyeing it in the washer, and then sewing on sequins or rickrack. Now Momo was not going to let her one and only new baby granddaughter wear a prefabricated Halloween costume.

"Danny wants Clara to be a blueberry," I told my mom. Within days, we received iPhone photos of prototypes made of blue fabric covering a foam sphere and trimmed with green ribbon shoulder ties.

The costume was perfect. Clara stepped into the sphere with her chubby legs, and I stuck a blue-striped onesie underneath and bought her some tiny blue tights online. She looked like a Wall Street fat cat reduced to wearing a barrel.

"Or," Danny recalled, "as if she was backstage at a pantomime of *Charlie and the Chocolate Factory*, hanging out between the matinee and evening performances." Her hair at that point had grown into a little Leslie Caron–like pixie, always over one eye. Too much.

Clara started walking exactly a week before her birthday. On the actual day, Danny and I took her to the Coney Island Aquarium. We bought a membership, good for the aquarium and all the New York City zoos. Now that we were parents of a toddler, we figured we would be visiting the zoo a lot.

A freak snowstorm hit the morning of the birthday party, with big wet flakes edged with ice. Even though Soda Bar was only two blocks away, my mother and I had to fight our way through the wind, laden with the hundred pumpkin cupcakes I'd stayed up until midnight baking and icing.

I was worried that no one would come in the inclement weather. For the first half hour, I hosted an empty room in my acid-green leather skirt that hadn't fit since before I was pregnant, and a Day of the Dead necklace of hot pink papier-mâché skulls. Soon enough, though, we got a crowd more suited to a house party than any baby soiree I'd attended.

Heidi, Josh, and Clay arrived first, with Clay dressed as a giraffe in a fuzzy suit. He greeted Clara with a kiss on the lips, tilting his head to the side.

"She's his girl next door!" Heidi giggled, clasping her hands. "The one who was there all along . . ."

The other Mommies arrived soon, with the kids all in costumes. Sofia was a sweet, if energetic, ladybug, and Emme was a bee. Antonia turned Gus out as a "zombie skate punk"— full monster makeup, skater gear, and his curls gelled into a fauxhawk (our first indication that Antonia was a serious costume mom). Anna showed up without Issie, which I thought was weird until I saw she was actually enjoying herself, gossiping with our friend Stephanie about divorce while knocking back glasses of wine. Jane arrived last, grumpy. "I don't believe in costumes for such small children!" she said. "They don't know the difference!" Still, she'd stuck a Carmen Miranda hat covered in fake fruit on Katie's head. Best of all: Katie was walking.

All of our babysitters showed up (the open bar helped) with their boyfriends or girlfriends, and a bunch of classical musicians who knew Clara solely from Danny's Facebook posts. A flutist brought a pumpkin pie and her dog. Clara kept petting the pup and then drawing her hand back, screaming and giggling.

Livy, one of my oldest friends from middle school, drove in from Philly, in the snow, scarfed down a beer and some fries, and drove home again. The mother of a ten-year-old son, she passed on to Clara one of his old favorite picture books, *Gluey and the Snail*, as a gift. "First birthdays are very important," she said.

Katie kept taking her fruit hat off and putting it back on, a tiny cowboy on a rubber horse bounced around at risk of concussion, and a three-year-old Laura Ingalls Wilder played hide-and-seek with Clara behind the bar's dusty curtains.

"They're going to pull them down!" my father worried, but I let the girls go. Clara loved the game, giggling wildly. She was social, her performer daddy's new soul of a child, tottering ten, even twenty steps at a time before crashing on her blueberry- and diaper-padded tush.

When Danny and I stood to make a toast, I looked at him and whispered, "I can't say anything. It's too much." It was the anniversary of Clara's birth, but also the anniversary of my major surgery, physical trauma, and the deep psychic disappointment I could at that point only begin to express.

Danny raised his glass and found the words I couldn't. "Everybody here is here because you've been a part of this last year, which has been the hardest and most magical of our lives. Thanks for helping us survive it."

Then Clara needed to nurse, crashing out from the excitement of the party and her first cupcake, my nipple still in her mouth.

"I'm so glad to see you're still breast-feeding," a friend said to me. It was Emily, the writer who told me to go to acupuncture when I first miscarried.

All I'd done with her was to speak my truth, to say what had happened to me and how I was feeling, and she became the first in my chosen community of mommies to help me, without fuss or feeling of imposition.

We've really come full circle, I thought. And I didn't fuck it all up. This feeling was my own first-birthday gift. I'd been in combat, on my quest, unrelenting, for four whole seasons. Now I could finally look around. The world was still standing, even if it was different from the one I knew before.

The Mommies all felt it with those important first birthdays. We had walking, talking toddlers, who developed so fast we had less time to obsess about our mothering. Now, I dared to hope, could we have time to develop ourselves?

12. From Meltdowns to Playgrounds

Welcome to Toddler Time

Facebook post from Elizabeth

April 24, 2012

Do I need to buy Clara a truck? She's obsessed with babies and tutus at only 18 months old. I only played dolls, dress up, and other girly things. Still, I worry I am not giving her enough options.

Sarah Jean Billeiter (aka amazing babysitter) replied:

She likes trucks, but she's not sure what to do with them. She always notices them at the sandbox and points and says, "Truck," but I never have a chance to encourage her to play with them because the boys are always hoggin' 'em.

Larry Gold replied:

What about a school bus? I mean a full size a la Ken Kesey.

Elizabeth Gold replied:

Dad, I thought we were hoping for a less Merry Prankster vibe this generation.

The second winter we were mothers, it didn't snow at all after the first fluke storm on Halloween. I bought Clara a wardrobe of gear for her first walking winter—boots, a snow bib, and pants—and she didn't wear any of it. It could have been a potent metaphor. Here we all were, preparing for the storm that never came. Instead, we rotated through the same five locations, over and over and over: home, the Underhill Playground, Blue Marble for coffee and a taste of ice cream, the supermarket, the pizza place.

Heidi and Clay made a daily "field trip" to Duane Reade, two blocks away, because he was obsessed with the revolving rack of toy cars and trucks between the greeting card and paper products sections. When they changed the store's layout, he was seriously upset.

Danny summed up the toddler-time ethos: "We used to eat at eight, now we ate at six. A baby *might* sleep more, but Clara needed to get out and move around. She just couldn't *do* much." Toddlers need to learn but are almost unteachable. They don't know what traffic is, but they want to run into it. Parents are still sleep-deprived zombies.

The kids were so freaking cute that it almost didn't matter. In spite of ourselves, and in spite of all the craziness, we were all starting to have fun. We had *people*.

At Clay's eighteen-month pediatrician checkup, he informed the doctor it was "Mommy turn now" to get a shot, not "Cway turn." The doctor, seasoned as she was, did a double take. Heidi took him to a music class and he ran rampant, interrupting the class to pull a soda bottle out of the trash and declare it "Mommy wine!" Heidi told us, "All the other mommies stared at me and didn't laugh. I was mortified."

Ironically, Heidi had been worried Clay would be a slow talker. A month before his first birthday in August, we took the kids to the Brooklyn Botanic Garden for an afternoon roll on the lawn. We were sitting, watching our little dough balls dig in the dirt, serious expressions on their faces, when a little girl, probably around two, came up to chat with us.

"I like your barrette," Heidi told her.

"Thank you," she said. "It's sparkly."

As she walked back to her family twenty feet away, Heidi turned to me with a sigh. "I guess it will be a while until Clay talks like that," she said. "Boys."

Clara already had quite the vocabulary (I thought). Her first word was *Hi!* which she used as greeting and punctuation. *Dada* came before *Mama*, much to my dismay; I worried it proved that I'd earned less love. "It's what they can say first. It's an easier syllable," Danny reassured me.

Clara liked to end words with the sound *du*, making *elephant* "e-du," *armadillo* "a-du-du," and *Clay* "Cw-du." All food was "teez," aka "cheese." As Heidi bemoaned Clay's verbal skills, I felt a little smug. I should have known. Whenever I pitied one of the Mommies, I was due for a comeuppance. Within weeks, Clay was correcting Clara's pronunciation of his name: "Cway, not Cw-du."

All the Mommy Group kids hit their milestones at different times and in different ways. When Gus, Emme, and Clara were around eighteen months old, Antonia, Renée, and I met up in the park. Clara was (and always will be) small for her age. Gus was tall, and Emme was right in the middle. We asked them to practice their jumps—a significant developmental milestone for just-turning-two-year-olds—and I filmed the adorable mayhem.

I still love rewatching the video. "Jump it, Gus! Jump it, Emme! Jump it, Clara!" I call out to each kid in turn, the other moms giggling in the background. Gus executes a lavish jump, with his usual bonhomie. Emme takes a moment from examining a flower to practice a small, less-powerful jump, and Clara, tiny and wearing the most adorable (I may be biased) gathered-at-the-ankle jeans, bounces up and down with her knees, her feet never lifting off the ground.

Gus didn't merely walk by the time he turned one—he *ran* like a little bear or a coyote. Over the summer, he'd started that crazy crawling on his knuckles, butt high in the air, fast, but nothing like once he went full biped. Adorable and terrifying, he'd run and run and run.

"Augustus, come back!" Antonia would yell frantically as he took off for the umpteenth time in one day. Chasing her son in a dramatic sprint over hillocks in the middle of Prospect Park's Long Meadow, she followed him as he made a quick splash through what appeared to be quicksand (mud), and receded into the distance, growing tinier and then . . . We couldn't see him at all. (Clara couldn't run yet, let alone run away.)

"Do you think he'd go in the street?" Renée asked.

"I dunno. Did Charlie ever do that?"

"No, running away was never Charlie's thing," she answered.

Four-year-old Charlie was with us on this Prospect Park outing. He had a day off from preschool and was happily playing in the overgrown grass with tiny LEGO guys. In about one minute, we all knew he'd lose a crucial piece, forcing Renée to comb the grass for it, *CSI*-style, reasoning with him, "Sometimes you lose things." But until that inevitable moment, she sat, legs stretched out to catch the full sun, on her striped waterproof blanket.

Antonia came back into view, appearing face first over a bump in the grass, eventually revealing that she was holding Gus, struggling and crying, lengthwise under her arm.

"Why does he do this?" Antonia asked, once she'd strapped Gus back into his stroller for a time-out. "Is he oblivious? Is it ADD? How can I tell?" She blew her bangs off her face. "I'm sweaty!"

We didn't have any answers for her. We didn't have any answers for ourselves. The kids had been mysterious enough when they were babies, loaves of bread lacking locomotion. They had all this power and strength. And *desires*, but we couldn't tell what they were. I wanted to know what Clara was thinking, because based on what she liked to talk about, it seemed her dominant preoccupation was yogurt.

We were rediscovering childhood through our children's eyes. Why and how did these little people make their choices? How much of their behavior was instinctual? Katie played pretend with her stuffed animals and dollies, though what she was saying sounded like "Kiki" and "Coco." (More than a year later, Jane would figure out those were Katie's words for *poop* and *pee*.) Emme didn't talk much yet, but she played hide-and-seek and fought with light sabers—real games she learned from her big brother. Clara loved music, mimicking songs with impressive pitch accuracy, even if she couldn't get the words. Katie and Gus weaned easily, and went down for three-hour naps in the afternoon. Clara slept through the night, and was still nursing, but she didn't nap.

Sofia and Clay talked in full, clear sentences. Clara was a fussy eater, and I didn't have the energy to diversify her food. Katie wolfed down broccoli and cauliflower as if they were mother's milk. Was that because Jane sautéed her greens in lumps of butter, or because Katie actually liked cruciferous veggies?

Clara never played by herself, screaming if we left her to her own devices for a second. Was Emme more independent as the second child, used to playing with older brother Charlie? Was she always going to be a more self-sufficient person, going on solo Outward Bound trips while Clara hung with the Drama Club?

The kids' toy preferences tended to fall along traditional gender lines. Trucks and balls all the way for Clay, dinosaurs for Gus, and babies, babies, and more babies for the girls. We did eventually buy Clara a truck, but she ignored it. She wasn't obsessed with pink and princesses yet, and we hoped she might skip that stage. (Little did we know that *Frozen* would transform all of our lives soon enough. Thank you, Elsa—at least you're a queen and not a pink-wearing princess.)

Were these preferences, quirks, and difficulties nature or nurture? How many of our theories were projections? And why were these kids so moody?

The first time I saw Katie melt down, her frustration was so palpable that I felt it in my own body. It was scary: her face turned magenta, then brick-red, and she screamed at her mother, hitting at her, tensing her body even more than usual. Clara sort of stepped back and watched her friend as Jane waded into the maelstrom of snot and tears to scoop her daughter up, holding her firmly, telling her, "Look in Mommy's eyes." After a while, Katie calmed down, and the girls went back to playing, but Jane and I were still shaky.

"I don't know what to do. I'd leave her alone, but I'm afraid she's going to hurt herself!" Katie's meltdowns got worse as she aged. Was it because of her physical difficulties? Jane couldn't figure it out.

My parents insist that I *never* threw a tantrum as a toddler. This seems impossible to me, though I remember my mother regarding my crying, screaming friends as sort of odd fauna, not knowing what to do when a playdate (known simply as "playing with a friend" back in the seventies) went south. When Clara made it through her first year virtually tantrum free, I figured she was a chip off my old block.

"Maybe she won't tantrum," I said to my therapist one day in a moment of extremely daffy hope. "Her needs for comfort are getting met—as long as I'm breast-feeding."

Ellen half-smiled. "It's more likely she hasn't grown into them yet."

When Clara and Katie started walking at almost the same time, they'd needed to concentrate so much on their weeble-wobble locomotion that they temporarily stopped interacting.

But now they *played*. Clara and I started playing "chase you" at home. It was her first game, and it was a big deal. The way it worked: I ran very, very slowly toward her, and she tottered away from me. Soon, she instigated it, calling out "Dase you, dase you," running to the other end of our apartment, chortling.

The next time we were visiting Jane and Katie, I showed them Clara's new party trick. "Chase you, chase you!" I shouted, and she waddled down the hall. At first I worried, because Katie's musculature was still weak—she was floppier than Clara. Then I realized this was good for both of them. Soon she and Clara were chasing each other, two little girls who couldn't even run yet, wobbly on their newly upright legs. They were laughing, screaming with joy. Watching them from the couch, Jane and I couldn't believe it. Even when they tripped each other up and fell down, they were still happy. Why didn't falling provoke a tantrum? Who knew?

In the last few years, there have been a slew of internet forwards, lists with titles like "Twenty Ways Your Toddler Is Like a Drunk Person," accompanied by photos of tykes who've dumped bowls of spaghetti over their heads and are grinning madly, or who've decided to put their puppy in the toilet.

When Clara was at the height of her Toddler Mystery Time, my favorite of these was "19 Surprising Facts About Toddlers" by Tracy Moore, for the website *Jezebel*. Moore's list was accompanied by a graphic of a toddler girl's pigtailed silhouette, with the words *Little Angels*, except *Angels* was crossed out to read *Monsters* in drippy bloody font.

The list runs from: "Did you know a toddler will kick you in the face and then laugh even when you are crying?" to "Did you know that a toddler needs to go back inside the house after you've left in the morning approximately three times because she forgot her 1.) string cheese, 2.) monkey, 3.) neck-a-lace?"

It says a lot about the state of mind I was in when Clara was in her ones-going-on-twos that I not only read that list repeatedly but guffawed out loud every time.

Alicia F. Lieberman's *The Emotional Life of the Toddler* was published in 1993 and is still one of the best books about this confusing time.

In a section titled "The Toddler's Wish to Have it All," Lieberman writes, "The toddler desires things . . . to enhance herself through her possessions." Great. But what do you do when they're melting down because you step in the way of that enhancement?

I wanted, both as a parent and as author of this book, to think about how other people parent toddlers. In January 2015, I knew I'd be in Southern California visiting Danny's family, and I decided to check out another style of mommy group.

LA is an alienating city. Strangers don't really talk to each other, because they spend all their time in their cars, because traffic is atrocious and unpredictable (one night I was able to listen to three hour-long episodes of *Serial* on what should have been a forty-five-minute drive) and because different ethic and economic groups rarely find themselves in the same place unless you count the freeways.

Echo Parenting & Education looked almost too good to be true. Philosophically based on the ideal of "a world of nonviolence," their mission is to "support and facilitate child raising rooted in connection and empathy." In practical terms, this means they lead targeted parenting workshops.

Echo Park is in Central LA—far enough from the beach to make it feel like a day trip from my in-laws' condo in Marina del Rey, but close to Griffith Park and the über-hip Silver Lake neighborhood. Within LA's general population and structure, Echo Park is both densely populated and poor. The majority of residents are Latino, predominantly from Mexico and El Salvador. However, like so many urban neighborhoods across the country, Echo Park has begun to gentrify. Hipster families renovate houses to eco-friendly standards, talk of urban farming, and glimpse scruffy celebrities at the local farmers' market. Still, the neighborhood doesn't "feel" fancy—yet.

Echo Parenting's office is not easy to find, especially in everything-is-a-mystery LA. It's on Sunset Boulevard, which sounds Hollywood glamorous, but is in fact an arterial main drag that feels, by East Coast standards, like a highway. I don't know what I imagined—something sophisticated, less like a small non-profit serving Latinas and their children? The building is a small two-story stucco office. The ground floor (where I wandered in initially) is a reporting center for parolees, with signs requesting that clients be substance free when they enter the facility. I finally found the right office, up a flight of stairs. It was homey, and clearly a women's space: bare bones but warm, with children's artwork on the walls and organic snacks on offer.

I was meeting with members of a parenting class, a diverse mix of voluntary attendees and mothers who'd "crossed a line" with a child and therefore were completing court orders to participate in group work of this kind.

Kim Pesati, the development and communications coordinator, greeted me warmly. At first impression, Kim seemed to fit neatly into the "new" Echo Park: white, dressed in clothes both expensive and subtly worn, and her seven-year-old son's name is a noun. Still, she was an active member of the Parenting Support Group.

The other group members were already waiting in the conference room. Pilar was the young mother of Angela, a rambunctious six-year-old, as well as being herself a domestic violence survivor. Naturally beautiful (think Lisa Bonet, circa 1989), she has participated in the parenting classes and support group since her daughter was an infant. Her demeanor felt deliberately calm, yet forceful. And Angela decided she was my official welcoming committee. All she needed to know was that I forgot to bring snacks (for which I was wildly apologetic), and that my iPhone doubled as a recording device. Pilar worked with her daughter's interruptions in a way that I initially found overly accommodating and then admired enough to try them out (successfully) on Clara later that afternoon.

"I'm feeling I need some support from you right now," she said to Angela as she squirmed. "You can participate, or you can go sit out and wait for me and play. You can't play with that phone, though. You can draw." That's not gonna work, I thought. Asking a child for "support" is wishy-washy. However, when Angela not only agreed but sat for about twenty minutes working on a picture of characters from *My Little Pony*, I realized she'd heard her mother's inclusive language and amended her behavior. If this was non-violent parenting in action, I wanted a piece of it.

The third Echo Parenting mommy in attendance was Lecia. Curvy and dressed for the unseasonably warm January weather, she had a tattoo inscribed on her inner arm in red script: *Hope for the best, prepare for the worst*. Her nails were hot-pink, with white, dagger-shaped tips. The whole effect was intimidating. Yet, of the three women, Lecia's story was the most self-sacrificing. At twenty-three, she has a six-year-old son, and she adopted a friend's seven-year-old daughter because her biological mother is "doing some time." Meanwhile, she recently graduated from California State University, Long Beach.

Lecia started coming to Echo at nineteen years old because, she explained, "I needed to make sure I keep sole legal custody from my daughter's dad because he's—" Here she paused and nodded at Pilar. "I'm also a survivor of domestic violence. He was physically abusing me, but I was emotionally abusing. I was going to end up being one of those parents using the belt—or, God forbid, something else. I didn't want to raise my kids to be fearful, but for them to know who they are and respect themselves. I learned here: how can you respect yourself if your own mother can't respect you? That's why I *had* to go to class and take counseling."

She continued, "I never liked seeing a mom walking away from her [screaming] kid, but I also didn't want to be my kids' shadow. At Echo I found a middle ground."

"What does nonviolent parenting actually involve," I asked, "beyond the obvious idea of, uh, not hitting your kids?"

Kim explained. "In the traditional way people raise their children, compliance is the goal. In nonviolent parenting, the goal is *connection.* Many people lead with evaluation and judgment of their children, we advocate leading with empathy, compassion, mutual respect, and connection."

"And addressing the child's core needs," Pilar added. "When Angel was [a toddler] things got difficult. She was saying no all the time, and she wasn't napping. I found myself doing things like holding the door shut, while she was pushing behind it."

"Which always works," I interjected. Pilar smiled.

"Right! You scream at them and get them all anxious. It felt horrible!" She continued, "But in class, we learn about child development and brain development. Consequential thinking comes in well after toddlerhood. I'm twenty-nine, and it was only a few years ago when *I* was able to say, *Oh, if I do that, this is gonna happen.* Now the support group helps me remember: *This is what my kids are capable of.*"

Toddlers are so busy because they're creating their *selves.* Ironically, this is exactly the moment when their mothers need to *re-*create their own selves as well. When I thought of the Mommies at this stage, I remembered how desperate we were to find our own time and space. Even if it cost us.

13. Schedules, Sitters, and Schools

Loco Parentis or Loco Parents?

From Elizabeth

November 16, 2011

Clara's with her new sitter today. Jen wears a lot of patchouli and those barefoot shoes, and I hope is not stoned while she's caring for the baby.

From Jane

December 5, 2010

Can someone remind me, where is the extended family that is dying to watch my child during the day??

As the second year progressed, time management became the major theme for all the Mommies. In the first year, we "knew" we'd never have time for anything but the baby again. We were holding on between feedings and diaper changes, catching sleep as if we were running point in a war zone. By year two, we were more organized, though we'd also learned what we each needed to give up for that organization.

Maybe we paid for more childcare and ate out less, buying more time for work or our marriages. Maybe our in-laws now took the kid one full day a week, and we had to finally make peace with their parenting style. Maybe we ordered takeout from the same Middle Eastern place three nights in a row to create some version of "family dinner" (guilty as charged).

We were all working more now, and for longer hours. Renée added a day and a half at the office to her week, making for almost full-time. At first she was happy, but then she quickly felt over-extended. Jane also went back, albeit cautiously, to work part-time—as much as she could between Katie's three-times-a-week midday therapy appointments. One day I ran into her on the street in Park Slope, on her way to a consulting appointment. In footless tights and a pretty dress, she looked great. We'd talked daily on the phone for almost a year now, knew the details of each other's breasts and C-section scars, but it was the first time I'd ever seen her in anything other than yoga pants and a hoodie.

Danny and I readjusted the way we worked, compartmental-izing tasks, letting go of all but the most important. Our house was always messy, we ate takeout almost every night, but we were making money and doing our "real" work of writing words and music. For other families, a neat house and home-cooked food might take priority, but this was our life and our family.

A year before, back when I first went on my medication, I'd needed so much help that I felt as if I'd been swinging on a trapeze with my eyes closed. I had to relinquish control: over who took care of my child when I couldn't, whether she ate formula or breast milk, whether Danny's parenting choices were exactly the same as mine. Michele the (future) doula was our first sitter, but she wasn't available 24/7. We hired more women to watch Clara, as many as we needed, trusting (rightly) that our daughter would adjust to a cast of thousands. We were lucky that she did.

Before we had Clara, Danny and I talked to every working artist-parent we knew. Danny was particularly concerned. Used to working through the night, on deadline, he couldn't imagine how he would ever compose with his new responsibilities. The advice he received was consistent. Find the time, and make that hour effective. Now we put this advice to the test. Babysitting was expensive. It only worked if we could justify it financially or creatively.

I added a new gig to my work life, though not without some drama. I was now a teaching artist at a venerable New York writing program for public school students.

My first residency was in the Bronx, which entailed a two-hour commute each way, two days a week, for a three-month chunk in the middle of winter. Breaking into any freelance teaching situation in New York City is extremely difficult, and this organization is known for its high-quality, flexible scheduling, and decent hourly rate. So, yes, the four hours on buses and trains seemed slightly insane, but this would, I hoped, lead to more work.

The wrinkle came when I had to explain to my (nonparent) supervisor that I couldn't get to the school by eight in the morning, the hour she thought my residency should commence.

"I'm still nursing in the mornings," I told her. "I need from around seven to eight to feed my kid and get the day started with her."

She looked confused. "That might be a problem," she said.

Again, this was a part-time job teaching creative writing; I wasn't exactly manning the nuclear phone. While I know my problem was small potatoes in the grand scheme of working-parent conflicts, it confirmed my liminal state. As a freelancer, I wasn't entitled to sick days or personal time, and Clara was a liability. The issue was less about what time I started and more about my boss's thinking that parenthood shouldn't affect the schedule. Parenthood always affects the schedule.

Eventually, we agreed that I could start later in the morning. After class, I wrote at a coffee shop on the Upper East Side, and then tutored for a few hours before falling asleep coming home on the subway. As soon as I walked in the door, Clara nursed until my nipples were as sore as when she'd been a newborn. It was exhausting, but we managed.

Then we all got sick. Antonia warned the Mommies that her whole family had gone down with a stomach bug in January. When it hit us in February, it was a horror show. Clara got it first, projectile-vomiting in (and on) Amorina Pizza, which meant all the servers *and* the busboys *and* the cooks caught it. Danny and I were next, with him barfing in the bathroom as I threw up in the kitchen sink. When Clara latched on, it felt vile, but it was the only way to keep her hydrated.

Then everyone at Blue Marble got the same flu, because the baristas were all our babysitters. We were vectors! My parents got it two weeks after we recovered, because rotavirus stays contagious up to two weeks after symptoms abate, contrary to what the internet says. They had to stay in their hotel in Brooklyn for an extra night.

Now, three years later, I wouldn't be so worried. Clara would be miserable, but she'd be able to tell us how she was feeling, I wouldn't be breast-feeding, and we'd have more confidence in our parenting. But that first family sickness felt so threatening.

At the end of the school year, I ended up getting a low assessment at my new teaching job. I'd had to call in sick three times. I looked flaky. And that was with our fantastic childcare.

. . . .

The Amazing Michele was from Colorado, where she'd gone to Waldorf School and then Naropa University.

"You mean the Jack Kerouac School of Disembodied Poetics?" Danny asked when she told us this during her interview.

"Where Allen Ginsburg taught and that Tom Waits attended?" I added. She nodded.

"You're hired," we both said simultaneously.

Well, not quite, actually. I still had one question for her.

"What do you *do* with a little baby?"

Michele has particularly round and innocent-looking blue eyes, and now she focused them on me with full intensity.

"You know, I hold the baby, and then sometimes I walk around, and maybe sing to her or put her in the swing . . ."

"That's it? That's all I do!" I started laughing. I'd been sure an expert sitter would have more tricks.

"They have a limited palette at this age," Michele said, dry. Hired for sure.

In her off time, Michele was (as many of our sitters turned out to be, oddly) a stand-up comedian. We didn't quite realize how her particular combination of Buddhism, humor, and performance skills would affect our child's care until she'd watched Clara a few times and we came to anticipate her highly colored blow-by-blow narrative.

"How'd it go?" we'd ask. Michele would sigh theatrically. "Well, that little baby gave me a run for my money today," she'd say. "I was like, *Baby, you need to go to sleep*, and she was like, *Uh-uh*." This was before Clara could utter more than a peep or coo, but Michele would give her a voice like a tween drama queen. She'd continue, "So I said, *Baby, I am not taking more of this bullshit. You are going to go to sleep.* And then I rocked her and sang her thirty-seven songs, and then she slept for like ten minutes and wouldn't eat anything." Clara would be sitting on Michele's knee, looking innocent as the day she was born. Michele would finish, "Don't trust her. She's got plans for us all."

Michele helped activate Clara for us, making her into a person more than a smush. She was just what we were looking for in a sitter: someone who'd admit when they didn't know better than us, someone who sometimes would, and someone who'd make our sleep-deprived, scared-new-parent selves guffaw in recognition.

But Michele couldn't work all the hours we needed, especially as our freelance schedules complicated everything. A typical scheduling text from me would read *We need an hour on Wednesday, then three on Thursday, from three to six, but actually more like three to seven thirty, if that's okay* . . .

Danny and I found our next batch of sitters through good old-fashioned gut. That is, he'd buy coffee from some nice girl at Blue Marble Ice Cream for a few weeks, strike up conversations, and then she'd become a babysitter. After a while, it was a running joke with the new hires. You're not a full Blue Marble employee until you've babysat Clara. Our daughter, in turn, became mascot of the place, comfortable behind the counter, demanding, as she got older, tastes of grass-fed vanilla. Danny and I both loved the ease of these relationships. It was a great strategy: hire people whom we liked to hang out with first, then check their baby-watching bona fides.

I'd actually thought this through years earlier. When I graduated from college, in the nineties, I worked as a nanny on the Upper West

Side of Manhattan. It was my first exposure to Nanny World, the kingdom of paid childcare. As a young, white sitter, I was privy to confidences from both the mommies (I supposed I reminded them of their younger selves), *and* the nannies (with whom I had working solidarity and whose company I usually preferred). I talked to sitters so resentful of their bosses' demands and laissez-faire parenting that they couldn't look them in the eyes. I saw mommies so suspicious of their nannies they'd follow them to the playground, lurking in the bushes to see if they were really pushing little Charlotte or Jordan on the swings, or secretly shopping and lunching with their nanny friends.

Back then I swore that when I had a family, I would not recreate this mistrustful nanny dynamic. When and if I hired childcare, I would ensure a decent and fair relationship, not expect unpaid overtime or unreasonable housekeeping feats, and always treat my child's sitters with the respect they deserved.

Since then, it's gotten easier in some ways to be a better nanny "boss." There are more than 200,000 paid childcare workers in New York City alone (by comparison, there are about 20,000 practicing female lawyers here). While they still work largely off the books, without benefits or formal organization, the sheer number of nannies in places like brownstone Brooklyn means that there is a powerful social contract. If you are a parent who's blown through many professional sitters due to your unreasonable behavior, the word will spread. Likewise, if a nanny is less than Mary Poppins—like or, God forbid, actually incompetent, a few bad references will put her off the market.

Park Slope Parents runs a comprehensive Nanny Survey every year, helping families and workers understand the conventions of salaries, raises, and vacation days. They offer contract templates, advising that families use them even for off-the-books hires. Using a contract or work agreement is a basic and brilliant tool; if a prospective nanny is unwilling to sign (or vice versa), it's a good indication that perhaps this might not be the right fit.

Most nannies in Brooklyn are immigrants, often mothers of their own small or grown children. It's crucial to acknowledge the difficulties involved in being a mother while watching someone else's kids. For example, when the nanny's charge has a snow day, her kids do as well. As a "boss," if possible, give your sitter that day off, or invite her to bring her own children to play with yours at your house. Don't expect that your sitter will come in if she can't get her own childcare; always have backup. And please—and I only mention this because I have seen and heard it in action—don't assume that nannies from specific countries or cultures will act in lockstep with each other. People are people. If this seems basic or overblown, spend a day on the playground and watch how nannies and parents interact with each other and among themselves.

The Mommy Group had different needs and approaches to childcare. Mine were for sure the loosest. The others tended, initially at least, toward more conventional solutions: professional nannies with childcare expertise and neighborhood networking.

No matter how it's organized, the nanny-parent relationship can be fraught, especially at first, when everyone's getting used to the system and the child is preverbal. Jane summed up the nanny-mommy insecurity perfectly. She wrote to us, *What's up with nannies saying, "I love you" to kids? I don't want Katie's sitter to say it unless she means it and I don't understand how she could mean it if she's only watched Katie five times.*

After her terrible initial experience with daycare, Heidi hired Lila, a middle-aged Guyanese woman, to take care of Clay. It was a stopgap measure; they wanted a nanny share, both to save money and to socialize their little guy. For now, though, one-on-one care seemed best and easiest. Lila was loving and sweet, but . . . she was staying later and later each day, hovering and chatting for half an hour after Heidi got home from work.

"I feel rude shoving her out the door," Heidi said, "but that's my only time with Clay in the whole day. I want to be alone with my baby."

Because she knew that Lila was booked to work with another family in a few months, Heidi didn't address the issue. But she did learn a lesson in communication: parents need to be very clear with their nannies and sitters about expectations, especially in a full-time situation.

Once again, Renée's previous experience with hiring childcare helped us all get some perspective. Her kids' nanny, Rose, was voluptuous, with a multicolored swirl of braids, and her presence—commanding yet fun-loving—matched her appearance.

"I *love* when Rose cooks for the kids or braids Emme's hair," she told us one afternoon as the kids attempted to finger paint. "Charlie eats her food more than mine, and Emme actually lets Rose comb her hair. It's not a competition. They just like some things she does better than when I do them. And thank God, because if I have to deal with one more hair-related temper tantrum from this little girl"—she gestured at Emme, who'd managed to get paint inside her diaper—"I'm gonna lose it."

Anna was having other issues with Amelia, the sitter she'd hired before Stephan left. She wrote to us: *I should value having a competent person, but it's like having a roommate. Like if she is in the bathroom and I have to use it. Or when she is looking for snacks that I don't have or sitting in my favorite chair.*

Maybe she was prescient, because her situation was about to crash hard. After Stephan left, Amelia had been a rock. Isabella had always been moody—tantrumming easily and needing extra cooling-off and adjustment times. Anna figured it was because of the divorce, and she felt grateful that Amelia was so good at "handling" her daughter.

Then things changed. Amelia started bossing Anna around, telling her what time she needed to be home and what was "best" for Issie. If Anna's off-work hours coincided with Issie's nap, Amelia refused to change *her* schedule, and Anna would arrive home to a sleeping baby and a crossed-armed, unyielding nanny. Amelia used the same logic about Issie's "needs" to stay at home all day, every day, never making friends or going on outings, not even to the park or bookstore, both a few blocks away.

Issie's tantrums worsened, especially when Amelia was due to arrive in the morning. Finally, Anna came home one day as a "surprise" and discovered Issie strapped into her baby seat—which she'd outgrown months before—wailing, while Amelia surfed the internet on Anna's computer.

Anna knew she needed to fire Amelia, but in the midst of her divorce, she felt so vulnerable. She told Amelia that her mother was moving to Brooklyn to help with the baby, which is why they would no longer need her services. Amelia retaliated, texting Anna multiple times a day, demanding six months of severance. She even threatened to intervene in Anna's custody battle, saying she would tell Stephan that Anna wasn't competent to care for her own child. It wasn't until Stephan himself confronted Amelia (at Anna's request) that she finally backed off. Anna changed the locks.

For her next sitter, Anna decided to go unconventional. She ended up with the world's funniest babysitter, surpassing even Danny and me in the "hippie realness" category with Clyde, a bass player who (among other quirks) didn't wear shoes unless there was actual snow on the ground. Looming over Issie like a benevolent, oversize Hobbit, he was just what that little girl needed: a man who didn't make her mother cry, who would roughhouse with her, carry her on his tall shoulders, and make her soup from a can. Issie adored him, thriving with him as she never had under Amelia's rigid rule. Anna could relax, staying late at work if she needed, even starting to date. *Date.* What a word for a mother!

What if childcare were a "right" in this country? Most Americans don't even know that other developed countries subsidize childcare. Women, mothers, need to make ends meet for their families, and they deserve to be professionally ambitious. In her book *Bringing Up Bébé: One American Mother Discovers the Wisdom of French Parenting*, Pamela Drucker writes about the French system of childcare. In France and many other European countries (with a special shout-out to the Scandinavian countries Denmark, Norway, and Sweden), the "village" exists in the form of subsidized childcare. Mothers are expected to want to go back to work. Almost more important, it is generally agreed that other people are well qualified to care for children.

It seemed as if we'd just gotten used to the hiring and choices involved in childcare for our under-twos when school became a topic.

246 E L I Z A B E T H I S A D O R A G O L D

> **From Jane**
>
> October 13, 2011
>
> I made the mistake of reading a Park Slope Parents
> discussion about the benefits/drawbacks of nursery school
> for two-year-olds and now have myself worrying, wondering,
> researching, etc., about what I want to do with Katie next
> year. Do any of you have thoughts about what you are going
> to do with your cuties?

Kids can start preschool at two years old, but the application process begins in the freezing cold, almost a year ahead of time. I couldn't imagine Clara amid activities, mats, and circle time. She'd only just learned to walk!

Our first decision: daycare or preschool? I didn't know the difference, but apparently, it was huge. Daycares, I was told, when I posed the question on the source of all knowledge, Park Slope Parents, were less like school and more like babysitting. They tended to be for younger children, and had extended hours to meet the needs of busy parents. Kids played all day, and there wasn't a "curriculum," necessarily. Ideally, a daycare would be a warm and easy way for a small child to acclimate to a group environment.

Preschools were what the name implied, with curricula and educational philosophies . . . Montessori, Waldorf, Emilia Reggio, inquiry-based, play-based, academic. The options were confusing. I remember, at my own nursery school (where I went part-time, on the days Yetta wasn't watching me), putting on a circus, reading books, and watching a boy pee into a small toilet. We went to city playgrounds, screaming and leaping off jungle gyms that must surely be condemned by now. Would that qualify as inquiry- or play-based?

Because Clara wouldn't turn two until late October, after the school year began, and kids couldn't attend an official preschool before their second birthdays, Danny and I decided we'd start by looking at daycares. I came up with a list of places, and we coordinated our schedules so we could both take the tours.

The first place we checked out was a couple of blocks from our house, in a dingy brownstone. At first, we couldn't figure out whether it was the right building—there was no sign for the school on the front door, merely a posted "No Loitering" notice. We were able to enter, finally, when another person left the building. At the bottom of the stairs, a painted arrow pointed up. Inside, the "school" was maybe twice the size of our apartment, with dirty plastic toys and books that looked as if they'd been bought in bulk at a dollar store. I'd read glowing reviews of this place online, in which the writers (supposedly parents at the school) praised the school's warm and loving teachers.

"Please take off shoes," the director told us, not even bothering to ask us our names. She showed us the week's lunch menu: chicken nuggets, french fries, and pasta, rotating every few days. "All organ-ique," she growled to us, as if it the designation was a species of South American bird. "Come see backyard."

The reviewers had also rhapsodized over the yard. We stepped out onto a freezing fire escape in our stocking feet, directly over a patch of AstroTurf scattered with a few lonely toys.

I asked about curriculum (admittedly, a leading question), and she told me they made an art project for Christmas.

"Your daughter is one?" she asked us.

We nodded.

"Is she toilet-trained?"

Huh? Clara was singing multiversed, in-tune versions of "Doe, a Deer" and "Singin' in the Rain," but we didn't even own a potty yet.

"Tank you for coming," the director said with a scowl. "If you want to enroll her, it will be a list."

Danny and I beat it out of there.

"No way," I said, once we were back on the street. "No. Way."

"Hey, I agree with you!" Danny looked even more freaked out than I felt. "There has to be a better solution."

"Not until she turns two!"

"Why?"

"It's the law!" (It was not, exactly, but there are regulations about the ratio of children to caregivers at different ages.)

"Sorry . . ." He grabbed my hand. "Thanks for doing the research. I wouldn't know where to start . . ."

"I don't know either!" I was freezing and miserable, convinced Clara was going to have to attend what I saw as a gulag-in-a-tenement. With my luck, it would be the only place that would take our brilliant, perfect child.

"Ask the Mommies," Danny said.

From Jane

January 4, 2012

I was similarly disappointed with the physical environs of the daycares I toured, even the ones that had great reputations. Can someone remind me, where is the extended family that is dying to watch my child during the day??

From Antonia

January 5, 2012

I am freaked out. Childcare is such an issue. Dillon said to me the other day: "I feel like I'm dealing with feminist issues in my

marriage!" No shit. Jane—I thought our extended family was
Mommy Group!

As a teacher herself, Heidi tried to calm us all down.

From Heidi

January 5, 2012

Schools in NYC are such a competitive and complicated (and
emotionally loaded) topic that it becomes a self-fulfilling
process. It's hard not to panic when you hear how competitive
everything is, which creates a climate of panicked mothers who
want to do the best thing for their kids. The difficulty is when
"the best thing" is presented as being a group of three or four
preschools that everyone wants to attend. There are many
good programs (many more for 3 year olds than for 2 year olds)
and whenever you decide to enroll your kid, it's going to be fine.

Heidi's wise words calmed me a bit. I would find a school for
Clara, someplace good enough for now, that wasn't terrible. Or
we'd do a nanny share. Something would work out. Clara's future
in kindergarten and high school and college wouldn't be doomed if
a year of preschool was less than perfect.

After a few more frustrating visits to places Danny and I did
not like (though none as bad as the first place), Melissa and I went
to look at a local preschool together. Five blocks from our house,
it was close enough to walk to but far enough to be a little adventure. When we arrived for the tour, I recognized a couple of the
families from the playground.

Children's artwork hung on the walls (the kids painted like mini
Jackson Pollocks—not a stretch for toddlers, but still, I was impressed). Students brought their own lunches every day, and each
classroom had a frog tank and a fishbowl.

Melissa and I walked next to each other, practically holding hands, we were so giddy. "This is it," we each whispered. "Clara and Sofia could go to school together!"

The application process was a little tricky, the director explained.

"You send us a check for your deposit by February first," she said, "and then we open them in the order we receive them, first come, first served."

"So, the more envelopes you send, the better your chances at the school?" I asked.

"Yes. One mother last year sent fifty letters," our guide said.

"Did her kid get in?"

"Oh yes."

I sent twelve letters. We got in. I bought Clara a tiny polka-dot backpack so she could practice going off to school. For a week, she insisted on wearing it every day, with rain boots and a hat, regardless of the weather.

"Skoo," she'd say. "I gonna go to *skoo*."

The most ridiculous irony: Clara wouldn't even be able to start school until after her second birthday. For the first two months of the year, we'd *still* have to find a sitter, *and* pay the preschool tuition in order to hold our place.

"We'll swing it," Danny said. "I have no idea how."

Money, money. I thought I'd conquered my envy of the other Mommies. But when it came to double-paying for school, I fell right back into my old resentments.

I remembered something a friend of mine, also a writer, whose children were a few years older than Clara, said to me: "It starts when you hear where other couples went out to dinner. Which restaurants they tried. Then you realize you don't have the same resources, the same life."

When Renée and Benji went out for the tasting menu at a Michelin-starred restaurant for their anniversary, I obsessed: they were *always* going to have better meals, better everything, as would Emme and Charlie. *The world will be their tasting menu*, I thought bitterly. It would be open to them in ever-arriving bites and sips.

I knew it was not that simple, and I realize how lucky I am. Even so, sometimes I wanted to live in a house where Danny and I would each have our own room to work, and Clara's bedroom would fit more than her . . . bed.

Then one day in Blue Marble, I realized Clara's babysitters surrounded me. Tyler (Tuesdays) had just arrived, and Sarah Jean (Thursdays), Coley (occasional nights and weekends), and Amanda (daytime at the backroom play space) were already working. Four adults who loved my child, all in a space not much bigger than a suburbanite's SUV. Danny and I had created a rich life for our child after all.

Now we had some other, more couple-oriented, issues to work out.

14. Sex and the Married Parents?

The Shortest Chapter in the Book

From Anna

September 15, 2011

I am going out on a date with a 25-year-old tomorrow. Crazy?

From Elizabeth

September 15, 2011

Only if you ask him to call you Mommy.

Of course, all the Mommies were dying to ask each other about sex, but we were uncharacteristically quiet on the topic. At a meeting back when most of the babies were around six months old, Antonia finally broke the conversational ice.

"My husband wants to have sex," she said. "But I find the very idea ridiculous."

Jane snorted in agreement. "Carl thinks it sounds fun, but I can't wrap my brain around it."

I stayed silent. Even though I heard what the other women were saying, I still worried. Clara was three months younger than their babies, and I could barely even think about revealing my still-scarred, stretched-out stomach to myself, let alone Danny. When would this change? Ever? Never?

Mommy groups have the potential to be fantastic resources for talking about sex and romance. The new-mother *omertà* on body issues is strong. I'll admit to wondering if another mother's flatter stomach or better-sleeping kid didn't lead to more romance with her partner. I'll also cop to the truth: for the first few months of Clara's life, I could have cared less about sex. There was too much else going on with my body, and I was too damn tired.

Postpartum and new-parent sex is a tough subject. The whole idea of married-with-child-nookie is a well-worn comic trope, to the point that when I posted on Facebook for stories from my network, I got this from a friend: "Last night I was so exhausted from the day of parenthood that I fell asleep and started snoring during sex . . . while I was on top."

The responses continued in kind.

From a friend whose kids are now in college: "I remember postpartum sex as being painful, sad, obligatory, and full of a silent despair."

From a prominent feminist poet: "I hated that, postpartum and throughout nursing, almost every time I'd orgasm I'd also experience milk letdown. I don't know how common this is, but I'd never seen it mentioned in any of the books."

From the mother of two children under the age of five: "IS there anything to talk about? I'm still waiting."

From an old friend of Danny's who, PS, does not have children: "Any discussion of intimacy building exercises other than sex? I know that there is a broad literature for sex therapists that addresses non-intercourse sexuality, and developing physical intimacy and emotional bonding in a variety of ways (partner yoga, eye contact exercises, breathing together, etc.)."

My husband's response to this one: "If you could keep your eyes open, you could maybe make some eye contact and this might work."

The post that brought the virtual house down was from my best friend's boyfriend's sister's sorority sister (whom I've never even met): "Are you asking more for stories of we-scoot-the-sleeping-toddler-out-of-the-way-and-that's-how-baby-sister-was-made? Or not-sure-who-was-more-afraid-of-what-was-sure-to-be-a-flabby-dry-gym-sock-mom-or-dad?"

Cue rim shot. *Ba-da-buh*. Ladies and gentlemen, thanks for coming to the Comedy Cellar for Clichés Ring True Night. Hope you used up your drink tickets.

Joking aside, why is postpartum sex such a bad joke? Isn't a healthy sexual relationship the cornerstone of a strong romantic partnership? Isn't physical intimacy what overtaxed couples need most to reconnect? Well, yes and no. Or rather: yes, but, as with everything after children, the definitions change. Welcome to the new normal.

I'll start at the beginning—as in, at six weeks after birth, when most women are "cleared" for sex. Yet, for many women, and all of the Mommies, frankly, the thought of anyone, let alone our husbands, touching *those* parts of our bodies seemed ludicrous and terrifying. Personally, I couldn't remember how my body worked sexually anymore. As I've already mentioned, at three months out, my stomach was still jiggly and puffy, and my scar tender to touch. My breasts were huge, leaky, and painful. Whether they were of erotic use was beside the point. Danny claimed that the potential for letdown at an intimate moment didn't bother him—but it bothered me (and I didn't know whether to believe him anyway).

Also, postpartum sex hurts. A lot. Especially at first. "It feels like broken glass," a friend said to me, regarding her first attempt at honest-to-Betsy penetration. There is a good biological reason for this, and it's not because you are somehow wrong or messed up. Plummeting estrogen creates vaginal dryness. You also just pushed a baby out of that thing, as well as that baby's toenails and *head*. If you're breast-feeding, this dryness is your body's way of keeping you from getting pregnant again. Thanks, body. Because we are not medieval farm wives, we can choose to buy some lube. Acupuncture is also excellent for increasing blood flow and promoting healing. And do those Kegels.

But for me—and for most of the Mommies—discomfort was the least of our postpartum sex issues. We were *tired*. Recent studies show that a return to previous sexual activity takes longer for women who are older, have had difficult deliveries, or experienced fertility issues. (In other words: all of us.) That didn't mean we didn't want to try, but more often than not, it felt like too much trouble for the first few months.

Melanie, an old friend from Seattle, wrote to me about her mommy group's discussions about "avoiding sex at all costs" in those early months of new motherhood, when exhaustion trumped sexual desire:

> One mom was talking about how she was going to have to have sex again that week (a few months into motherhood) because it was her husband's birthday and that was his request. Another woman was going on about toe contact in bed—once she and her husband touched toes, sex was soon to

follow. A third mother said she tried to be careful about taking showers only when her husband was otherwise occupied. She was "screwed" if he saw her naked.

Her "light" anecdote became more of a confession. Her email continued:

I was in a relationship with someone whom I almost never had sex with. Like, once to conceive and probably not for a full year before that. The women normalizing not wanting or not having sex was a relief, but for a different reason for me. I was in a sexless, unhappy marriage.

Oh. That's where you want your mommy group to notice that something bigger is wrong, and ask if you're okay. Melanie didn't stay in her group—and she got divorced.

The big takeaway (and one that we did end up talking about, albeit with some embarrassed reticence) in Mommy Group: if you want to get that mojo back, make the time, and exercise a little creativity while you're at it. A shade on our living room window markedly improved Danny's and my romantic life. Clara's bedroom is five feet from ours, and she's an irritatingly light sleeper.

I bumped into Dillon one night at the local bodega, buying flowers for Antonia. When I mentioned it to her the next day, she said, "I think he was trying to get laid." Did it work? "Not really."

Dillon, who remembers that night, still protests, "I was just being nice! Really!"

Melissa was the most open of the Mommies when it came to talk about rekindling her sex life. She told us when she decided to "spice things up" by taking Patrick to a shooting range for their anniversary. While she recommended it highly, I went to Quaker school and Danny is a pacifist. Neither of us wants to touch a gun, least of all erotically.

At a Mommy Group dinner I held strictly for talking about things people didn't want to talk about—that is, sex—the ladies got down, briefly.

Anna kicked it off.

"All my married people, you gotta tell me: do married people have sex after their kids are born?"

Now that the kids were four years old, we were less self-conscious than we'd been back in the early days. We went bananas.

"All the time! Night and day!" Melissa shouted.

"Be honest! I really want to know," Anna said.

"Once every three weeks," Heidi said, to general agreement.

"If you're dealing with fertility stuff, it makes sex feel awful emotionally," Jane volunteered. "But even if we weren't, we wouldn't have sex once a week. We *want* to have sex once a week."

"A lot of the time, I feel like I *have* to do it," Heidi added. "Though we like each other much more when we're having sex, for sure."

That brought general yeses from the gang. And an anonymous recollection of a "couples" visit to the Toys in Babeland, our local (very woman friendly, not at all sleazy) sex shop. Purchases were adorably his 'n' hers: a cock ring and a vibrator.

"Porn," another she-shall-not-be-named source said. "And I like to cruise the craigslist 'seeking partners' ads for inspiration."

Heidi went on in her determinedly serious vein. "After we have sex, I feel really good! And I actually enjoy it so much more than I did, like, twenty years ago."

"True."

"True."

"True that."

We turned to (and on) Anna. "You had *way* more sex than any-body did during the first two years of your child's life," I said to her. "Also, my child climbs into my bed every night."

"My child's in my bed too!" Anna said. (This was an ongoing issue for both of us.)

"Anna, I think a child being in *your* bed is okay. A child being in Elizabeth's bed is less okay," Jane declared. "I slept in bed with my mom, and she was a single mom."

"I want Danny in and Clara out," I protested. "I want to sleep with my husband!"

"You gotta reclaim this." Melissa was now eating pad Thai out of the carton, her usual manners left behind with the words *cock ring*.

"Okay, okay . . ."

"It wasn't easy for me, girls. I had to have sex. Otherwise I was going to be too depressed to function," Anna said.

"We remember," I said.

Anna's lack of "official" sexual partner meant that she ended up pursuing romance with a single girl's single-mindedness. It made her feel less lonely.

After Stephan stood up for her through the nanny drama, Anna's hopes rose. She was willing to reconcile, but Stephan had other plans.

One September morning I got a text: *Can you come over with Clara right now? Stephan's new girlfriend is picking up Isabella, and I don't want to be by myself with her. She'll be here at 11.*

I checked the clock. It was 10:40, a half hour walk to Anna's, and Clara and I were both still in our PJs. I dressed us at record speed, practically throwing the stroller down the steps, and jogging most of the way as Clara screamed with laughter: "Fast! *Fast!*"

As we rounded the corner of her block, I saw that Anna was already in front of her house. Holding Isabella in her arms, she rocked her gently, stroller and diaper bag sitting neatly on the sidewalk next to them. It was 11:03.

"We're here!" I shouted, still running.

Anna had dressed up, in a wraparound silk frock, pumps, and full makeup. She'd even curled her hair.

"It's cool. She's running late," she said.

I unbuckled Clara, who jumped out of her stroller and started to play on the sidewalk. She looked up at Isabella, waiting for her friend to join, but Anna kept her daughter close to her chest. After a few minutes, a car service pulled up. I shouldn't have been surprised when the woman who emerged looked as if she could be Anna's younger sister.

There was little small talk. "Ready to go, Issie?" she said.

Clutching Isabella in her arms, Anna looked as if *she* was never going to be ready. I watched her take a deep breath, give the baby an extra squeeze and kiss, and then finally pass her into the other woman's arms. Isabella whimpered a little, keeping her eyes focused on her mother. "Bye-bye, baby, Mama loves you. See you tomorrow."

Until the car service pulled around the corner, Anna stood tall, waving, bright smile on her face. Then she slumped against me, wiping the corners of her eyes.

"I don't know how you did that," I said.

"Me neither," she said. "Okay, okay." A deep breath, and she straightened, throwing back her shoulders like a gymnast, flashing me a sly grin. "So, what'd you think?"

"She's totally not as pretty as you."

"Awww, you're sweet. Let's go get a croissant. Better than crawling back into bed and crying all day."

By the time Clara and I strolled home, brushing buttery crumbs off my T-shirt, I was relatively confident that Anna was okay.

The next morning I realized, checking my email, that I should have known better.

From Anna

September 17, 2011

Sometimes it feels impossible. Last night, when I was falling asleep, I felt so angry that Isabella was not in her nursery and that I had to be separated from her so unnaturally. I wanted to send Stephan a barrage of texts telling him that one day I would tell our baby the horrible story of how he left me to date other women when she was a few weeks old. I still don't understand how he could be so cruel after seeming so loving and caring for so many years.

A few days later, another text: *I met a guy. He's young, cute, and totally into me.*

Be careful, I responded. *But have fun. You deserve it.*

What I didn't say is that I was a tiny little bit jealous. Not of her heartbreak or divorce (obviously), but Anna was having *adventures*, nights off from childcare without having to pay a sitter, while I didn't fit into any of my old high-heeled shoes and my still-lactating boobs created freak-show cleavage rather than a sexy peekaboo. Unless Danny and I really made a concerted effort at romance, I often felt as if we were coworkers as much as partners, giving each other the occasional high five as we passed each other between shifts.

A bigger issue for me was the larger (in every way) one of post-pregnancy body issues. As in: what was this new body and why did I have it? We are so inundated with the idea that women get back to their "bikini bodies" after losing the "baby bump" that even if we are grown-ups with reasonable expectations, it can be hard to accept that things . . . aren't where they used to be.

The Mommies were not, in general, terrifically concerned about weight loss. We're New Yorkers, and we walk a lot; it's easy enough to stay fit-ish here. Occasionally, one of us would brag about hitting the gym or a class, and the rest of us would say, "Good for you," and continue eating cookies.

Ideally, fitness is something to return to naturally post-baby. Jane and Carl had been avid bikers. Now they got a seat for Katie and went on rides around Prospect Park. Anna played tennis. Renée ate pounds of chocolate and stayed unreasonably thin. The rest of us struggled and tried to decide how much we cared.

Pooja Makhijani is an American living in Singapore. She joined a mommy group specifically for expatriates, founded by local doula Ginny Phang. At the weekly gathering, Pooja was able to escape Singapore's intense pressure to be perfect. On a phone call, she explained to me that in Singapore's expat community, "They have this whole idea of the yummy mummy—and getting back to being a sex object for a man." She joined her mommy group in part to get away from this idea.

Many new mothers fear they'll never find their old shape, internally or externally, after childbirth.

When Clara was a toddler, I attended a few boot camp classes with a local mom and trainer named Chana Balk. The classes kicked my ass, and then I hurt my knee. I wish I'd hired Chana to work with me privately, because once I stopped her classes, I fell off the fitness wagon for a loooong time.

Finally ready (with an almost-five-year-old) to learn exactly how to treat my "new" body, I interviewed Chana about her techniques—and fished for some free advice. (I've since hired her and she's changed my life.)

"Getting fit postpartum is twofold," she explained. We were sitting at a local café, and I was proud of myself because I'd just chosen a "healthy" salad for lunch rather than a sandwich. Chana was sitting on the floor, wrestling her adorable sixteen-month-old daughter, Addie, into some version of submission. A mother of three (!), Chana left a lucrative life as a firm lawyer to raise her kids and pursue her dream of building her own training business. She's tiny and ferociously fit, with long curly hair and a frank, hilarious demeanor. At boot camp class, she'd often advise us to "tooch the tush"—a potent combination of Tyra Banks and Yiddish.

"I'd been very into fitness my whole life, but after I had my first kid, it took me a year of very hard work to get my body back—though it will never be the same," she said to me. "I'd gained eighty pounds."

"Whoa." I couldn't imagine this lithe woman with an additional eighty pounds on her.

"Postpartum, women need to get an okay from their doctors to exercise, usually at about six weeks. But there's things they can do the day the baby's born, to help their abdominals heal and get the muscles back into place."

"Like Kegels?"

"Yes."

"Did you do any of that?"

"No."

We both broke into laughter. Addie screamed with joy.

"With her, I really ate nutrient-dense food when I was pregnant, and I didn't gain much weight at all. I felt as if I was feeding her," she said, patting her daughter on the butt.

"Once you're ready to exercise, there are two different post-partum issues. First, getting rid of the fat you might have gained, so you do cardiovascular exercise for that. Second is healing your abdominals and retraining your pelvic floor."

She mentioned diastasis recti (a condition that many women don't even know they have), when the abdominal muscles split during pregnancy. "Then you have this permanent pregnancy pooch. Doing specific abdominal breathing really helps," she continued. "The pelvic floor is like a hammock. You pull up, and pull in your vagina. People who have eight-year-olds are walking around thinking it's too late for them. But it's not."

"What about our idea that women should be back in bikini shape, like, six weeks later? I mean, I know that's ridiculous, but it still affects my thinking," I said.

Chana rolled her eyes. "The women who are celebrities and look so perfect might have gotten a tummy tuck on the table after a C-section. From the moment their babies are out, they have phys-ical therapists coming to work with them, a nutritionist, and a chef preparing all their meals. They have baby nurses so they can get a good night's sleep, and then at six weeks they have trainers come in to work with them."

"I'm doing Kegels as we're talking," I said.

"Good."

"What would you tell a typical mom who comes in to see you?"

"If you want to lose weight, the first thing I look at is diet. Eighty percent of weight loss is diet. Exercise is crucial for so many reasons, for feeling good about yourself again, but diet is really most of it."

"What about wine?" I ask.

"It's sugar," she said. "If you drink two glasses of wine and you want to lose weight, you can't. Say one glass a week."

I grimaced.

"Well, balance it," she said. "It's all about making choices."

She pointed at herself for emphasis. "I'm not in the gym nine hours a day, and I do go out for ice cream with my kids—though not every week. I don't ration healthy foods like avocados or cherries."

"I used to be great at making myself good food, and now I'm bad at it," I confessed to her.

"Don't be all or nothing," she said. "As mothers, we can't go to Pilates in the morning and then have brunch. You have to fit exercise and food preparation in. Exercise will make you feel good, will make you eat better, and will make your sex life better."

How should a busy parent make time for exercise?

"If I have a client a neighborhood away, I'll run to my appointment. I take my sons to the park to ride their bikes and I jog alongside them. I fit it in."

Ugh, I thought, when Chana and Addie toddled off. More work, less fun. But I didn't order a cookie after my salad, that day or for the next week (and counting). One day at a time.

It's the same with sex. You find the time with your partner, because you need intimacy, even if it feels like a lot of work at first.

A few weeks ago, Danny and I were simply trying to discuss the issue of me writing this chapter. We were lying on our bed, door closed, as Clara watched TV in the living room. But she had evidently gotten bored with her show, because the doorknob started to rattle.

"It's like the raptor in *Jurassic Park*," Danny said, flopping onto his back. "After you have a kid, the raptor is always at the door!"

The knob continued to jiggle, until Clara finally got a better grip.

"I want snuggles!" she demanded, jumping onto the bed, right between us. We gave her snuggles.

15. Hillary Was Right

It Takes a Village

From Liza

Monroe, North Carolina

Why can't new mothers today just relax? Surprise, you are exhausted, your body is unfamiliar and everything doesn't always go the way it's described in the books, but oddly enough, women have been managing for centuries.

From Antonia

April 11, 2012

I'M PREGNANT. This is not a joke. Found out yesterday morning. I'm only four weeks so it's way too early to be telling people, but I figure I'd tell you all, as you have been my comrades on this journey thus far. Anyone free this afternoon?

It was Clara's second spring, and I was ready to understand what had happened to me. Coincidentally, the *New York Times* was running a personal essay series for their online Opinionator section about what was apparently the new "it" psychiatric illness: anxiety.

In some ways, it would have been easier not to tell my story. What would Clara think when she was grown up, reading about my struggle when she was such a little baby? I still felt guilty. I wanted to be a voice for women who were as lost and terrified as I had been. As a writer, I understand my own experience through my work. At that point, I expected rejection for all of my work, and so I was shocked when they accepted it.

My essay "Meltdown in Motherland" came out in May 2012 and received hundreds of online comments. Many readers seemed to think that my experience was bullshit, explaining to the internet that loss of independence and of physical well-being was part of the deal with motherhood. These same commenters seemed to think that my—or any mother's—desire to return to personal and professional satisfaction was bellyaching and that I should change my attitude.

Still others confirmed what I already suspected: having a baby has always been harder than people want to admit. One woman explained—specifically for the less sympathetic among the commenters—that in the bad old days, women with postpartum mental illnesses might never have recovered.

From Debnev

Reading, Connecticut

After each of my two children was born, I felt a powerful need to tell my story. Self-centered? Maybe. Many mothers apparently feel the same way. We need to share our stories of pregnancy and birth. From our combined personal stories emerges a larger picture of women's experience and motherhood.

As I reacted to the reaction to my piece, I realized I wanted to write another story about parenthood: about the Mommy Group. After a great deal of thought and consideration, I approached the group with my idea for a book about . . . us. I was sure they wouldn't approve. Instead, they surprised me, offering me full access.

That summer passed much as the previous one had: playgrounds and sprinklers, trips to the beach and the zoo. Renée hosted a joint second birthday party for Emme and Katie. The kids scribbled on huge sheets of paper with crayons and smashed cupcakes into their faces.

In August, Anna wrote to all of us:

> I'm signing the divorce agreement in the next week or so. I'm moving on, dating, and thinking forward, but I'm still so sad, missing the family I thought I was set up to have. Life brings about so many changes. It has been nearly two years. Thank you all for helping me so much. You all are great friends.

Fall came fast. Clara still had that two months before she could go to school, but the other kids were starting. She wore her new "skoo" backpack every day until she actually started, and then she didn't want to wear it ever again. Toddler logic.

Sofia was in her class. Sarah Jean, a Blue Marble babysitter, would pick both of them up and bring them home to play two days a week. By the time Clara was ready to start at the end of October, she already thought of herself as a schoolgirl.

All the Mommies worked on Mondays now, and with the kids in school, meetings were trickier to coordinate. Renée started hosting us on Friday afternoons. The kids chomped ravioli while we (surprise) drank wine and ate a fancier version of the kids' food— cheese and crackers. Now we talked less about problems with the kids and more about issues surrounding life with them: husbands and aging parents, in-laws, and work.

Antonia told everyone she suspected she might be pregnant at a

Mommy Group dinner in the spring. Most of the babies were on the cusp of turning two. I had the stomach flu *again*, and didn't even want to imagine their fun night out at a new Italian restaurant in the neighborhood. I heard about it, though.

"You missed some big news!" Jane said to me later than night on the phone. "We told her to drink up while she could!"

Antonia went home that night, tipsy, and took a pregnancy test. The positive result sobered her right up. I was somewhat glad I hadn't been there, I realized, when I read Antonia's email that morning. Talk of second babies freaked me out.

I always thought I'd have more than one child. In fact, I always *planned* on more than one child. I also thought I'd write a bestselling novel while I was still in college, live in Paris in my twenties, and have an affair with Roald Dahl.

Then I had my real life. Meeting Danny, waiting until we were ready to get married and pregnant, the miscarriages, my crummy pregnancy, postpartum anxiety. I couldn't go through that again. Not for Danny or my parents, not for Clara, and not for me. My mental health is nonnegotiable.

Yet I felt sad when my period arrived on time every month. Since having Clara, I could tell when I was ovulating—I get *mittelschmertz* and other, less Germanic signs. Every month, I'd think, well, maybe? Should we? And then what if: we'd started earlier, I'd stayed pregnant the first time, been "better" at pregnancy, hadn't developed postpartum anxiety? But I did. I'm working, loving my life with Clara and Danny. *Dayenu.* Enough. Or as my grandmother Yetta would say, "Enough already."

. . . .

Lauren Sandler's book *One and Only: the Freedom of Having an Only Child, and the Joy of Being One* sat on my research shelf for a year. Sandler is my age, an only daughter of liberal feminist Jewish parents, the mother of an only daughter, and she lives in Brooklyn. Theoretically, her bona fides should at least have made me receptive to the book. Instead, even opening it felt like too much of an admission: we were one and done.

When I finally read *One and Only*, I learned that at least our decision to have one child would not hurt Clara professionally or intellectually. According to Sandler's research, only children are more successful than those with sibs. If this finding seems fishy (or at least like wishful thinking), she points to China as an example of "a nation composed mainly of only children [that] has succeeded in lifting an impoverished agrarian economy toward the possibility of world domination in a single generation."

I still have trouble discerning how much of Sandler's work is anecdotal, in spite of all her data. In the end, families are different, sibling relationships vary, and there's only so much parents can predict for their children. Danny, who has a younger sister, is a high achiever who found his love of books at an early age—a typical "singleton" characteristic. My best friend, Chris, as the second of five siblings, is as emotionally enmeshed with his family as I am with mine. The point—as always—is finding fulfillment and emotional and physical health, in whatever kind of family you get.

We had another Mommy Group night out in October when most of the kids had already turned two, at a farm-to-table restaurant near Antonia's new apartment (so Brooklyn, we joked, ordering the grass-fed hamburgers and artisanal rosemary-infused cock-tails). Antonia was due in less than a month, and she almost didn't make it to meet us. She rallied, though, and then we were all there, dressed up, wearing lipstick—except Heidi. She was home with morning (and all-day and evening) sickness; she was due in February. Looking around the table, I saw five beautiful women I loved.

"We're not having another kid," I told everyone. "It's definitive."

"Well, that's why we have each other," Jane broke in. It was her role, to reassure us—me—when things got too heavy. "Clara won't be lonely." As she spoke, I remembered one afternoon when Jane and I were sitting at the kitchen table in her house. The girls were playing with Magna-Tiles and were getting along.

When Jane told me they'd also decided to try for another child, I must have looked visibly upset. "That baby will be part of your family too," she said, "like Clara is in ours. This won't be a loss. It will be a gain."

It was one of the nicest things anyone had ever said to me.

Melissa stayed quiet through the conversation, but now took a gulp of her drink. "I had another miscarriage, guys," she told everyone.

"Oh God, I'm sorry," we all said.

"What are you going to do?" Antonia asked, her hand involun-tarily touching her about-to-pop belly.

"I don't know if I can go through it again," Melissa said. "I'm working on my career. I'm painting, sending my portfolio to galler-ies. Patrick is bummed, but I'm forty-three—"

"You are?" we chorused. "How on earth do you look this good?"

"I'd love to have another, but with who?" Anna said.

Jane changed the subject again—to Katie's interventions. "She's almost all caught up! She'll still need physical therapy, and I worry about her falling all the time, but remember how scary we thought it could be? Oh—and we're looking for a house. We saved enough." Her news was the mood lightener we needed. Falling down, getting up, moving on.

I hadn't been surprised when Heidi told me she was pregnant. She'd been having a great—what she later called a "gold"—year.

"I went on Weight Watchers and lost twenty pounds," she reminisced. "Work was really good. We had a wonderful nanny. I was like, *I feel so good. I should have another baby!* I thought we really had everything under control. So we quit the nanny we loved, put Clay in school full-time, and I got pregnant."

Heidi's first pregnancy had been ideal. Conveniently off from teaching during her last trimester, she loved her daily ice cream and nap. Old ladies smiled at her, subway conductors held the train for her as she waddled down the stairs. Before I even met her, Danny told me about seeing this pregnant woman walking down our block, her belly stretching a foot in front of her, stopping to, quite literally, smell the roses in our neighbor's garden. When he described this glowing person to me, it was all I could do to keep from throwing the TV remote at his head (I didn't want to have to get up and take it back, though). Later, when I realized he was describing my new friend, I forgave him for her unseemly pregnant joy—almost.

This pregnancy was a whole other deal. She texted me one night in a panic. *I'm pregnant and spotting. Didn't that happen to you? What happened?*

I reassured her but remembered how freaked out I'd been in the same situation.

Her doctor confirmed that she was fine the next day. But this wouldn't be the easy pregnancy she'd had with Clay.

Clara's second birthday party turned out to be on the eve of Hurricane Sandy. We booked the back room play space at good old Blue Marble ice cream. On the day of the party I was certain the dire weather predictions would keep everyone home. Instead, it was a last hurrah before what would turn out to be a sad and stressful week indoors.

I made pizza, like a real mom, patting flat the lumps of store-bought dough, pouring on spaghetti sauce from a jar, dumping on cheese, and then, once it was cooked, carrying the baking sheets straight into the party. I had bought the cake and felt guilty about it. My pièce de résistance, however, which I had obsessed over for weeks before, was our activity: decorating mini pumpkins with facial-feature stickers. I imagined it all, the cute little pumpkins, and the kids carefully decorating. That morning, I went to the Greenmarket at Grand Army Plaza and bought what I thought should have been twenty dollars' worth of small pumpkins (but in fact was more like sixty dollars) and carried them home, limping from that knee injury I'd sustained at mommy-toddler boot camp a few weeks earlier.

I'd decided on Clara's costume this year based on what we had around the house and what I thought she'd like: Curious George in a tutu. It was easy. Brown onesie and tights, and her fave poufy skirt. I'd tried to jazz it up, going to a notions store in the fabric district near Times Square and buying furry trim. The texture sent Clara screaming into the other room. She was scared of fur.

As with Clara's first birthday, the party grew into a rager. Kids and parents whom I hardly knew but had invited last-minute showed up. Old friends whom I hadn't seen in years brought new babies and toddlers. My friend Marco, who owns a *New York Times*–starred Italian restaurant, deemed my pizzas excellent. The food was gobbled, the baby pumpkins were covered in stickers, and Danny and I totally forgot to take photos.

I only really cared that the Mommy Group was there. As this second year of Clara's life ended and folded into the third, I felt the powerful urge to make sure they were witnesses to the changes we were all making.

The other Mommies had been at the party for an hour, costumed kids running amuck, when Antonia arrived. Due in less than a month, she'd still MacGyvered the best outfit for Gus. Capitalizing on his curls and high energy, she dressed him as Richard Simmons, complete with purple tights and a headband. Well, there was supposed to be a headband. By the time she arrived, she was crying too much for us to understand her or to produce the headband. Then she barricaded herself in the single bathroom.

Heidi, a few months less pregnant, took charge.

Renée kept track of Gus, Jane made up a plate of food, and Heidi brought it into the bathroom. Eventually, Antonia got herself together enough to leave the loo.

I don't think anyone else at the insane party noticed the drama with Antonia, but we were acutely aware. We took care of each other, each protecting the others from our own blowing storm.

Mayor Bloomberg suspended all MTA service later that night, soon after the final party guests made their way home.

Heidi texted me that night: *If we get to leave the house tomorrow, do you want to come over and put Clara in the bathtub with Clay and a bunch of shaving cream? Yes, the fear of being shut in is getting to me. The birthday party was great, though!*

Our apartments were only twenty feet away from each other on the block, but the airborne tree limbs and glass and windows somehow sucking our children out into a raging *Wizard of Oz* storm meant that we couldn't even get that far for several days.

As the week continued, we watched news reports of how devastating the storm was for our neighbors, some only a few miles away. We were snug in our top-floor apartment in a neighborhood out of the flood zone, with power, heat, and whatever else we needed, but rumors of looting in Coney Island and disaster in Staten Island kept coming. People weren't able to reach the neighborhoods to assess the damage. There were no streetlights, no running water, and no basic services. We didn't know if people had died. We didn't know if there was going to be large-scale chaos.

When we finally left the house and made it to Heidi's, it was as if Clay and Clara had matured in the two days. They played in a tent fort Heidi and I made for them out of blankets and couch pillows. We took turns reading them stories, both kids snuggling together into one of our laps. They watched TV together, sitting side by side on the couch for back-to-back episode of their mutual favorite, *Curious George*.

The next day was Halloween. This was the first year Clara had even a cursory understanding of the concept: she dressed in her costume, walked up and down the street, and gave people candy from a bucket, right? Wait, no, that wasn't right. She walked up and down the street, took candy from other people, and then gave it back. Wait, no . . .

Clay didn't share Clara's confusion. He was a fierce trick-or-treater, correcting grown-ups when they said his costume was a Brontosaurus ("No, *Brachiosaurus*") and amassing a jack-o'-lantern overflowing with candy.

"She's a monkey in a tutu in a hurricane," I said to Danny as Clara trick-or-treated. "It's like a line from Bob Dylan." He laughed, and as always, I loved it. We still had the same weirdo sense of humor.

Later, when I thought about the last two years, the hurricane hitting on Clara's birthday felt so apt. The storm raged whether we were prepared or not. We had battened down the hatches and survived. All of us.

Antonia had Verne, her second boy (this time, her labor was so fast she almost had him in the cab on the way to the hospital), right before Thanksgiving; Heidi gave birth to Walker (unmedicated VBAC—Walker does not have Clay's melon-head) in February. The Clay family moved soon after that. They were only about a twenty-minute walk away, but Underhill wasn't their home playground anymore, and we couldn't go knock on their new window. Anna started seeing a guy—her first real, serious relationship after Stephan—and she bumped up her work hours. Renée put Emme in school five days a week, as did Melissa with Sofia.

It wasn't that we didn't see each other anymore, but that journey with the original fellowship—mothership—was over. We'd made it home.

Epilogue

There and Back Again

ME: WHAT DID YOU DO AT SCHOOL TODAY?
CLARA: IT'S A SECRET. I CAN'T TELL YOU SECRET STUFF.

—EVERY DAY, 2012–2015

These days, when Clara is in school, I often write in local coffee shops. Whichever one I choose, whatever the time of day, I share the space with mommy groups. The babies are tiny; the moms' bodies still soft and swollen. I watch them stir extra packets of sugar into their cappuccinos, listen to them talk too loudly and with too much detail. They're exchanging freshman-year confidences, telling their most basic stories along with anecdotes about naps.

I want to tell them it gets better. Really.

About a month before I finished writing this book, we had an official Mommy Group dinner at Anna's swanky new apartment. Everyone knew I'd be taping the proceedings. I had a bunch of last-minute questions, and it seemed easier—and more fun—to do it together. I ordered in way too much Thai food and wine, pressed

Record on my phone app, and let everyone have at it, which they did (this was the night of the cock ring confession).

Finally, as we were winding down, Anna asked, "Are you gonna have an epilogue with the girls in violin class?"

"I thought my epilogue would be my fortieth birthday," I said. It had been the previous July, and everyone who was in town came. I showed off the tattoo I'd bought myself as a birthday present: a lavender-and-turquoise starfish, with Clara's initials along the side of one of its legs in tiny script. I got that specific tattoo because Clara belted out a song about starfish that she learned in school every day for the last year. Also, starfish regenerate. If they lose an arm, it grows back. Just like my life had regenerated after . . . everything.

Listening to Anna, I changed my mind. My birthday wasn't the end of the story. The true epilogue for the Mommy Group was Gus, Clay, and Clara going to the same amazing preschool, and talk of where we're all applying to kindergarten, and who's playing at whose house after Katie, Clara, and Emme take ballet that Saturday, and whether Sofia will be Queen Elsa and Clara will be Princess Anna this time when they hang out after school.

And the epilogue is violin class. Anna had been teaching Katie, Issie, and Clara for months, every Monday. Now about two heads taller than Clara, Issie played with a strong, sure bow, already scratching out "Twinkle, Twinkle." Katie was serious and composed while she played, listening, wanting to do well, strawberry-blond hair pushed back from her face with a barrette. Clara, the musician's daughter and granddaughter, hated to practice but loved to sing. She always ran out of the lesson, busting into Anna's spare room, where Jane and I lounged on an unmade bed, talking,

talking, our conversation picking up where it left off weeks before, always interrupted by the girls, the children. The rhythm of our talk will always be like the murmur of a mother soothing a baby. Is that too corny an analogy? No, like Baby Bear's bed in "Goldilocks and the Three Bears," it's just right.

Acknowledgments

You don't get to publish your first book, after age forty and with a small child, writing about community and motherhood and your own nervous breakdown, without having a gazillion people to thank. So please bear with me.

Thank you:

To Terra Chalberg, my smart, patient, and rather chic agent. Your faith and excitement about this book and my work has helped with each sentence. To Sarah Branham (and, of course, Sarah Durand) at Atria, thank you as well for your patience, attention, and enthusiasm. There is so much in this manuscript that would be less nuanced and more clichéd if you hadn't asked so many questions. To my publicity and marketing team at Atria: Lisa Sciambra, Kathryn Santora, Arielle Kane, and Jin Yu. To Haley Weaver for all the emails. To Kathy Daneman for being hot stuff.

To Audrey Schomer for transcription, assistance, and fascination with all the gory details.

To the people, named and pseudonymous, whom I interviewed, including Rachel Carlson Burns, Peggy Francois, Susan Fox, Dr. T. J. Gold, Susanne Milenkevich, Stephanie Mortimore, Leigh Anne Prescott, Eida Ulen Richardson, Freda Rosenfeld, Abigail

Shaw, Katherine Stone, and Stephanie Wright, as well as many others.

To Ellen Krug, Jessica Silver, Dr. Michael McIntosh, and Dr. Katrina Bradley: thank you for Clara, and for the health of my body and mind.

To Richard Locke, Patricia O'Toole, and most of all to Lis Harris (and Marty Washburn), my teachers and mentors at Columbia's School of the Arts. I hear your voices in my head every time I sit down to write (often in chorus).

Over the last two years, I have been part of a brilliant writing group (all Brooklyn mommies!). For chocolate and tissues: Laura Allen, Suzanne Cope, Lisa Selin Davis, Katherine Dykstra, and Abby Sher. Most of all to Nancy Rawlinson. All books have one person who reads more drafts, tolerates more questions, and offers more insights. For this book, I was beyond lucky to have Nancy in that role. Your turn.

To my larger writing, parenting, and friend community: Janet Grillo and Matthew Grillo Russell (the Godfather), Brenda Shaughnessy and Craig Teicher, Julia Fierro, Emily Barton, Liz Edmund and Howard Slatkin, Sonya and Andrew Glazer, Kari Groff, Dana Miller and Ryan Kovalak, Lucas Thorpe, Karina Moltz and Pete Robbins, Livy Snyder, Serena Jones, Peter Catapano, Onika Simon, Simone Dinnerstein and Jeremy Greensmith, Stew, Amanda Filley and Marco Canora, Paola Prestini and Jeffrey Ziegler, Adaline Frelinghuysen (and company), Sharon Scott (and company), Amy Osborn, Rebecca Davis, Kate Gale, Millree Hughes and Sarah Davis, Jennie Ketcham, Joyce Maynard, Ed, Lyn, and Jessie Tettemer (and the Octagon), the legendary Bob Levine, Alison McGhee, and landlord extraordinaire Earlton Singleton.

To the babysitters: Michele Arrieta, Jennifer Arlia, Sarah Jean Billeiter, Jacob Basri, Anne Lind, Chelsea Feltman, Tyler Fischer, Emma Tattenbaum-Fine, Chloe King, nicHi douglas.

To everyone at the Maple Street School, and particularly to Wendy Cole for the pink computer and fairy dust.

Special lifelong thanks to Christopher Milenkevich and Randy Hartwell, and to Tara Smith and Thomas Struth.

To my cousins (cuz-lings?): Russell (with especial mention for draft reading, sanity saving, and straight talking), Rachel, and Lily Gold.

To my uncle Steve and aunt Barbara Gold, for teaching me about justice and for telling us that it's perfectly normal for an infant to fall off the sofa once or twice.

To my uncle Richard and aunt Cheryl Gold (and Kritz), for laughter and listening.

To my aunt Hettie Maidman, for Pucci and common sense.

To Alan and Shirley Felsenfeld, for support, care, and the use of their upstairs bedroom as a writing studio.

To Miriam and Paul Jacobsen, my grandparents who didn't live long enough to know me as an adult. Miriam would have fixed my hair and Jake would have been tickled pink and taken credit.

To Len and Yetta. Yetta, I wish I could give you the first copy of this book, hot as a fresh soft pretzel off the press. Lenny would have asked for a couple dozen to sell in the lobby—and he would have too, at almost full price. We'll all always live behind the store.

To my parents, Larry and Vicky Gold: for teaching me that love and art and partnership and parenthood are not mutually exclusive ambitions. For showing me what to look for in a partner and marriage. Most of all for being Momo and Lala.

And to my brilliant, kind, hilarious Capricornian husband,

Daniel Felsenfeld. For your clarity of expression and dedication to the creation of honest notes and words. For being the only person who's ever wanted more parentheticals. For knowing a house needs a piano. For repeating till funny. For driving through the night.

To Clara, aka Elsa, Violet, Sophia, and whoever else it is by now. I love you more than anything. I really, really hope you sleep through the night in your own bed someday.

To all the women suffering and wondering if they can do this: Yes, you can, but not alone. Find help and friends. It will get better.

Finally: to Stacy, Jayson, and Greta Greene. About a month before I turned in this manuscript, something terrible happened. Our dear friends Stacy and Jayson (who are mentioned throughout this book) lost their two-year-old daughter, Greta. Months ago, I dedicated this book to Clara, Danny, and my parents. I'm also dedicating it, now, in the moments of completion, to our beloved Greta Greene.

A Note on Sources and Research

I used many resources for this book. Much of my data comes from official sites, such as the US Census and the Bureau of Labor Statistics. I consulted polls and surveys conducted by the Pew Research Center. Other sources included professional organizations such as the American College of Obstetricians and Gynecologists (whose articles are also accessible to the general reader wanting to, for example, bolster her desire to labor for a longer time before having a C-section). I found important resources in popular newspapers and magazines. Many excellent nonfiction books examine contemporary parenting.

Throughout this manuscript, I, for the most part, credited or mentioned sources as they occurred.

I conducted many interviews with mothers and experts on various issues and professions related to parenting. Because so much maternal community building takes place online, I relied extensively on results from questions I posed on social networking sites, as well as blogs, responses to my email newsletters, and personal referrals. I am very grateful that so many women shared such private information with me, and with such spirit, candor, and humor. In most cases, I have changed their names and identifying details.

I did my best to reach out to people from various demographic categories, especially in terms of race, economic level, and social class. By its nature, any work such as this is incomplete. I dearly wanted to include as many mothers' voices as possible. I hope I have made good on that effort. All mistakes and inaccuracies are my own.